SONG OF THE PADDLE

An Illustrated Guide to Wilderness Camping

A falls on the Hood River

SONG OF THE PADDLE

An Illustrated Guide to Wilderness Camping

BILL MASON

KEY PORTER BOOKS

Canadian Cataloguing in Publication Data

Mason, Bill, 1929–
 Song of the paddle

ISBN 1-55013-079-X (bound) ISBN 1-55013-082-X
(pbk.)

1. Camping — Canada.   2. Camping — United
States.   3. Canoes and canoeing — Canada.
4. Canoes and canoeing — United States.   I. Title.

GV790.M37 1988   796.54   C88-093163-9

Page vi: Morning mist in the Petawawa Gorge,
Ontario.

Key Porter Books Limited
70 The Esplanade
Toronto, Ontario
Canada M5E 1R2

Printed and Bound in Canada

92   6 5 4

CONTENTS

INTRODUCTION

Odysseus ordered his men to plug their ears when they sailed by the island of the Sirens so they would not be lured to their destruction on the offshore rocks by the sea nymphs' irresistible song. In order to hear the song, Odysseus asked his men to lash him to the mast. I know all about this sort of thing because I hear a song like that of the Sirens every spring when the ice on the rivers begins to break up. Years ago in the heart of Winnipeg, Manitoba, I would be working at my desk in a commercial art studio, hear the song, hand in my two weeks' notice and get my outfit ready. My parents thought I would outgrow it but I never did. If anything, the song is becoming louder and more insistent with the passing years.

Some people hear the song in the quiet mist of a cold morning; others hear it in the middle of a roaring rapids. Sometimes the excitement drowns out the song. The thrills become all that matter as we seek one rapid after another. Sleeping, eating and living outdoors become something we do between rapids. But for other people the song is loudest in the evening when they are sitting in front of the tent, basking in the camp fire's warmth. This is when I hear it loudest, after I have paddled and portaged for many miles to some distant, hidden place.

I probably heard the song for the first time as a child playing among the canoes pulled up on the sand at Grand Beach on Lake Winnipeg. My parents tell me that they couldn't get me away from the canoes. I climbed over and in them by the hour. They couldn't have known it but, in my imagination, I was journeying to faroff places where only a canoe could go.

When I was about nine years old, a huge storm broke up the pier at Grand Beach. Everyone thought it was a great disaster, but I knew it for what it really was: a miracle. All my life, as short as it then was, I had been trying to build a canoe by nailing driftwood together. Every time I grabbed my homemade paddle and climbed on board, it sank. I could never find enough wood to make a raft that would float with me on board. And now, as far along the beach as the eye could see, there was wood.

With considerable effort, I nailed together two timbers and set them afloat. A feeling of euphoria came over me as I hopped on and felt myself buoyed up by the water. Paddling away from the beach, I watched fascinated as the ripples in the sand dropped away beneath me. The water gradually darkened until I could no longer see the bottom. I was afloat on water that was deeper than I was tall. I loved the feeling of danger, excitement and adventure. For the first time in my life, I was no longer bound to the land; now I could reach the offshore rocks that had seemed so far away.

Mine was the most beautiful canoe ever made because it was mine. I hated it when people called it a raft, so I hacked away at the ends with my penknife to create some semblance of a bow. I would paddle over to what was left of the pier and tie my canoe to the ladder along with the other canoes. Tying and untying the knot was a wonderful ritual. It was a way of affirming ownership: this was my canoe, and I could paddle it anywhere, anytime I wanted. Just belonging to a canoe is a large part of being a canoeist.

After my journeys, I would sometimes hang around the boat livery at Grand Beach. The owner had a great fleet of canoes and rowboats, and sometimes I would see this kid bailing the rainwater out of them. I figured he must be very rich to own so many canoes. Occasionally my father would rent one for what seemed like the world's shortest hour. I loved being in a real canoe, and yet it wasn't quite the same as paddling my timber canoe alone. Even though Dad let me decide where to go, he did the steering. Already I had fallen in love with solo paddling.

The first thing I ever owned, that was related to a real canoe, was a paddle. On one of our excursions, Dad and I found a paddle floating in the weeds. It had probably belonged to two canoeists who had tipped and drowned in the lagoon a couple of weeks before. I also suspected that their canoe had been rented from the boat livery. My father threw the paddle up on shore. After returning the canoe, we went back to retrieve it. Although I knew at some level that the paddle was tainted, my conscience was clear. Dad did it, not me. Anyway, even if it did belong to the rich kid at the livery, I figured he would never miss it. That paddle became my most cherished possession.

Many years later, I learned that your sins always find you out. Barrie Nelson, a good friend with whom I had worked in an animation studio, and canoed with on many enjoyable trips, picked an old paddle out of my paddle rack. He studied it for a long time, then turned to me and asked, "Where did you get this paddle?" I explained how we had found it in the lagoon at Grand Beach. A smile crossed his face as he looked at me and said, "You crooks! This paddle belonged to my grandmother's boat livery. I used to spend the summers there looking after the canoes." I could hardly believe it. My best friend had spent his childhood wallowing in a canoe mecca and had never invited me to go for a ride! I'd have sold my grandmother just for the privilege of sitting in those canoes, let alone paddling them.

Many people have asked me, "What came first? Your love for the canoe or the land?" It was definitely the canoe. The canoe took me away from the crowds and introduced me to places that had remained unchanged for centuries. And in the going I discovered a sense of freedom that has never been equalled in any other way. When I was 11 years old, I began work on what would be my first real canoe. Of course I had no idea how to build a real canoe, so it was built with a kayak construction using formers and stringers. It took a full winter to complete the job. In the spring, we hauled it down to the Red River that flows through Winnipeg and, much to the surprise of my parents, it actually floated upright. I grabbed my ill-gotten, oversized paddle and headed off. I was elated with my new-found freedom. I was no longer just listening to the song. I was singing it!

1

1 PLAYING THE SONG

Most people call it "camping" but I prefer "living outdoors." "Camping" is what you do when you spend a few nights outdoors. You don't hear the song nearly as clearly as when you are living outdoors. "Living outdoors" suggests a much closer relationship with the land. It is an art, but it is even more than that. It is the beginning of a relationship with the world of nature, a world of lakes and rivers, rocky, pine-covered shores and plunging rapids.

Films, books and stories almost always portray wilderness as dangerous. Even children's stories are loaded with all the terrible things that can happen to you in the deep, dark forest, from being turned into ginger-bread to being attacked by a big, bad wolf. For some reason, we enjoy scaring ourselves half to death. We love to watch or read about other people enduring all kinds of adversity. I've seen films in which the hero breaks his leg in a plane crash, goes over a waterfall, and is attacked by a grizzly and a pack of wolves. Our culture calls it adventure, but really, it's adversity.

I have always loved doing adventurous things, sometimes walking that thin edge, but I'm not all that keen on adversity. It's not much fun being cold, miserable, hungry and lost. Adversity is usually the result of poor planning, inadequate equipment, incompetence or a combination of all three. Occasionally, through circumstances beyond our control, we do run into difficulties. I've been uncomfortable many times. I've suffered because of bugs, cold, heat, wind, rain and exhaustion, but none of these rates as adversity unless it is sustained over a long period of time. It's the contrast between an arduous day and the sheer comfort of the camp that makes living out-doors interesting and exciting.

One way to avoid adversity is to stay home. Another way is to learn the skills and acquire the equipment that will make adversity a remote possibility. Much of the hardship experienced in North America by early European explorers could have been avoided if they had adopted the ways of the native people. The polar explorers, Robert Scott and Roald Amundsen, illustrate the point very well. Scott dressed his men in clothes that were best suited to sailing. He and his men perished. Amundsen had great respect for the native people and marvelled that they could survive in so harsh a climate. He paid close attention to how they clothed themselves. He made loose-fitting clothes of fur like theirs, using the layering principle. Their clothing was drafty, but that allowed moisture to escape. Amundsen made it to the Pole and back.

On my first canoe trip in 1946, we camped on an island almost a mile from the children's camp. Although the counsellors were nice people, they had never been in a canoe before and had probably never seen a tent. The island they chose could have passed for Devil's Island. It had been burned over several years before and was a tangled mass of brush. We arrived after dark and found the mosquitoes in a ravenous frenzy for blood. The counsellors managed to get a lantern going, but it was so thickly covered by mosquitoes that we couldn't see much any-way. During a hasty meal of bread, jam, peanut butter and mosquitoes, it started to rain. We dragged out the tents, but nobody knew how to put them up in the dark. In desperation, we crawled under the overturned canoes and pulled the tents over us. This was my introduction to adversity and I didn't like it.

My acquaintance with adversity was fol-lowed the next morning by an introduction to rigor. The trip back to camp took place in pouring rain against a headwind; most of us were without raincoats. The experience rated very high on the rigor scale. In the evening, when I was asked to give the trip report, I summed it up with one word, "rigorous."

I'm sure many of the kids on that trip never set foot in a canoe or slept under canvas again. I just knew there had to be another way. Things have improved since then; that camp now has one of the best canoe-tripping programs in Canada. And I, personally, have been trying to stamp out adversity and rigor in all kinds of canoe camping ever since, be it solo, group, family or guided trips.

The adversity of arctic exploration (Metropolitan Toronto Reference Library) ———

Living in luxury ———

Adversity in the extreme (Public Archives Canada)

3

Travelling solo

On my first solo canoe trip, I used a borrowed tent that filled up half the canoe. The canoe was rented, the only one available in the whole country. I paid nine dollars for three days, which was more than the canoe was worth. The canvas was falling off, the gunwales were rotted and the bow was split. I could actually see where I was going by looking through the crack. Laden with layer after layer of paint, the canoe was so waterlogged that I could only lift up one end at a time. To portage, I had to find a tree with a notch, drag the canoe to the tree and hoist one end up into the notch. Then I ducked underneath, lifted it and staggered until I found another tree with a notch.

I eventually put two portages behind me and reached a lake that had no cottages, no roads and no people, only me. I had been alone many times before, on the edge of the lake at camp or at the beach, but this was different. I paddled to the most distant bay on the lake and set up camp. Ravenous after the strenuous portage, I caught a fish and fried it for supper. It was the best meal I'd ever eaten. The camp fire was alive; it kept me company. And although I felt completely alone, I was not the least bit lonely.

I would be irresponsible in encouraging people to canoe and camp alone if I didn't also point out the dangers. I have always been aware that any mishap that renders me immobile will almost certainly lead to my death unless I am on a well-travelled route. This is particularly true of an open-ended trip with no set return date after which someone is going to miss me. If someone does, by chance, find and help me, my injury or need for assistance will probably spoil their trip. If no one finds me, and my family begins to worry, someone has to look for me, which can be expensive and troublesome.

This raises the question of whether to carry a location-finding device (see page 134). Does carrying such a device detract somehow from the wilderness experience, the feeling of severance from the man-made world? Is the inherent danger of solo travel an integral part of the journey? Is it foolish romanticising?

These are questions that we must answer for ourselves.

If you do decide to go solo, go prepared. Think about everything you do. Think about the possibility of injury even from routine actions, such as picking up and carrying the canoe over a muddy trail, chopping wood or running rock-studded rapids. Close your eyes and imagine yourself pinned helplessly between your canoe and a rock in the middle of a rapid. You might decide to portage the rapids. When you are chopping or splitting your firewood, imagine sinking the axe into your foot and then notice how carefully you position the safety log.

When travelling alone, there is no one to share the work. Everything takes longer. Keep this in mind when choosing a destination. A solo paddler can't travel as fast as two paddlers. It's especially difficult to paddle against a strong headwind for any length of time. When paddling a straight course, where no quick maneuvers are necessary, I sometimes sit in the stern with the weight up front so the trim is level. In the stern position, less steering is required at the end of each stroke. In waves, I prefer to kneel closer to the center of the canoe.

I have never hesitated to travel solo, mostly because I am careful and take precautions. I have also been lucky. I have totalled a canoe and survived several swims down rapids. Once I was standing about 8 ft. (2 m) above the ground, on a fallen tree, to take a photograph. I stepped on a hornets' nest. When they attacked, I panicked and jumped to the rocks below. The ground was uneven and I could have broken a leg or ankle, or had a reaction to the bites. An unforeseen hazard can materialize at any time. Maybe that's why travelling alone is not only a journey, but also an adventure. There is nothing comparable.

Travelling with a group

Six is just about the right number of people for a fun trip. It is also considered the safest number for travelling on a remote wilderness river, where a lot of manpower or woman-power is sometimes needed for hauling pinned canoes off rocks. If a canoe is lost, it is possible to travel with three people to a canoe. And if a canoe gets swept away on a fast current after a dump, there is one canoe left to rescue the swimmers and one to chase after the missing canoe.

When I travel with family and friends it's for the joy, the camaraderie and adventure of the trip. Sometimes the joy comes from sharing places we all love. The most exciting trips are those on which we see a river for the first time, when every bend is a surprise. But first you have to agree on a trip and on duties in preparation for it. This is what winters are for.

Trip preparations for a wilderness journey
Most people take a certain amount of pleasure in the dreaming, planning and preparation of their canoe trip. Some aspects are more fun than others. Some of my favorites are poring over maps on long, cold winter evenings, and trading trip information with other canoeists. Although making arrangements for car shuttles or flights isn't quite as much fun and can be complicated, it's all part of the adventure. The following is a checklist of all the things that have to be done:

1. Put together a group of canoeists who are compatible. A balance of skills within the group, including whitewater experience and knowledge of first aid, navigation and natural history is desirable on long, difficult trips. On unguided trips there are no rules as to who should be in charge, but ideally it should be the person with the most experience, knowledge or skill, or better yet, a combination of all three. Sometimes leadership falls to several different people. For example, if one member has travelled the route and is a skilled canoeist, he or she should logically be the leader while on the water. Someone who enjoys cooking might take over the kitchen.

2. Research possible trips by scanning maps, reading trip reports, magazines and books, or looking at the slide shows of other canoeists. Another good source for potential trips is the *Wild Rivers Survey of Canada* available from Parks Canada, Ottawa, Ontario, K1A 1G2.

3. Decide which trip you will take, purchase the required maps and mark them up with whatever information you can get. Friends and acquaintances will do this for nothing; commercial outfitters and guides charge a fee —but it's usually worth it.

4. Select a departure date and agree on the length of the trip.

5. If a car shuttle is used, make arrangements for drop off and pick up. If flying in, make charter flight arrangements.

6. Make arrangements for transporting your canoes (which can't always travel with you) or make rental arrangements with an outfitter.

7. Secure travel permits where necessary.

8. Buy fishing licence(s).

9. Obtain special information such as fire hazard conditions and expected water levels. Some rivers dry up in late summer when there has been little rain.

10. Decide whether or not you will be using the services of a commercial outfitter for flight arrangements, shuttle services, canoes, equipment or guide.

11. The skill level of each group member should be given careful consideration. Personal instruction or a whitewater course might be advisable for some of the members.

12. Make up a menu and decide who will buy the food and who will pack it. Also decide who will bring pot sets, utensils, stove, food wanigan and packs.

13. Will everybody be using their own tent or will people be teaming up?

14. Put together personal equipment, clothing, and so on.

Canoe camping with friends

Travelling with a group . . .

Renting canoes and equipment

If you are in the early stages of checking out canoeing and wilderness living, there are some advantages in renting the canoe and equipment. It gives you a chance to check out the various types of canoes and tents before settling on equipment you will have for many years. Some rental places will apply the rental fee or part of it to the purchase of new equipment. There's also the possibility that once is enough and you won't be going again.

Many people buy a nice canoe for their pleasure canoeing and rent a tougher one for running rapids. A friend, who is an outfitter, makes a point of asking the client whether he or she intends to use the canoe on flat water or in big whitewater. One day I was at the back of his store when two clients drove up and returned what was left of their rental canoe. They hastened to explain, ''We want you to know that we did not abuse that canoe.'' And it was true. All they had done was upset the canoe, broadsiding it on a rock. The current destroyed the canoe. The real problem was that they had told my friend they would be using it on flat water. If they had taken an older, well-worn canoe, the replacement cost would have been much less.

Canoes and camping equipment are heavily booked on weekends. Be sure to order ahead so you have a wider choice. The staff of a good outfitter have likely been where you intend to go and might be able to offer valuable advice. They are able to assist you better in the middle of the week. It's unreasonable to expect the same kind of service late Friday afternoon when everybody is picking up their equipment. There is usually a deposit against damage to the canoe. Check over the canoe before using it and list the damage, if any, for later reference. If you are not familiar with carrying a canoe on your car, be sure to ask for advice from the outfitter. They will be glad to help if only out of self-interest.

In many areas much of the local canoeing activity centers around the outfitter. They have a good idea of who is going where and when. Sometimes they even have a club operating out of the store. Many also run training clinics ranging in length from one day to several days. These clinics not only teach you how to paddle safely, but also introduce you to like-minded people. You have a chance to check them out, and they have an opportunity to look you over. This is very important if you are going to sign up for an extended wilderness trip.

For information on Canadian clubs in your area, write to the Canadian Recreational Canoeing Association, P.O. Box 500, Hyde Park, Ontario N0M 1Z0. In the United States, write to the American Canoe Association, Box 248, Lorton, Virginia 22079.

Aircraft charters

The problem with the fly-in trip is that the pick-up date puts pressure on you. If you and your friends miss the flight, it can cost a small fortune. It means the pilot has to come looking for you, which is why it's important that he or she knows your route. With aircraft, as with most shuttles, it's pay before you go, so have the cheque or money in your hand at pick-up time!

As a rule of thumb, Beaver aircraft can carry one canoe on the floats, or if previously arranged, a 16-ft. (4.8 m) canoe nested inside a 17-ft. (5 m) one which has had the thwarts, seats and decks removed. Cessnas, Piper Cubs and other small aircraft carry only one canoe. On our Hood River trip (see page 83), a single-engine Otter carried two nested canoes on one side and a third canoe on the other. With the Twin Otter's large doors and cargo space, the three canoes are carried inside along with six passengers and all the camping gear. A lot depends on the pilot. In some areas, the pilot might refuse to take more than one canoe inside.

On distant northern trips, it's cheaper to rent canoes from outfitters who have canoes on location than to fly yours in. In other situations, it is more expensive to fly your canoe home than it is to buy a new one.

Dressing adequately

It's in the interest of the group that each member be suitably clothed. If all but one person are equipped with wet suits or water-proof paddling jackets for Class 3 rapids, then you've got a problem. Every time a big rapids is run, that one person's life is in danger. Sometimes it is possible for one or two canoes to run rapids while one or two portage, but this should be agreed upon beforehand. Some rivers have so many rapids that you have to run most of them.

Waterproofing the packs is a must (see page 97). The whole group suffers if some poor soul has to climb into a soggy sleeping bag. Everyone should have at least one complete change of warm clothing. Some trips need a leader to check on these things.

Filming your trip

I receive many requests for advice on filming canoe trips or expeditions. Usually, the would-be filmmaker wants to film the trip in order to make enough money to pay for it. The members express great enthusiasm for take one, less for take two, and rebellion sets in on take three. This sort of approach usually results in no film, a spoiled trip and disgruntled canoeists. My advice is to forget it. If the purpose of the expedition is to make a film, that's different. Film is a demanding medium and requires the total cooperation and dedication of all the expedition members. When I was filming my *Path of the Paddle* series, I would run the same rapids as many as ten times so the cameraman could catch the different angles. We would arrive at a key location and wait for the weather to clear, even if it took three or four days. Shooting videos requires a similar degree of dedication; without it you end up with a mediocre video. Still photography is a better bet for group trips (see page 92).

Family canoe camping

North of Lake Huron's Georgian Bay there lies a range of bald, rocky hills of pure white rock. Lakes of crystal-clear blue water nestle in the deep valley between the hills. It is magnificent country for families or novice canoeists. The rivers are small and meandering. Although portages are necessary, they are not excessively long or rugged. The lakes are not too large and afford excellent campsites, with beautiful little beaches.

It was for these reasons that my wife, Joyce, and I selected Ontario's Killarney region for our year-old son's first long canoe trip. We knew from our previous trips with Paul that we would have no difficulty keeping him still in a canoe as long as he was able to reach the water with one hand. The fascination of watching the cool water trickle through his fingers, or the bubbles form in the wake of his miniature paddle, kept him happy by the hour.

We slid our canoe into the water on George Lake at the government campground, loaded in the packs, put Paul into position encased in his life jacket and pushed off. At the end of the lake we landed, hoisted the packs on our shoulders and headed over the portage trail. I went ahead with my packs, set them down at the end of the portage and returned for the canoe. I met Joyce and Paul halfway. They were meandering along, Paul dragging his paddle and picking blueberries. Often he employed the paddle as a shovel to unearth something of particular interest. At the end of the portage his worldly goods included pine cones, pebbles, bits of moss and fungi, all of which were proudly displayed and commented upon.

There was a different feeling after the portage. We were in a world that had remained unchanged for thousands of years; its treasures were ours to search out and enjoy. Before us lay a winding river, beaver dams and a wide swamp. We had been told that beyond the swamp lay a portage that led to an alpine lake nestled among high cliffs. When we finally reached it, we knew we had hit the jackpot. White rock escarpments towered above the water's edge and folded back into treeless ridges where one could wander at will.

For our campsite we chose a low, rocky point with a white, sandy beach. There was a lot to be done in preparation for a chilly night and we set about making a comfortable home. I used to cut tent poles in the bush but, with the increased use of the wilderness, this is no longer appropriate. Now I carry them with me. Joyce cleared roots from a small area and gathered sticks for the fire. Paul, who constantly tripped and fell on the uneven ground, helped. We constructed a fireplace of rocks, put the supper on to cook and erected the tent just as the sun started to meet the top of the hills above us. After supper, we popped Paul into his sleeping bag, and sat for a long time in a silence broken only by the crackling of the fire and the occasional wail of the loons.

Paul stirred with the first light and was raring to go. After a morning dip at our private beach, we decided to make this our base camp. In the ensuing days we walked the portages into the surrounding lakes, traversed the high rocky ridges and paddled the bays and inlets searching for their hidden beauty.

Paul collected twigs for the fire, pine cones, worms and frogs. He took on a blacker and blacker appearance because, whenever he tripped, his skin picked up the pine gum from the drippings on the ground, and then the dirt stuck to the gum. We agreed that it was clean dirt and he was none the worse for it. Strict boundaries for his play area were established, away from the fire and shoreline. It was an invisible line that he could not cross and, in all the time we were there, he never did.

Running an easy rapid, Blue Chute, French River, Ontario ───────

Family canoe camping . . .

Your child's first trip
Time and again parents tell me they can hardly wait until their kids are old enough so they can take up canoeing again. Then they ask how old a child should be before getting into a canoe. If I know the parents are skilled canoeists, I always say, "On the way home from the hospital should be just fine." (Of course, I would never suggest this to people who are still learning to handle a canoe.)

In cold-water conditions it's prudent to stay a couple of canoe lengths from shore. This is just common sense. Assume the worst and ask yourself if you could get the child to shore immediately in the event of an upset. If you are far from shore, do you have floatation in the canoe so you can right it and climb back in quickly? Experienced canoeists are very unlikely to upset on calm water, but an inexperienced paddler in the bow or stern constitutes a risk. I would never have taken my children in a canoe with an inexperienced paddler. Our children were on their first real canoe trip at about a year and a half. Paul was an ideal passenger, and Becky was like a jack-in-the-box. Your knowledge and skill as a canoeist and camper are the decisive factors in judging how old a child should be before riding in a canoe.

Preparing for a family trip
The most important thing about family camping is to make sure everybody has a good time so they will want to go again. Otherwise, you will end up camping by yourself. Children will like canoeing and camping if you do, and if you introduce them to it at an early age. Children are perceptive: if you take them camping for their benefit, or as a duty, they will know it.

You and your children will enjoy yourselves most if you pick your trip and plan the distance to cover that's right for you. No one can tell you what that distance is and it will probably take some experimentation to discover it. The distance you can travel with young children is limited. Plan your route so the portages are short. Many wives, husbands and children have been dragged out over the years on "death march" endurance trips by well-meaning spouses, parents or counsellors. They never heard the song, and sadly, probably never will.

It's important to involve children in the preparations for the trip. On the trip, they must feel needed or they will become bored. Involve them in the cooking, gathering wood, finding rocks for the fireplace, rolling out their sleeping bags and other camp chores. When you start your trip, keep the time in the canoe short. Make the children comfortable; if they are very young, the motion will almost certainly put them to sleep.

When we are on a holiday, we get up when we feel like it, eat when hungry and sleep when tired. When it's rainy, we enjoy the scenery from the door of our tent, a cheery camp fire in front of us and the teapot warming beside it. It's a mistake to set a rigid schedule that doesn't allow time for swimming, or for collecting pebbles, leaves and other important items. Stop early in the day so that you can set up camp at a leisurely pace. On many of our best trips with the children we retraced some of my old trips, because I knew where all the best camp spots were. I would try to camp on a sandy or shallow beach because time in the water is always a highlight of any trip. We never believed in a schedule according to which we had to travel every day. It was being outdoors that mattered, not the destination.

Clothing
Your children's clothing, rain gear and footwear should be as good as your own. I've seen people decked out in the latest rain gear whose kids were draped in plastic sheets. If children are inactive — for example, when sitting in the middle of the canoe — they will need to be dressed more warmly than someone who is paddling. If you are wearing pile or wool on a cold, rainy day, they should be wearing the equivalent.

Avoiding sunburns, bug bites and scary things
Overexposure to the sun can be very serious. If the children don't have a tan before you leave, expose them gradually. Remember that half the burn will come from the reflection of the sun on the water.

There were a few trips on which the black flies and mosquitoes were merciless, but we all survived. We didn't camp in late May or early June when the bugs are at their worst. We never used bug repellent on our children's skin; just a little on their clothes. Bugs were never much of a problem in the canoe, and we could get relief from them inside the tent.

If you or your spouse has a fear of lightning, snakes, spiders, wind or waves, never let your children see it, or you will pass it on. Whenever we saw lightning, we oohed and aahed as though we were watching fireworks. The kids joined in and loved it. Obviously, we made sure we weren't standing on an exposed point or under the tallest tree in the vicinity. Our favorite saying when we saw an insect of any kind in our tent was, "Never mind, it won't eat much." Then we would gently remove it from the tent. Fear of animals, insects and snakes is simply unnecessary. If you are apprehensive about waves, don't make a big deal about it; just get off the lake and make camp.

Starting them early

Fun things to do

It helps if your tent is big enough to allow room for play on rainy days and evenings. With our Campfire tent, Joyce and I could read and sip tea in front of the fire under the protection of the canopy, while the kids played in the tent. Here is a short list of suggestions for keeping children amused:

- Carry paper, pencils and crayons.
- Draw or arrange pebbles or stick patterns in the sand.
- Carry Plasticine. On rainy days, Joyce would set Paul, Becky and me up in a corner of the tent with a box of colored Plasticine, and she wouldn't hear a peep out of us for hours.
- Carve canoes out of wood.
- Introduce children to field glasses for studying birds, animals and the landscape.
- Becky enjoyed saddling up a crook in a tree as a horse. We always made sure she fed and watered it.
- Build sand castles.
- Make a bow and some arrows.
- And finally, there are very few children who don't enjoy fishing.

Family canoe camping, Georgian Bay, Ontario

Collecting frogs

A play horse

9

Guided trips

There was a time when I believed that the wilderness adventure should be limited to those who were willing to take the time and effort to acquire the necessary skills and proper equipment. Now I'm not so sure. I have met people who have been on guided northern trips, on the Nahanni River in the Northwest Territories for example, listened to their enthusiastic descriptions and seen the delight and joy that it brought to their lives. Professional guides can bring wild places within reach of people who would never otherwise experience them.

I had a friend who had canoed on short trips of her own for many years. At the age of 60 she took her first guided trip (to the Arctic), and for years after took a guided wilderness trip every summer. She canoed down the Coppermine, Nahanni, Dumoine and many other rivers. Her enthusiasm for the land and joy in whitewater never diminished.

You can employ a commercial outfitter in varying capacities. Some canoeists leave everything except personal clothing to the outfitter. Others hire the outfitter for one or two jobs: to rent canoes, for example, or to make charter flight arrangements. The most common situation is one in which the individual or group selects a trip from an outfitter's brochure. Some people hesitate to join a trip on their own for fear of getting into an incompatible group. I have talked to my son and other guides about this and, to my surprise, have been told that it rarely happens. There seems to be something about wilderness living that brings people together.

The professional guide or experienced friend who knows the river

Running a river for the first time is always exciting. Every bend is a surprise. But if you can't see the flat water or a shore eddy before the river disappears around a corner, you have to land and scout the shoreline. There is no way to know if the rapids end in a falls. If you have detailed trip notes, you *might* be willing to trust them. However, notes can be inaccurate; your reading of them might be mistaken, and rivers change dramatically as the water level rises and falls. I have carried excellent notes prepared by Parks Canada Wild Rivers Survey, yet on blind corners with our lives in jeopardy, I haven't been keen to trust them.

It's different running a river with a guide or friend who has been down it before. The guide not only knows what's around the corner, but also on which side of the river to run each set of rapids and where the escape eddies are. They also know what kind of water is downstream of any given rapids. For example, a difficult rapids can be run if it's followed by flat water which allows a recovery in case of an upset or swamping. If the rapids is followed by more rapids, it might be desirable to line the worst sections to assure a safe run. Without a guide or a friend who has been on the river before, you would have to scout downstream to the next flat section before attempting it, making progress much slower.

Some people prefer to have a guide not only for safety, but also to allow more time to enjoy side trips or leisure activities. One of the few rivers where I had the luxury of a professional guide was on the Little Nahanni in the Northwest Territories. It was reassuring to follow my guide into some of the biggest high volume rapids I had ever seen. There were a couple of canyons where there was no turning back. It gives an added feeling of security to know that someone has an overall picture of the river.

Short takeoff bushplane ——————

Guides learn rescue procedures ——————

The one that got away, Little Nahanni, NWT

A rain squall sweeps across the landscape along the headwaters of the Mountain River, NWT

The warm glow of an arctic evening bathes Second Canyon, Mountain River, in warm light

An A+ campsite faces the mouth of Second Canyon, Mountain River

Living outdoors on a family trip, Magnetawan River, Ontario

Over a leisurely lunch, the pros and cons of running the last stretch of rapids are debated, Hood River, NWT —————

◀ A kite soars above our island campsite, headwaters of the Mountain River

The ominous maw of First Canyon looms beyond our campsite, Mountain River ————

Camping above a falls on the Hood River

The second drop of Wilberforce Falls plunges into the depths of the canyon

We pass the point of no return as the downstream run through Wilberforce Canyon begins ⸺

Paul and Becky run their first rapids, Blue Chute, French River, Ontario

A floatation-equipped canoe ventures where open canoes were never meant to go, Black Chute, Ottawa River, Ontario

◀ **Canoeing the line between the onshore surf and waves breaking over a shoal, west coast, Vancouver Island, B.C.**

The end of the portage around a falls that remains nameless on our map, Hood River ─────────────

◄ **The apprehension of entering Second Canyon turns into exhilaration, Mountain River**

A guide describes what's around the bend, Little Nahanni River ————————————————

Guided trips. . .

In addition to ensuring an enjoyable experience, a professional accepts responsibility for getting his or her clients to the destination safely. You have to give up a certain amount of freedom, once you place this responsibility in the hands of the guide, since the abilities of the entire group determine how things are done. For example, although you may be longing to paddle on the outside of the islands instead of the lee, you might have to stay in the lee for the sake of the group. It helps if everyone possesses about the same skills, as the group has to travel at the pace of the slowest or least experienced person. If there is only one inexperienced paddler, compensation can be made by teaming him or her with the guide.

In my early years, the only guides available were hunting and fishing guides who operated out of lodges. They were exceptionally skilled at running rapids but mostly in motor boats. The hunting and fishing guides are still out there, but the new breed of whitewater canoe guide is usually young and highly skilled in handling canoes. We usually think of guides as being male, but over the past several years the proportion of women to men guides has been steadily increasing. If you are putting together an all-women trip, this is something you might want to keep in mind.

The skill, knowledge and experience of a guide can vary, so it is important to know who you are getting. Good outfitters will be happy to list the qualifications of their guides. Canoeing guides should have appropriate certification in life saving, river rescue, CPR, first aid and white water paddling. The prerequisites can vary from place to place depending on the regional organization. Some of the questions to ask about your guide are: How familiar is he or she with the river to be travelled? Does the organization have annual staff training courses? What other leadership courses has the guide taken? (Courses in crisis management, rescue techniques and group management may all be useful.) And what is his or her experience in the sport?

To run Class 3 rapids safely requires considerable training, even with a guide. Many commercial guiding companies offer pre-trip training sessions ranging from beginning to advanced whitewater. Even if you are a moderately proficient paddler, taking a whitewater course enables the guide to assess your level of skill.

My son, Paul, has been guiding wilderness canoe trips for many years with Black Feather Wilderness Adventures. He has had several experiences that illustrate the necessity of assessing a person's skill level for a wilderness trip. I'll let him describe one:

I was organizing a trip on a northern river which had Class 2, 3 and 4 rapids. We were using spray covers, although I had no intention of running Class 4 rapids. We were checking the skill level of the participants. There was only one person whom we couldn't assess, since he had come from the mid-West, but he had listed some week-long trips that included Class 2 rapids. We allow for some pre-trip instruction at the start of the trip, so that seemed fine. After loading up the canoes, we proceeded to wallow down a 5 ft. (1.5 m) stream that carried us 300 ft. (91 m) to a lake, the headwaters of our trip. My partner, the fellow from the mid-West, grasped his paddle with two hands in the center, and frantically splashed his way down the little stream, narrowly maneuvering through the willow branches and 3 to 4 in. (7 to 10 cm) high waves. I managed to do a few strokes while staring in amazement and disbelief.

When we came to the lake, he noticed my silence and asked, "How was that?" and, in the same breath, "Does it get any harder?" I casually answered, "Yes, it does get a little harder," all the while picturing the back ferry in 3 to 4 ft. (1 to 1.2 m) waves above a substantial hole in canyon number two. I suggested that perhaps we could take a little time to practice. To his credit, he was one of the fastest learners I've taught, and we had a great trip. After such a positive experience, it's hard to turn someone away because of a lack of skill. Perceived risk makes the trip exciting

for the client. Actual risk is what the guide should be able to assess and, of course, it should be very low.

Paul's story had a happy ending, but if there had been several clients who had overestimated their skill, they could have been in trouble. On one or two weekend clinics you can learn basic skills which can enhance your enjoyment of a trip. It's more difficult to learn as you go because the beginning of any whitewater trip is always the most difficult. The canoes are heavily loaded, the river is studded with rocks and everybody is a bit rusty in their skills.

I have little enthusiasm for the type of trip in which the clients allow the guide to act as a servant. Most professional guides find that it's easier to do the work themselves than to cajole people into doing chores. However, they usually welcome assistance: it gives them more time to do the little extras that enhance the trip for everyone. And for the members of the group, there is satisfaction in sharing the responsibility of cooking, washing up and leaving a spotless campsite. On a wilderness trip, anyone who sits back and allows the guide to do all the work is not getting his or her money's worth.

Voyageur canoes

In 1963, I became involved in a film called *The Voyageurs*, produced by the National Film Board of Canada. It was great fun dressing up as a voyageur and imagining myself as a part of that era. I was one of the paddlers, as well as second cameraman. That film was on the leading edge of a great explosion of interest in the big voyageur canoes, and it is now possible to go on a guided trip in one.

It doesn't take much experience to enjoy paddling amidship in a voyageur canoe, as long as a skilled paddler is in the bow and stern. Ralph Frese of Chicagoland Canoe Base Inc. has been making replicas of voyageur canoes, and staging pageants of voyageur days in Chicago, for many years. His canoes are made of fiberglass, but you would never know it because of the finishing. He puts cedar planking and ribs inside the canoes, and lashes the gunwales to the hull. Glenn Fallis of the Voyageur Canoe Company Ltd. in Millbrook, Ontario, not only makes voyageur canoes, but also trains skilled paddlers for paddling these canoes in whitewater. In western Canada, Neil Hartling of Nahanni River Adventures in Edmonton, Alberta, has pioneered the use of the voyageur canoe for trips down the canyons of the Nahanni. He has overcome the difficulty of transporting them, by designing and making them to be taken apart for stowing inside an aircraft. For their maiden voyage, Neil and his guides did a journey up the Nahanni River to Virginia Falls, a truly amazing feat against the 8 to 10 mph (12 to 16 km/hr) current.

Portaging the take-apart Voyageur canoe, Nahanni River, NWT ——————————

Voyageur canoe, Virginia Falls, NWT ——————

2 CAMPSITES

Many of my most memorable campsites were established on perches beside a spectacular waterfall, canyon or some other fascinating landform. Some of my best photographs and paintings were accomplished from the door of my tent in such places. It is ironic that the very publicizing of these magnificent scenes has led to increased traffic and even crowding, making camping beside them undesirable. When travelling a wilderness river, it is proper etiquette to choose a campsite that does not spoil the view of a spectacular scene for your fellow travellers.

I would love to set up my tent on the brink of Virginia Falls on the Nahanni River, but I'm ten years too late. Virginia Falls has become the most popular viewpoint in Canada and once you've seen it, you will understand why. By contrast, Wilberforce Falls on the Hood River in the Northwest Territories, while just as spectacular as Virginia Falls, will never be crowded. The remoteness of the location, the inclement weather, the difficult terrain and, worst of all, the mosquitoes, put it beyond the reach of all but a few dedicated wilderness enthusiasts. We enjoyed the luxury of camping right on the brink of Wilberforce Falls. It was the coldest, the soggiest, the most windswept campsite I have ever endured, but it was worth it. The mosquitoes and weather are the guardians of this incredible scene, and I hope it stays that way. The earth is being overrun by mankind and his machines. There will always be a need for quiet places that can only be reached by physical effort, skill and endurance.

Choosing a campsite

My idea of an A+ campsite is a flat spot on a rock close to the water's edge with a scenic view. It has a sharp drop-off for swimming and towering pines—as long as they are neither dead nor the tallest in the area. I'm not afraid of lightning, but you won't catch me standing on the highest hill, under the tallest tree or out on the lake in a thunderstorm. In summer, a windy point to catch the cooling breezes and avoid the bugs is ideal. In cold weather, the lee of a hill or trees makes a snug campsite. Finally, the perfect campsite has an unlimited supply of firewood and water you can drink right from the lake or river.

When you travel in a park or on a well-travelled route, you will find all the best campsites already established. Cutting and clearing new ones is illegal in parks and not recommended on most rivers. On seldom-travelled wilderness rivers, you have to create your own campsite and leave it as undisturbed as possible.

Location of tent

Because of the comfort of sleeping pads, I like camping on flat rock. Pitching the tent on a layer of moss is nice, but moss is fragile. Nor do I believe in digging up moss from other areas to put under the tent. Cutting bough beds is also a thing of the past. With the increasing number of people, the ever-decreasing wilderness can't tolerate these abuses anymore. The less you disturb the land, the better.

Location of camp fire

Rock is the safest place for the camp fire. A fire should never be kindled on mossy or organic soil. The fire can work its way underground and spring up again hours, or even days, after being doused. If there is no rock or sandy soil near the tent, I cook down at the water's edge. If there is no safe place for the fire, it is necessary to do without. It isn't worth the risk of starting a forest fire. Strong on-shore winds can cause problems with sparks, but sometimes the wind will die down around sunset.

It is always frustrating to come upon a campsite where someone has thrown all the available boulders into the lake. Some no-trace camping enthusiasts have been known to do this because the rocks were blackened by the camp fire. This is carrying the no-trace camping concept to a ridiculous extreme. There is nothing objectionable about a previously-used camp fire spot as long as it is spotlessly clean.

No-trace camping

The proper disposal of human waste is an important aspect of outdoor living—even more important than garbage disposal and the proper use of camp fires. On the well-travelled routes in many parks, simple but adequate toilets are provided. Sometimes it takes a little effort to find them. They consist of a box with a hinged lid. For privacy the lid opens away from the direction of the path. The box is superior to the outhouse because it does not require cleaning and maintenance as the outhouse does. Incredibly, some people are reluctant to use these boxes, probably because they are weather-beaten. They prefer to leave their contribution on the ground, often in sight of the tent area. There is nothing that does more violence to a wilderness campsite. A pristine waterway can be turned into a dump overnight by one group of inexperienced or thoughtless campers.

Last summer we were canoeing the Petawawa River that flows out of the northern part of Algonquin Park in Ontario. When we arrived at one of my favorite campsites on a beautiful little island, we were confronted by the sight of 26 individual dumps, and toilet paper blowing everywhere. The island is predominantly Precambrian rock, so the cleanup took an hour and a half. It took much longer for the rage to subside. The toilet provided by the park was opposite the campsite on the mainland. Unfortunately, the Parks Department will probably have to post no-camping signs on this lovely island.

Where no toilets are provided, opinion varies in regard to toilet facilities for a group; that is, more than two. Some people feel everyone should take responsibility for digging and covering their own toilet. Others believe it's better to make one toilet for the group. Equipping each person with a small trowel encourages them to dig a proper hole. For an individual, the hole should be about 6 in. (15 cm) deep. If you go for the group toilet, the size depends on how big the group is and how long the stay. Sprinkling pine needles or ashes over the excrement seems to work well for the duration of your visit. If the hole is dug between two trees, a log can be tied between them to sit on. Don't forget to reclaim your rope and fill in the hole before leaving.

Toilets should be located well away from the campsite and water. Much of the terrain that canoeists enjoy is poor in topsoil, so runoff flushes waste into the water before it decomposes. Beaver have been blamed for outbreaks of giardiasis, a debilitating sickness that is becoming common, but human waste in the water supply could also be the cause.

Washing dishes in a lake or stream should also be avoided. Your small contribution of soap and waste might seem insignificant, but it all adds up. The dishwater should be discarded well away from the shore. The same applies to bathing. Soap up with biodegradable soap and pour a pail of water over yourself, away from shore, before diving into the lake.

A few years ago, we were camping above the tree line in the Monashees, in the British Columbia interior, with my friend and guide Neil Hartling. When it came time to answer nature's call, I grabbed the toilet paper and headed for the door. Neil looked up and handed me the matches. He could tell by my expression that I was puzzled. ''It's to burn the paper,'' he said. ''Before, during or after?'' I replied. He laughed and told me of the designated area for the toilet. If you can't bury it, the toilet paper should be burned after use.

In winter, it's tough to dig a hole. It might be possible to dent the ground a little with the back side of the axe, or scuff up enough soil for a light covering before you leave. There are some places, such as the Grand Canyon, where the traffic is so heavy and the terrain so rocky that human waste has to be carried out. This is the final reality we face with the hordes of people who are descending on wild places.

For a while we are the only visitors, Mountain River, NWT

3 TENTS   Roughing it

As I see it, camping can be divided into three basic categories: (1) roughing it or camping without a tent; (2) camping with a small, lightweight tent, usually of nylon; (3) camping in a tent that is high enough to stand in. There is one other category, but it's not the subject of this book. I'm referring to camping in car tents, tent trailers and mobile homes. I've done more than my share of this, mostly in the back of a Land Rover while on film trips; it's simply an alternative to staying in motels or hotels.

Camping without a tent is only fun in idyllic weather. When it's raining or the bugs are bad, it can definitely be classified as adversity. Many people dislike camping because they have had bad experiences while roughing it. Nowadays, very few people rough it by choice. Generally, only those who are lost, the survivors of plane crashes, or the victims of other unforeseen circumstances set out without tents.

In 1966, I was filming wolves on Baffin Island. We were crossing a range of hills to a valley where a wolf den had been sighted the year before by Dr. Douglas Pimlott, a wildlife biologist. I was travelling with a young student biologist, Pascal Grenier. We were carrying only our sleeping bags, a small amount of food and camera gear, because there was a cache with a tent, food and fuel at our destination beside a lake. The question was, which lake? There was a whole chain of lakes and we couldn't find the right one.

It was early June, the worst time of year for travelling in the far north. In the depressions between the hills, the snow was strong enough to support us for about nine out of ten steps. On that tenth step we would break through the crust and be in snow up to our hips. The packs made it very difficult to climb back onto the surface. We couldn't follow the rocky, snow-free ridges because our direction of travel was at right angles to them. We were soaking wet from perspiration when moving, and chilled by intermittent rain when we stopped to rest or eat. I wasn't wearing wool under my raincoat and hadn't yet heard of polypropylene. To avoid hypothermia we knew we had to eat often, in order to keep our core temperature up. We were only warm when travelling.

Finally, we were forced to camp, but the only flat spots on that rugged terrain were clay boils. They looked inviting. When we walked on them they were as hard as concrete, but when we jumped on them, they turned into quagmires. There was no alternative, however, so choosing a boil about 6 ft. (2 m) in diameter, we placed our sleeping bags on groundsheets, crawled in, and pulled the corners of the groundsheets over us. We were very tired and fell asleep quickly.

In the middle of the night, I was suddenly wakened by a knife-like cold. After a moment, I realized that I was not only freezing, but also soaking wet. Pascal woke up at the same time. We leaped up to find that we had sunk almost a foot (30 cm) into the clay boil. Once the groundsheets had sunk low enough, the water in the clay had poured in, turning our improvised beds into baths of ice-cold water.

We grabbed our gear and headed off. It was about 3:00 AM, but there is no darkness at that time of year in the far north. Although we were cold and miserable to begin with, once again the effort of walking generated body heat and we were soon warm. We searched the shores of lake after lake, looking for the cache. We ate as we travelled. All the creeks were full of meltwater and there was no choice but to wade across them. Some were too deep to cross safely where we found them, and we had to travel upstream until they were smaller. The water was so cold, it numbed and almost paralyzed our legs. Fortunately the air temperature hovered just above freezing. If it had dropped below, we would have been in serious trouble.

We finally found the cache but, as we approached it, we saw to our horror that it had been broken into by wolves. Empty dehydrated food packages, clothing and camping gear were strewn all over the place. To our relief, the tent was undamaged. We hastily put it up and set up the stove. It was a Yukon stove, capable of burning any fuel, but we only had stove oil. But where was the hose? The stove was useless without it. In that whole sodden landscape there was not one scrap of anything that would burn. The Inuit would have used seal oil. We searched the remnants of the cache, then widened our search outward. We finally found the hose — or what was left of it. The wolves had chewed it up; there wasn't a piece longer than 2 in. (5 cm). By feeding the fuel directly onto the burner a teaspoonful at a time, we were finally able to boil water for tea.

That was adversity in the extreme. The experience left me with some fine film footage of wolves, and a lasting friendship. If you're going to walk a thin edge, the ideal companion is someone like Pascal Grenier. It wasn't fun at the time, but I don't regret the experience and I'm sure Pascal doesn't either.

Most camping books explain in detail how to rig a shelter with a tarp over a canoe, but even when backpacking there is no reason to be without a tent. There are tents on the market that weigh no more than a tarp.

Roughing it without a tent

Modern free-standing tent, Georgian Bay

Living outdoors in a Campfire tent, Lake Superior

17

Light tents for hiking and canoeing

New materials and designs have resulted in some very practical and comfortable tents in recent years. Small, external-frame, freestanding tents are the most popular. There is, however, no such thing as a tent that is ideal for all types of camping. Different tents are designed for different purposes. Generally the more comfortable the tent, the heavier it is, so everything is a compromise.

Material

A tent should keep you dry from the outside and dry from the inside. A completely waterproof tent would keep out the water, but would also keep in the moisture from your body. This would condense on the relatively cooler roof and run down to form puddles on the floor. The air inside the tent would also be damp and clammy. So the ideal tent material sheds the rain and still allows moisture to escape through the walls. A light cotton with a high

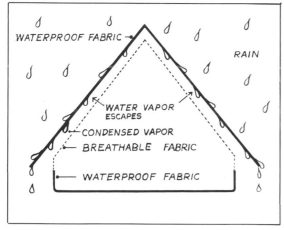

Breathable tent material

thread count, such as Egyptian cotton (sailcloth) or poplin, and uncoated ripstop nylon nearly meet these criteria. They breathe well when dry, but they all lose this property to some degree when wet. Another slight defect of these materials becomes apparent when it's raining very hard: a fine spray of water may penetrate uncoated material. If anything touches or rubs against the roof or walls, the

material becomes saturated, and droplets form on the inside. Fabric manufacturers have spent fortunes trying to invent a material that solves all these problems. It's unlikely that they ever will.

Most tent manufacturers solve the condensation problem by using two materials. The tent material is porous in order to allow water vapor to escape. It condenses on the underside of a waterproof, coated nylon fly and runs down onto the ground outside the tent. The fly also keeps rain from coming in contact with the inner walls of the tent, so you remain dry regardless of the weather. The tent floor is made of coated or treated material that extends 8 in. (20 cm) or more up the sides to form a shallow bathtub. The upper sidewalls are often uncoated or panelled with no-see-um netting.

In cold weather, if you use a gas stove for heat, the warm air that escapes through the walls and open vent of your tent will carry moisture away with it. However, operating a gas stove inside a tent is dangerous, because of the possibility of carbon monoxide poisoning. Unfortunately, the problem is not necessarily solved by building an open fire near the tent. One of the salient features of many synthetic materials is that they melt if a spark touches them.

Size

A tent should be comfortable. You should be able to sit up even in a backpacking tent. For canoeing trips, when weight is less of a problem, a tent that you can stand up in is desirable. A so-called two-person tent, 4½ by 7 ft. (1.3 by 2.1 m), is usually fine for a solo trip or a weekend for two. On an extended trip a so-called four-person tent, 7 by 8 ft. (2.1 by 2.4 m), is ideal for two, leaving room for a couple of packs and the dispersal of damp clothing.

Design

The design of a tent can make the difference between a comfortable camping trip and an uncomfortable one. Here's what to look for in

a light tent.

The fly sheet should not touch the sides and ends of your inner tent and should extend far enough over the door to prevent rain from entering. A tent that must have the door closed in a rainstorm is a hovel. If the fly sheet is extra big, you can leave your packs, shoes and damp clothing under it to keep them from getting any wetter. Some manufacturers provide a floorless vestibule for this purpose and for cooking over a stove.

Netting is an absolute must. Fine mesh netting keeps out the sand flies; at night they can be the most miserable of all flies, making sleep impossible. Netting, unfortunately, may interfere with the view and tends to keep out fresh air as well as insects; however, almost all tents now have no-see-um netting.

For a free passage of air, it's essential to have a full-size door in one end of the tent and a large window in the other. This also makes it possible to enjoy the view in both directions. This is very important to me. I don't live outdoors to stare at four canvas or nylon walls. If the rain is sweeping across the landscape and the surf is crashing onto the rocky shore, I want to see it.

Dome tents, while more roomy and aerodynamically superior for withstanding high winds, generally provide only a limited view. The A-frame design, when equipped with a large door and window in the ends, or preferably a door in each end, is better for viewing and for ventilation. An advantage of the two-door tent is that, in the event of a !**!! zipper jamming or refusing to stay closed, you can seal the offending door with duct tape and use the other.

The two-door tent is also handy for wildlife photography: you can stick your lens out one door and come and go through the other without your subject seeing you. When I was making my series of films on wolves, I pitched my tent high on the brow of a hill, so the wolves couldn't see me enter or leave. Although the tent was in full view, they came to accept it, and fed on my bait without too much concern.

Breathable inner part of tent, Mountain River —————————

Waterproof outer fly —————————

Dome tent and low-profile wind-resistant tent, tributary Mountain River —————————

Light tents. . .

Freestanding tents

Self-supporting tents have become very popular. You can move them or turn them around with ease if the wind changes or if you want to change the view. Also, you can houseclean by lifting them up and shaking sand and leaves out the door! These tents have an exterior, light tubular metal or fiberglass frame. No pegs or guy ropes are necessary except to keep the tent from blowing away in strong winds. However, if you erect the tent and put it down with nothing in it, even a moderate wind can blow it away.

One of the funniest and saddest stories I've ever heard was about a fellow who was canoeing the Fildegrand in spring flood. The Fildegrand is a wild little river in Quebec that flows into the better-known Dumoine River. He was setting up camp above one of its many falls. After erecting his brand-new, freestanding dome tent, he put it down exactly where he wanted it and then turned to reach for his pack. The wind picked up the tent, bounced it over the rocks and into the river above the falls. It hung there for a moment in the current, then disappeared over the brink and was seen no more.

Pegs

Tent pegs come in a great variety of designs and materials. All tend to bend, break or shatter. Without doubt, the peg most useful in everything from sand to scree is a 12 in. (30 cm) galvanized spiral spike. It's even usable on rock—it can be forced into a crack. It's also long enough to be held firmly by rocks or logs on a guy rope. The only drawback is weight, but for many modern tents, only two to four spikes are needed either to hold them down or pull out sidewalls. The spikes are stored by dropping each one into a section of tent pole. This way, only the head is exposed and the tent cloth and bag are protected from the point.

Campfire tent

There is a world of difference between camping and living outdoors. By living outdoors I mean sleeping, cooking, eating, reading, sketching, relaxing, chatting and looking at the scenery, all from under the protection of my tent. When I am filming, writing or painting, I spend a lot of time sitting in camp. On filming trips I've sat for as long as eight or nine days waiting for the sun. So a tent that is comfortable in any weather is essential to me.

A comfortable tent is a tent that you can stand up in, and walk into and out of freely. It's a tent that will shelter you while cooking over an open fire, regardless of weather, and from which you have a full view of the scenery at all times. It also gives complete protection from bugs. Camping in such a tent is the very opposite of roughing it.

The origins of my Campfire tent go back a long way. A few years ago, someone at Woods Bag and Canvas Ltd., one of Canada's earliest tentmakers, dug through their files and found their 1909 catalog. Some of the items shown are wonderful. If the Herders' tent, for example, doesn't make you long for the good old days, its price certainly will. A 7½ ft. (2.2 m) square tent cost $10.50! The bad news was that the poles cost $2 extra, but that included pegs. The information I enjoyed the most was the maximum width. They made an $80 tent for logging crews that was 50 ft. (15.2 m) wide.

I first saw something like the Campfire tent in Calvin Rutstrum's book, *The Way of the Wilderness*, later published as *The New Way of the Wilderness*. This book became my camping bible, and Rutstrum was my hero. I devoured everything he wrote and lived many of his wilderness journeys vicariously through his books. Rutstrum called his tent the All-Weather tent or Reflector tent. He took the basic Shed tent and made a few changes. Like most tents in those days, his did not have a floor. It had what was called a "sod cloth," a strip of material that was folded inside the tent around the base of the walls. Rutstrum added a ground cloth, which was laid over the sod cloth to keep out dirt, wind and insects. It

could easily be taken outside and cleaned, a necessary feature since it was customary in those days to wear your boots inside.

Since people first started building fires, they discovered that a piece of skin or bark rigged at an angle would reflect some of the heat. However, the rain could still blow in under the front or at the ends and there was no protection from biting insects. The most important modification that Rutstrum made to the Shed tent was the addition of two wings for protection from side winds and blowing rain. They also served to reflect the heat from the fire into the tent. This is what gave the tent its amazing versatility.

The Campfire tent is known by many other names. I've seen it referred to as the Baker, Lean-To, Reflector, Herders', Shed, and All-Weather tent. In 1962, I used the tent while acting as the canoeist in the film *Quetico*, which was made by Chris Chapman for the Quetico Foundation. It subsequently appeared in a tent catalog as the Quetico tent.

I've added a floor to the basic design, and a bug flap, plus a few other improvements. The result is called the Campfire tent because it is designed to have the fire in front of it. Cooking and eating are done under the protection of the canopy.

The Shed tent and Herders' tent from the 1909 Woods Bag and Canvas Ltd. catalogue

Today's Campfire tent

Campfire tent . . .

The Campfire tent is basically a lean-to with sides (photograph 1). The roof slopes at a 45° angle, the perfect angle for maximum reflection of heat. There is a low wall at the back to increase head room and sidewalls to keep heat in and rain out. Mosquito netting with ties on the sides can be pulled back when not needed. A 12 in. (30 cm) floor flap can be tied up to keep insects and dirt out. There are loops around the bottom of the tent for stakes, but I rarely use them as the sleeping bags and equipment are adequate to hold the tent down. The guy ropes are all that are needed. I often don't bother carrying poles for the canopy as there is always something lying around to hold it up without resorting to cutting green poles.

In clear weather, you can sit before the Campfire tent enjoying the warmth of your fire and the view in all directions except behind you. You seldom need to enter the tent area during the day unless it's to relax, read or escape the bugs. Shoes are removed to keep the floor clean. When you crawl into your bag at night, you can look up at the stars, northern lights or the moon rising behind the trees. After a hard day of paddling and portaging, I cherish these moments before dropping off to sleep.

The joking about my "circus tent" dies down after the first wet spell. If it rains during the night, all I have to do is pull the canopy out and tie it to two rocks which I have left conveniently in position for that purpose (photograph 2). It's not much of an inconvenience, but I know people who wouldn't get out of a warm sleeping bag if the world was coming to an end! If there is any possibility that it might rain, I extend the fly slanted down at the front, and fold the two wings over the packs, loose gear and the supply of dry firewood (photograph 6). This arrangement keeps everything dry in any normal rainfall. If the rain is accompanied by wind, I lower the canopy to within two feet (60 cm) of the ground. If it's raining in the morning, I rig a pole at each corner to raise the canopy (photograph 3). I am careful to leave one corner low enough so the water will drain off.

I build the fire just beyond the edge of the canopy, using my canoe as a backlog (see page 43). In certain wind conditions, the fire can be placed off to one side leaving one of the wings extended. A brisk fire can be kept going all day in the rain by leaving all the pots uncovered on the fire with water in them so they don't burn. This way the fire is protected from the rain and the rain adds more water to the pots. The fire's warmth radiates into the tent removing that damp, clammy feeling. Even wet clothes from the day before can be dried.

It's on such days that I may bake bread or a cake while reading, writing or sketching, all in complete comfort. I admit that I may be exaggerating the comfort a bit — rain rarely falls straight down! Rain driven by a strong wind tends to find its way under a canopy, making us wet no matter how we arrange it.

If the wind is coming from the right, the right wing can be pulled out and secured to the pole (photograph 4). When the wind comes from the left, the left wing is extended. If it's one of those gusty days, with the wind coming from all angles, both wings can be extended (photograph 5) and the corners weighted to form a cozy area 9 by 7 ft. (2.7 by 2.1 m) in which to sit and work. When I do have to batten down the hatches, it's a comfort to know that all I have to do in the morning is slide some dry kindling under the pots on the grate and light it, without even leaving the tent.

I have had to deal with hurricane-force winds on many occasions because of my affinity for high, windswept rocks, where I can survey the land around me from the front of my tent. I'm especially partial to the shores of Lake Superior which is notorious for its squalls and storms. To hold the tent down, I lower the canopy and cross over the wings (photograph 6). I secure the corners with large rocks and string guy ropes from the peak of the poles to take the strain off the tent.

The one time that I hesitated about taking the Campfire tent was on the Hood River trip (see page 83). The entire trip is far to the north of the tree line. Everyone said that my tent would be flattened or torn to shreds or blown away by the winds. However, I decided to take the Campfire, but with a small dome tent as a backup. As it turned out, we used the Campfire tent and, securely fastened, there wasn't anything in the way of winds that it couldn't handle. In 35 years of camping, my tent has been blown down only twice.

One of the things I particularly like about the Campfire tent is the ventilation. On hot, humid nights, you still feel the slightest breeze, because the largest side of the tent is all door. One friend had windows installed in the back of his Campfire tent for cross-ventilation. It seemed unnecessary to me, but a recent trip to the sun-baked islands of Georgian Bay convinced me it's a good idea. The windows can be zippered closed from inside.

Another great thing about the Campfire tent is the protection it gives from the sun. You extend the canopy and sit in the shade enjoying the gentle breezes off the lake. After a day in the sun, cooking and eating supper in the shade is a welcome relief.

Another test for a good tent is whether you can leave it completely open to get rid of the damp atmosphere that sets in after a day or so of rain. Can you hang up the sleeping bags and wet clothes under the protection of the tent, but in the breeze? Can you go off to sketch, film, write, fish or collect firewood with the full assurance that if it rains nothing will get wet? Yesterday, I left the canopy up and the whole front of the tent open with the sleeping bag hanging up to air in the door, along with some damp clothing. I went off for the day. It poured off-and-on all day. When I returned in the evening, everything was dry. I've seen tents that allow the water to drain off the roof and straight through the door into the tent when it's left open. Then there's the tent that has the door facing up. When you open the door to get in or out, the rain falls straight in. To be fair, the tent was designed this way to survive hurricane-force winds on mountain-tops. Since you rarely face these kinds of winds on a canoe trip, it makes sense to place

1 Tent only

2 Canopy extended, wings over packs

3 Canopy angled to shed rain, canoe as backlog

4 Canopy up, one wing out

5 Canopy up, both wings out

6 Battened down for storm

Campfire tent . . .

comfort before protection from hurricanes.

With a certain amount of effort and skill, the Campfire tent becomes a versatile and comfortable shelter for a wide range of weather conditions. If used badly, it can present problems. For example, if you don't secure the tent properly and a storm hits from the front, the whole tent can become a huge spinnaker, and you might find yourself setting sail for parts unknown. On the other hand, if you are sitting in one of those miserable little dog-houses in the pouring rain, and you see a guy basking in the heat of his fire in front of his Campfire, come on over and have a cup of tea. I've always got room for a couple more.

The Campfire tent is at its best where fuel is available for the open fire. For above the tree line, or on the tundra where wood is not readily available, it might not be the best choice, although I have used it in these conditions on several occasions. In the High Arctic or at high altitudes, I reluctantly move into a ground-hugging mountain tent.

When backpacking, I am as much a fanatic about going light as anybody. The design of some of these light, freestanding tents, and the technology employed in making them, is superb. While I'll use one for backpacking, you won't catch me with one when I'm travelling by canoe. The number of people I'm travelling with is also a factor to be taken into account. I once calculated that the weight of my four-person Campfire tent is about the same as two two-person tents of average weight, equipped with fly sheets and one lightweight tarp for the cooking fire. Small tents used to be known as "pup tents." Pup tents are best suited for just what the name suggests.

Campfire tents pitched side by side
Anyone who has done much camping with me has invariably ended up buying their own Campfire tent. However, it is not a great tent for large groups if yours is the only one. As soon as it starts to rain, everyone piles into it along with all their wet, soggy clothes. It isn't long before you can't even see the scenery

through the forest of clothes under the canopy. Two Campfire tents can be pitched side by side to provide a 14 × 7 ft. (4.2 × 2.1 m) cooking and eating area for six people. Given the right mix of companions, this is my personal choice. A word of warning though: snoring can be a problem; similarly, companions who dig endlessly in noisy plastic bags.

Material for the Campfire tent
I have had several Campfire tents over the years and have tried various materials. It is difficult to find Egyptian cotton with a weave that is tight enough to prevent leaking in a downpour. You also have to treat the tent to prevent mildew and to waterproof it. Waterproofing inhibits the breathability of a tent, but with the Campfire tent that's not important. I never close the door at the front completely, even when the temperature is below freezing, as I like fresh air and the view. If you cannot get the right materials, then you have to use a fly over the tent.

My first Campfire tent lasted 15 years before it started falling apart. It was often used for five or six months at a time. That's a lot of use! My next tent was also Egyptian cotton treated with waterproofing at the factory. It mildewed and sprayed me in a downpour until I treated it with Preservo. This tent is 9 ft. (2.7 m) wide and has been used on all our family and filming trips. After 25 years it is weakening, and this year I have resorted to using a fly.

Fifteen years ago I had a 6 ft. (2.1 m) Campfire tent made for solo trips. For this tent, Egyptian cotton treated for mildew and waterproofing at the factory was used, with nylon for the floor. One night on Lake Superior, a friend, Alan Whatmough, and I were hit by a gale. I didn't even wake up until Alan nudged me and said, "Mason! We're drowning. Wake up. There's water in here." I said, "No way! My tents never leak! It's not possible." Alan replied, "Well, if it's not water, I'd sure like to know what it is because I'm lying in six inches of it." I sat up and sure enough, there it was: a good six inches and the end of my bag was soaked. I was furious. A Campfire tent had

never let me down before. I grabbed my knife and stabbed ten or twelve holes in the floor to let the water out. I said, "Well, at least the floor was waterproof." When I got home, I decided to try a commercial brand of waterproofing, other than Preservo. It isn't bad, but it isn't foolproof. I now use a light fly over this tent.

Several years ago, I had a Campfire tent made in coated nylon as an experiment. I wanted to try cutting down on weight. It was a disaster. The coating began to peel off within a year and all the seams leaked like a sieve. I occasionally use it for winter camping because its silver surface reflects heat well. Otherwise it's a dud.

Much of this chapter deals with the Campfire tent and how to use it safely and efficiently. Although cotton is far superior to synthetics such as nylon for a tent that is designed to be used beside the open camp fire, it is flammable, particularly when treated with a mildew preservative and wax-base waterproofing. Those who legislate safety laws have to assume that people will make mistakes and set their tent ablaze if they pitch it near a camp fire. For this reason, commercially manufactured cotton tents must now be treated with a fire retardant and bear a label stating that the tent must be positioned several yards from an open fire.

Ironically, fireproof synthetics are even less suitable beside an open fire because they melt in intense heat. Cotton will withstand an amazing amount of heat without damage as long as it doesn't come into direct contact with an open flame. In 35 years of living in cotton Campfire tents, the number of burn holes I've seen wouldn't add up to the fingers on one hand. However, my synthetic nylon mosquito netting regularly suffers holes from wayward sparks. I patch the holes with duct tape and eventually replace the netting. Here is an example of how spark-resistant waterproofed cotton compares to synthetics. Look at the winter camping shot on page 35. To do a night shot like this I cheated a little! I picked a windless night and loaded newspapers on the fire. They burned very brightly and supplied

Two Campfire tents rigged for rain, Mountain River

Campfire tent . . .

sufficient light. After the photograph was taken, the whole mass of flaming newspapers rose in the upcurrent and drifted right into the tent. I batted at it in an attempt to propel it out of the tent, but instead it disintegrated into thousands of flaming fragments that scattered over the interior of the tent. I thought, ''There goes my tent. It's going to look like Swiss cheese.'' After I had extinguished the last spark, I examined the tent and found that there was not one burn hole; however, the mosquito netting material was full of holes and had to be replaced. The answer to the dangers of the cotton tent is to use it with skill and that's what this book is all about. Unfortunately, the government cannot legislate a level of skill, so they have outlawed flammable materials in favor of synthetic materials that melt.

I find this rather ironic because one of the greatest dangers facing mankind is the contamination of our environment from chemicals used in the manufacture of synthetics. There is sound evidence that synthetic chemicals are causing a hole in the ozone layer. It's not even safe to go out in the sun anymore. So what do they pick on? My natural fiber cotton Campfire tent! Legally anyone can make their own Campfire tent, but it creates a problem for commercial tent manufacturers. They may be held liable for any accidents that result from tents that are not of a fire retardent material. If you do purchase a synthetic Campfire tent, skillful use can prevent the meltdown syndrome. For example, the environmental fireplace (see page 45) is a great asset in avoiding problems from open fires. But then the Campfire tent is only for those who are willing to put some effort into learning the skills of outdoor living.

Dimensions
Although the Campfire tent can be made in any dimensions, the recommended height is 6 ft. (1.8 m) and the depth 7 ft. (2.1 m). The width depends on the number of people you intend to accommodate: one or two people, 6 ft. (1.8 m); two or three, 7 ft. (2.1 m); three or four, 9 ft. (2.7 m). The nine-foot tent can sleep five, although cooking and eating get a bit crowded when it's raining. For five or more people I would choose my Campfire tent for my companion and myself and let the rest use whatever they wanted. I suggest a tarp for cooking and eating. Without a large tarp, everyone will be jammed under the tent canopy when it rains.

Two Campfire tents side by side, Mountain River

Pitching the Campfire tent

If someone handed you a Campfire tent to put up for the first time, you would be in big trouble. Lying on the ground it looks like a rat's nest. Once you get the hang of it, though, you can put it up almost as fast as most freestanding tents. The tent is laid on the ground with the floor down.

1. Find the two back corner ropes (they are color-coded) and tie to trees or stakes. If to trees, don't tie higher than about a foot (30 cm) off the ground. Be careful to tie out at an angle. Place the ridge of the tent along the back wall of the tent.

2. Fit the lower end of the side poles through the loops at the corners of the door near the ground.

3. Tie the tent ridge corners to the poles where the upright joins the crossbar. Then tie the tent to the crossbar at three points.

4. Now, with assistance from someone on the opposite side, raise the tent and tie the guy ropes out from each side at an angle to a tree or stake or a pile of rocks. If your partner is busy or you are on a solo trip, tie the ends of the two ridge ropes to trees or rocks and tighten the ropes in stages with the slide tighteners until the tent is fully erect. If you just tie one rope at a time, you will bend the spikes on the tops of the poles. To lower, use the reverse procedure by loosening the slide tighteners.

5. Considerable adjustments are required to get the tent taut and square. One trick is to move the base of the poles around until the tent is square, then finally tighten all four ropes.

6. Pull the poles apart and the bug flap will tighten.

7. You can stake the lower back corners down if there is a wind, but I rarely do. This is all the tent you need in sunny weather. To raise the canopy, tie the ropes out to a tree or use the canopy poles with the rope tied down to a stake or rock.

8. On the Precambrian Shield, it is rare that you can drive tent pegs into the ground. I try to tie to trees or shrubs or ground plants. Most of the time I use large rocks. Always tie the rope to the rock with the Mason rock hitch (see page 39). The slide tighteners should be near the tent grommets, not at the tie-down end.

9. Never tie to a rock with one of those fancy tautline hitch knots that you tie at chest level so you don't have to bend down.

10. If the rock pivots, the rope will slip off and the tent will fall down.

11. Always back up the rock you have tied to with at least one other rock.

12. In hurricane-force winds, I tie extra ropes from the top of the ridge poles to anchor points behind the tent to take some of the strain off the back corner grommets.

All of my Campfire tents and those of my friends were made by Black's in Ottawa, but they don't make them anymore. You either have to make your own from the accompanying plan (see page 29) or order one specially made from a tent manufacturer. Several small tentmakers have shown some interest in the tent and have come up with prototypes. Horizons Unlimited, an outfitter in Saskatchewan, made my last tent. It is the small version (see page 31), but they also will make the standard size in 7 ft. (2.1 m) and 9 ft. (2.7 m) widths. The cost comes out at about twice the price of your average tent, which is understandable, because of the high cost of cotton and because they are not made on an assembly line. For information and prices, write to Horizons Unlimited, Box 1110, La Ronge, Saskatchewan, S0J 1L0.

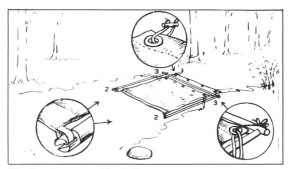

Tie back ropes first, then corners

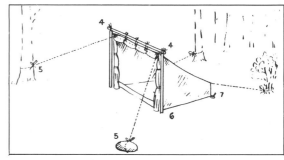

Erect and tie front ropes

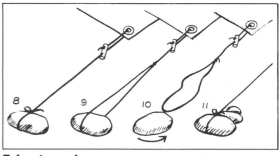

Tying to rock

Making a Campfire tent

Many people get a great sense of satisfaction out of making their own canoe, packs and tent. I enjoy patching them but I've never started from scratch. Although my first Campfire tent was retired years ago, I can't bear to part with it. Every five years I roll it out, look it over to see if it can be patched again, then roll it up for another five years.

I have friends who have made their own Campfire tents and are happy with them. You might find it fun to cut out a cardboard tent from the plans and rig it up and play with it to understand all the possibilities. Finding the material is the toughest part. To further complicate matters, there are many grades of Egyptian cotton and many kinds of water-proofing. You could use a synthetic material. Whatever your choice, experiment with a square of your proposed material before buying enough to do the tent.

Plans

Reinforcing in a Campfire tent is important because of the large surface area. Some people like the idea of sleeves for the ridge pole and side poles, but I've found them a bother; ties are faster and simpler to make. The tent plans are for a normal floor, but some people prefer the bathtub style of tent floor, in which the waterproof material comes up the sides about a foot (30 cm). The problem with mixing materials is that with synthetics the needle-holes leak; with cotton, the needle-holes swell and thus become waterproof. The different materials also expand and contract at different rates causing puckering.

The first step in making the tent is to prepare a full-size paper pattern from the plans. It's possible to make the tent on an ordinary sewing machine, but a double-needle machine is obviously better. Use linen thread. Allow extra material for the double seams. Note all the reinforcing points for strength. If you don't know how to make a strong, waterproof seam, you should consult an expert. The grommets can be installed by hand or you can have a tentmaker do it for you.

If you do make a Campfire tent, and it leaks, you will have to resort to using a fly over the roof. The lightest material possible should work just fine. Tie it down at several points or it will flap in the wind. Install extra grommets in it if necessary.

Half the fun of making your own Campfire tent is personalization and experimentation. Be careful, though; the plans shown here are well-proven and may save you some time and money.

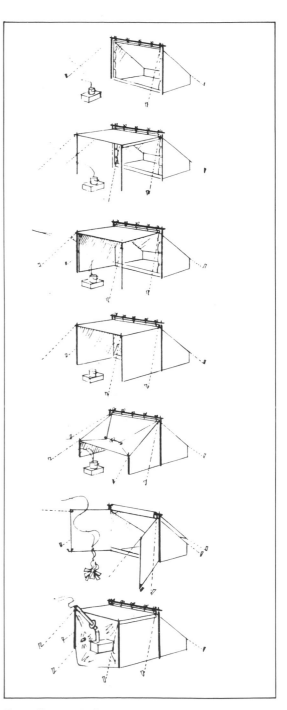

Campfire tent plans

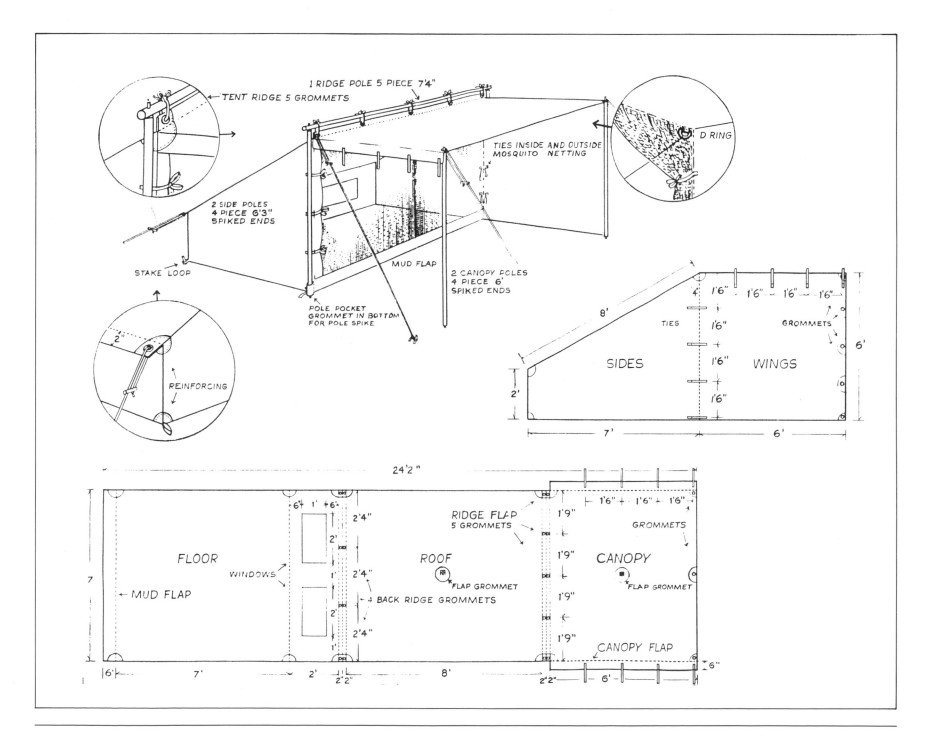

TENT RIDGE 5 GROMMETS

1 RIDGE POLE 5 PIECE 7'4"

TIES INSIDE AND OUTSIDE
MOSQUITO NETTING

D RING

2 SIDE POLES
4 PIECE 6'3"
SPIKED ENDS

STAKE LOOP

MUD FLAP

2 CANOPY POLES
4 PIECE 6'
SPIKED ENDS

POLE POCKET
GROMMET IN BOTTOM
FOR POLE SPIKE

REINFORCING

2"

SIDES   WINGS

8'   6'

TIES

1'6"   1'6"   1'6"   1'6"

1'6"

GROMMETS

1'6"

2'

1'6"

7'   6'

24'2"

FLOOR

WINDOWS

MUD FLAP

6' 1' 6'

2'4"

2'

2'4"

1'

2'

2'4"

1'

BACK RIDGE GROMMETS

RIDGE FLAP
5 GROMMETS

ROOF

FLAP GROMMET

1'9"

1'9"

1'9"

1'9"

CANOPY

GROMMETS

1'6" 1'6" 1'6"

FLAP GROMMET

CANOPY FLAP

7

6'   7'   2'   8'   2'2"   6'

2'2"

6'

Mini Campfire tent

Many people like the basic idea of the Campfire tent, but feel it's just too much to handle in weight and complexity of use. They also feel it's too vulnerable to adverse weather conditions. I can appreciate these concerns; it's a big step to go from the small, light, simple tents to the complex-but-versatile Campfire tent.

After many years of camping with the full-size Campfire tent, I recently decided to use a smaller version for my solo painting trips. It is lighter to carry on portages and is less susceptible to high winds on exposed lakeshores and above the tree line. This lower, narrower tent has turned out to be a very nice compromise. The width is the same at 7 ft. (2.1 m), but the depth is only 4½ ft. (1.4 m), so you sleep across the tent. It's very roomy for one person and will easily sleep two. The tent is equipped with a window in the back for cross-ventilation. Although the height, at 4 ft. 3 in. (127 cm) means you can't stand up in the tent, its cleverly designed canopy rises to 6 ft. (1.8 m) at the outer edge. This enables you to stand upright, or nearly upright if you are tall, while tending the fire in the rain. With the canopy rising gradually from the back, the rain runs right down the roof to the ground. The wings can also be raised to 6 ft. (1.8 m) to close off the sides from wind and rain. In high winds, the canopy can be lowered and the wings crossed over and secured to make a weatherproof, low-profile and cozy tent for efficient use of a small fire. And finally, if desired, the tent can be closed completely.

The accompanying plans describe how to make a mini Campfire tent and the photographs explain its use. But the tent is so versatile that you will figure out many more variations.

Tent only

Canopy fully raised and one wing

Canopy lowered and both wings extended

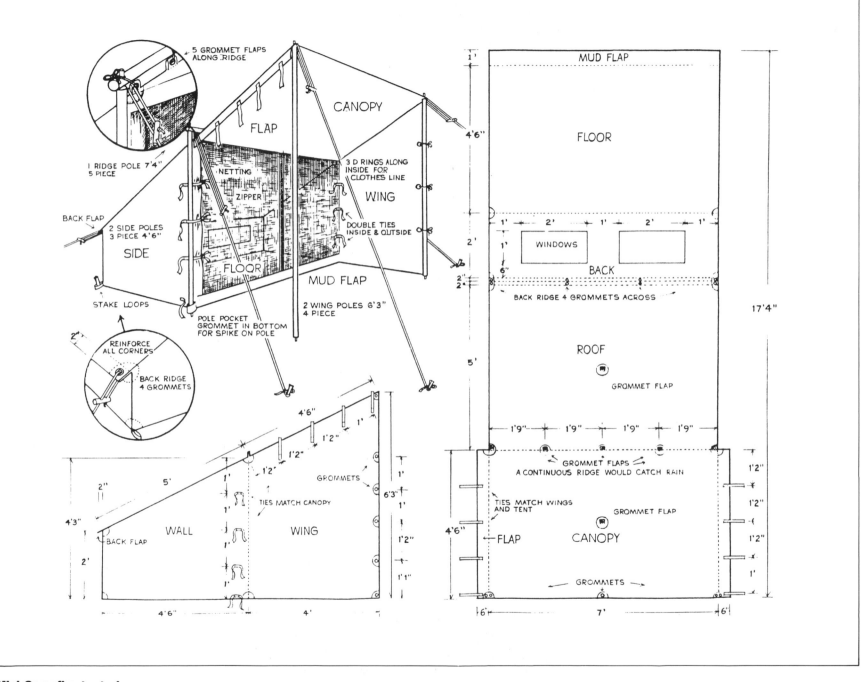

5 GROMMET FLAPS ALONG RIDGE

CANOPY

FLAP

1 RIDGE POLE 7'4"
5 PIECE

NETTING

ZIPPER

3 D RINGS ALONG INSIDE FOR CLOTHES LINE

WING

BACK FLAP

2 SIDE POLES
3 PIECE 4'6"

SIDE

FLOOR

FLOOR

DOUBLE TIES
INSIDE & OUTSIDE

STAKE LOOPS

MUD FLAP

2 WING POLES 6'3"
4 PIECE

POLE POCKET
GROMMET IN BOTTOM
FOR SPIKE ON POLE

2'

REINFORCE
ALL CORNERS

BACK RIDGE
4 GROMMETS

MUD FLAP

1'

4'6"

2'

1'

6"

2"
2"

FLOOR

WINDOWS

BACK

BACK RIDGE 4 GROMMETS ACROSS

17'4"

5'

ROOF

GROMMET FLAP

1' 2' 1' 2' 1'

4'6"

5'

2"

4'3"

2'

WALL

BACK FLAP

4'6"

5'

1'2"

1'2"

1'2"

1'

1'

1'

TIES MATCH CANOPY

WING

4'

GROMMETS

6'3"

1'

1'

1'2"

1'1"

1'9" 1'9" 1'9" 1'9"

GROMMET FLAPS
A CONTINUOUS RIDGE WOULD CATCH RAIN

TIES MATCH WINGS
AND TENT

GROMMET FLAP

FLAP

CANOPY

GROMMETS

6"

7'

6"

1'2"

1'2"

1'2"

1'

4'6"

Mini Campfire tent plans

31

Tarps

I have seen and used some pretty weird-looking tarps in my day. They are usually too small and there are never enough trees in the right places to pitch one properly. And no matter what you do, you find yourself huddling under it to avoid the rain that always seems to blow in from all sides.

One of the few times this did not happen was when I travelled with Gilles Couët on the Hood River. Gilles brought along the biggest, the best, and the most ingenious tarp arrangement I have ever seen. For groups of six or more it is an excellent arrangement.

On that trip the weather conditions were just about the worst I have ever experienced for canoeing. At the end of the day we were nearly hypothermic. There was no wood for a warming fire because we were far above the tree line. We used our Primus stove for cooking. Within minutes Gilles Couët and Gilles Lévesque would have their huge tarp up. With a change of clothes and a hot cup of tea in our hands, the landscape didn't look as bleak anymore. Preparations for supper could proceed in relative comfort.

The manner in which the tarp was pitched cut the wind completely. Designed by Gilles Couët and manufactured by his Chlorophylle company, it is certainly the answer for group camping. A well-rigged tarp can do wonders for flagging spirits after a day of paddling in the rain. Without shelter, the standard procedure is to throw together a cold meal as fast as you can, and crawl into the sleeping bag. Then you lie there all night, dreading breaking camp if the rain doesn't stop by morning. It is not a cheery prospect.

The secret to Gilles' tarp is using two canoes to hold down two sides close to the ground, while the other two sides are raised on a pole. A third canoe is overturned across the opening and used as a table. It is possible to turn the setup around if the wind changes. The tarp can also be pitched without the use of canoes by weighting the two sides down with rocks. With Gilles' tarp, we were completely protected from the wind and rain. After supper the kitchen was turned into a den of

Chlorophylle tarp erected using two canoes

Tarp rigged for large group, no wind

iniquity as Wally Schaber broke out the cards and the food barrels were pulled up to serve as a table. I sat off to one side sketching. After about an hour, Wally leaned over to inform me that he had lost our Campfire tent to Gilles but not to worry, he'd win it back with our canoe. The whole evening was in sharp contrast to the usual scene.

A well-designed tarp must be completely waterproof and large enough to accommodate your group. It must have plenty of tie points along the four sides, and a reinforcing square or pocket to receive a center pole. It's also a good idea to have a loop in the center on the opposite side of the center pocket in case you want to raise the tarp with a rope tied to a tree branch. These modifications allow many variations to cope with all kinds of wind and rain conditions. You'll also need an ample supply of cord.

The tarp can be used as an emergency shelter if the tent is lost in an upset. This is a distinct possibility on rivers that flow at 8 to 10 miles (13 to 16 km) an hour and never slow down. Always pack the tent and tarp in separate packs and put them in different canoes if there is more than one.

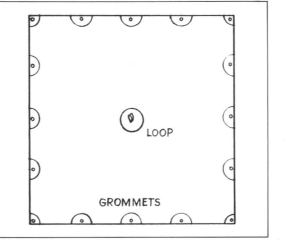

Tarp plans

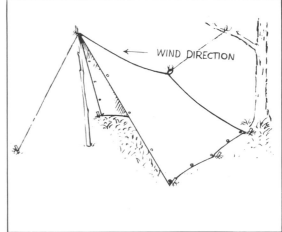

Pitched for protection from wind

A comfortable shelter in adverse conditions

33

Open Campfire tent in winter

Basking in warmth of fire

The Campfire tent is ideal for living outdoors in the winter. It can be used either open or closed. In the open mode, the camp fire is positioned about 4 ft. (1.2 m) in front of the open tent. The canopy is thrown back over the roof, and the wings are pulled out at a 45° angle to reflect the heat into the tent. The tent is pitched with the back toward the wind. A back log behind the fire reflects the heat into the tent, increasing the efficiency of the fire to an amazing degree. Tinfoil stretched between two sticks in the snow is also a marvellous reflector. You can even bring the tinfoil halfway around the fire to concentrate all the heat. The tinfoil can be used again and again.

Fires can be controlled if the firewood is cut short and split. The cooking pot can be suspended over the fire by driving a stick into the snowbank. To use a frying pan, I balance it on some burning embers pulled off to one side, as the main body of the fire is too hot. Sparks can be a problem, so it is not advisable to leave your camp unattended. If your gear is full of holes, then you must be doing something wrong. When you are breaking camp, finish burning all the logs down to ashes and extinguish the fire completely.

One disadvantage of the Campfire tent is that, if the wind swings around 180°, the whole camp has to be moved. The other disadvan-

tage is the great amount of wood that is consumed to stay warm. A large, open fire soon denudes the area of dry wood. But in a remote wilderness area, it is a wonderful way to enjoy the outdoors. When I was filming wolves in the Northwest Territories, I had unlimited time on my hands, and an unlimited wood supply; hauling and cutting wood for the hungry fire was no hardship at all. In fact, a fire keeps you warm in two ways. It keeps you warm while you're hauling and cutting, and it keeps you warm when you burn it.

Position of camp fire ——————————

The base for the fire is a more serious problem. If you are camping on 3 ft. (1 m) of snow, dig out the working area to a depth of about 18 in. (45 cm) and cover the bottom of your firepit with deadwood and several layers of tinfoil; otherwise your fire will melt a hole in the snow and drop to ground level very quickly. Alternatively, carry a sheet of aluminum or light metal to lay over the base logs. The final and best solution is to dig your whole camp down to ground level.

You should take into consideration what kind of soil your fire is on. On organic soil, the fire can destroy the ground cover; it may even smolder away all winter, and burst into flame the following summer.

Open fire with tinfoil reflector ——————————

Closed Campfire tent in winter

Above the tree line, and for a quick assault on a mountain peak, very light, high-tech equipment is in order. You need a liquid- or gas-fuelled stove. Because the fuel has to be carried with you, the stove is used sparingly, for cooking and for melting snow to drink. Any heat is strictly a by-product of cooking. Comfort depends on warm sleeping bags and clothing. Moisture is a constant problem in these conditions because, with such a limited source of heat, it is difficult to dry clothes properly.

The closed Campfire or wall tent heated with a wood stove provides a level of comfort which, in striking contrast to mountaintop conditions, can border on downright decadence. I could never figure out why anybody would want to use the alpine style of camping in a treed area, where there is an abundant supply of firewood. The closed tent with the wood stove is much more efficient and comfortable if you are out for extended periods.

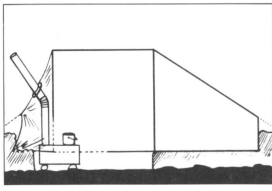

Closed Campfire tent on snow ────────

Plastic closure with hole for stove pipe ────────

For years I have used my Campfire tent, in winter, in a modified form. First I dig my work area down into the snow about 18 in. (45 cm). If the snow isn't too deep, I dig the snow down to ground level. I extend the wings and canopy, and hang a sheet of clear 6 mil polyethylene in the opening to close the tent. The one problem is securing the polyethylene sheet to the canopy and wings in such a way as to keep out the drafts. Metal spring-loaded clips work well.

The sheet is equipped with a metal ring through which the stove pipe is inserted. To do this, a hole is cut in the sheet about 1 ft. (30 cm) from the top. The hole is surrounded by duct tape, then two pieces of light metal, with a hole to receive the stove pipe, are bolted together on each side of the sheet. Unless the duct tape extends out past the metal ring, the hot metal eventually will melt the sheet. Some strings are taped in the middle of the sheet to pull it away from the stove. The stove pipe has a 45° section so it will stick out through the polyethylene sheet. The pipe should be secured to the crosspole with wire to prevent the flapping of the polyethylene sheet from working the pipe loose.

Because this is a makeshift arrangement, there are many little adjustments that have to be made to keep the drafts out. Zippers on the wings and canopy, and a polyethylene closure, would be ideal. I like this arrangement, because the sun shines through the polyethylene making a bright, cheerful work area.

Heating with a wood stove in the winter is efficient. The air is kept fresh and dry, because the stove takes in air for combustion, which is replaced with air from outside, coming in through any openings or the pores of the tent material. The cold air coming in from outside is not noticeable because of the amount of heat radiating from the stove. The stove can vary in size from 12 in. to 2 ft. (30 to 60 cm). A rectangular one is better than a round one, so you can set your pots on it for cooking. You can make it yourself, or buy a commercially made one (see pages 46 to 47).

Trail stove

Work area

37

Knots and ropes

Every book I've ever read on camping has a section on how to tie knots. The bad news is, I don't know how to tie knots. Whenever I need to tie a knot I just make one up. Well, that's not quite true. I know a granny knot and a square knot. But when I'm in a hurry I never know which one it will be. When I'm tying a really important one—for example, when I'm filming out of a helicopter and I'm leaning halfway out the door and if it comes undone I'm dead—I tie a lot of knots. Like maybe a hundred of them. But I've never been killed because I don't know how to tie knots. In film work you need knots. I've leaned out of 200 ft. (60 m) towers, hung off 1000 ft. (300 m) cliffs, sat in the doors of airplanes and helicopters, suspended myself out over the brink of Niagara Falls (I must have tied a thousand knots in that one), and never have I had a knot come undone.

If you want to talk about rope, that's another matter. I know a lot of things about rope. For example, ropes are always too short or too long. If the rope is too short and you tie two lengths together, you'll find that the knot is always in the wrong place and won't go through the pulley or gets caught on a branch. If the rope is too long and you cut it, you'll find that the next time you need it, both pieces will be too short.

Another thing about rope is that you always have less than you thought you had. You're always wondering where the right piece is. It's gone, right? And when you get home you never have as many pieces as when you left. I've come to the conclusion that every time I go canoeing my friends steal it. You can never catch them at it, but I know they've got it. And it's always the best stuff. The one piece that would have been just the right length. But the worst part is they always accuse me of taking their rope.

So why have I never learned to tie knots? I have a theory that you have to learn when you are a kid. I was never in the Boy Scouts, and at camp, I was always off in the canoe classes instead of knot class. I could see through their plan. I knew that they had a limited number of canoes and to keep the kids occupied they had knot classes. With a nickel's worth of rope you could keep a bunch of kids out of trouble for a couple of hours a day, or for two whole weeks. Not me, though. I knew where the action was. It was down there in the canoes. Even the names of the various knots confirmed my suspicion that it was nothing more than a make-work project. Take the sheepshank for example. I knew right from the start that I was never going to need that one. Another one that really cracked me up was rope splicing. I'll bet not one of those kids ever made it on board a sailing ship, and even if one did, I'll bet the captain never asked him to splice a rope.

In the rockbound Precambrian Shield country, it's seldom possible to drive a tent peg into the ground, so you have to tie your tent to whatever tree, shrub or rock is available.

Because these can be far from the tent, extra-long guy ropes are useful. However, with long ropes and varying distances, what do you do with the extra rope when it's not needed? You need a knot that's easy to tie and untie with a doubled rope. With all of the hundreds of knots that have been invented, the world had to wait until I came along with the fastest, easiest knot! I wouldn't trust my life to it, but my tent has never fallen down because this knot has let go. I have humbly named it the Mason tree, shrub, or rock hitch (illustration 1) depending on what it's tied to. You can forget all those other knots you wasted your childhood years learning to tie when you could have been out in a canoe. If the only thing you learn from this book is how to tie and untie this knot, your money will have been well spent.

The only other knots I've ever needed are the bowline (illustration 2) and the trucker's hitch (illustration 3). The bowline is a great knot if you need to haul a canoe off a rock or tow your car. No matter how much stress it's under, it's always easy to untie. I use it about once every five years, so I have to refer to my *Klutz Book of Knots*. Here it is stolen off page 3. There is one other knot that is a must for canoeists. The trucker's hitch or power cinch is not so much a knot as a method of securing your canoe on the car. Its combination of self-releasing loop and two half hitches provides considerable mechanical advantage for tightening the rope. Be careful you don't pull the decks off your canoe when you secure the bow and stern to your car bumpers. This knot is also featured in *The Klutz Book of Knots*.

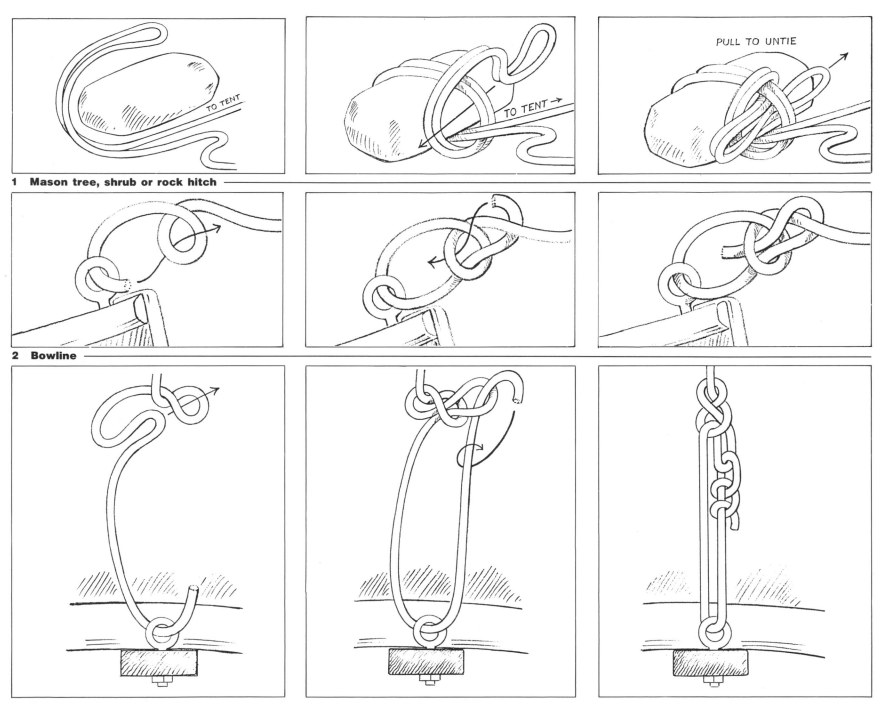

TO TENT

TO TENT →

PULL TO UNTIE

1 Mason tree, shrub or rock hitch

2 Bowline

3 Trucker's hitch or power cinch

4 CAMP FIRES, FIREPLACES AND STOVES

Camping at the mouth of Second Canyon, Mountain River

Camp Fires

Sometimes my camping trips are an excuse to satisfy the urge to sit and stare into the flames of a camp fire. There is life in a camp fire, and a primitive pleasure in watching it come alive. One of the most beautiful comments I've ever read about camp fires is in Sigurd Olson's book, *The Singing Wilderness*. He described his memories of all the camp fires he had sat staring into as a string of pearls. The more recent ones shone the brightest in his memory, but when he blew on the more distant ones, they sprang to life and the memories of a place and time came flooding back.

Not everyone shares my love of camp fires. Some outdoor enthusiasts prefer the convenience of the stove. Others only use the fire for light and warmth. For some people, the open fire means black greasy pots; sooty clothes, tents and sleeping bags; burned food and watering eyes. There are ways to avoid all this. However, to be able to enjoy good meals prepared over the open fire in all weather conditions, and without degrading the environment, does require considerable skill.

From many readers, the suggestion that fires are part of modern camping will elicit cries of outrage. But to me, doing away with camp fires to save the wilderness environment is like throwing the baby out with the bathwater. I cannot bear to think of a time when the camp fire will be a luxury we can no longer afford. Of course, as greater numbers of people explore the wilderness, we all have a responsibility to learn to tread softly.

One way is to know how to handle fires safely and efficiently. Some people leave tinfoil, bits of half-burned plastic, leftover food and even cans and glass in the fireplace. Mounds of soggy ashes and half-burned logs also destroy a wilderness mood. People who don't carry a saw or axe sometimes put a long log across the fire to burn it in half, and then push the ends in as it burns. They often end up dousing the partly-burned log, which leaves an awful mess for the next camper. This abuse is particularly evident on the once-pristine shores of Lake Superior. Its almost unlimited supply of driftwood is resulting in many half-consumed bonfires left to mar the beaches. Throwing the logs into the water or bushes to get rid of them is no solution, because charred logs take years to break down. Cutting and splitting them makes a mess of the area as well as of the person doing the cutting.

A basic courtesy and good camping ethic is to make sure anything you put onto the fire is completely consumed. No-trace camping means leaving no evidence of anyone having been there. The exception, on the well-travelled routes, should be the flat, cleared area, the fireplace, and maybe a little kindling for the next camper. You can tell a great deal about a person by the campsite that he or she leaves.

Partly burned logs

Garbage in fireplace

Clean, tidy fireplace

Collecting firewood

Firewood should be collected selectively to leave the scenery undisturbed. When we look up at an old dead tree, we see a lot of firewood. But if we look again, we might see an apartment block for a myriad of creatures. The large holes are where the pileated wood-peckers come regularly to feed on grubs. Some of the older holes might house chicka-dees, smaller woodpeckers or squirrels. The branches could be used as a perch for a family of kingfishers or even a great blue heron. And if you look again, through the eyes of a painter, you might see something that is very beautiful and an integral part of the scene. It is far better to select some smaller standing or leaning deadwood. Dead trees that are not lying on the ground are often firm and make excellent firewood.

I have read books that go into great detail about how to choose wood for a hot, efficient fire. I find that you usually don't have much choice: you take what you can get. If you have a choice, use cedar to start the fire, then after the fire is established put on hardwoods, which burn much longer. Keep an eye on cedar and pine; they both spark a lot.

In country such as the Precambrian Shield, where the cycle of growth is quite rapid, the open fire can still be an important part of a journey by canoe. Backpacking in the moun-tains is different: the land is fragile and the growing cycle is very slow. To kill the ground cover means erosion and destruction. The important thing is to be able to differentiate between the two types of land. There are encouraging signs that people are becoming aware of this and of the no-trace camping ethic. Birch trees and standing dead trees stripped of their bark to light fires are not as common as they once were. With skill, care and concern for the next person, the camp fire can still be very much a part of the wilderness experience.

Feather stick

A candle makes a great fire starter

Starting the fire

If the weather is dry, I use pine needles, a handful of grass, paper or twigs to start the fire. If the weather is wet, logs cut into 12 in. (30 cm) lengths are split to get at the dry wood. A knife is used to make feather sticks. One trick is to carry a candle. You light it, lay it on the ground, pile sticks on the flame and as it grows the wax melts onto the wood turning each piece into a candle. When the fire is going sufficiently, remove the candle for use at another time.

I wish I could say that I can light a fire without matches or a lighter. If I were desper-ate enough and given reasonable conditions, I think I could, but hope I never have to find out. I have strike-anywhere matches stashed throughout my gear, in my first-aid kit, repair kit, food box, fishing gear, and so on. Replace unused matches once a year because, in time, they become difficult to light.

Controlling smoke

To the questions "What happens to the smoke?" and, "Doesn't it get into your tent, not to mention your eyes?" the answer is an emphatic, "Yes!" But there are ways to cope with it. If the tent is pitched across the wind, the smoke will usually blow away. A good trick is to prop the canoe up at an angle, at a reasonable distance from the fire. The cavity of the canoe creates a vacuum and sucks the smoke away from the tent. If it's aluminum, the canoe will reflect the heat very efficiently into the tent. If wood and canvas, the canoe will be dried by the fire. This makes the canoe lighter. Of course, you must use common sense as to how close you put the canoe to the fire and must never leave it unattended. The ABS canoe is the most susceptible to heat damage, as it will melt. If the canoe is more than warm to the touch, it is too close to the fire.

Sometimes the wind and rain are very difficult to cope with and it seems, no matter what you try, the smoke persists in getting into your eyes. Maybe the wood is lousy. Maybe the lay of the land is causing a backdraft. However, these conditions are rare in my experience.

Fireplaces

The best method of building a fireplace to cook on is to arrange the rocks to accommodate either fire irons or a grate. Fire irons consist of two 3 ft. (1 m) lengths of angle iron laid between two rocks. One end is spread wider than the other to accommodate the widest pot. I prefer a grate, but fire irons work well for a large group. You can put more pots on the fire and it's easier to arrange the rocks.

Because most of my trips are by myself, or with a maximum of four people, the grate is lighter and more convenient. Arranging the rocks is a little more trouble. I need two rows with a level edge to suspend the grate on. Two to four stones to hold the grate or fire irons are much more practical and easier to clean than a fire ring. Although a ring of stones is supposed to keep the fire from spreading when it's built on combustible soils, a fire shouldn't be built there in the first place. If the only place to build the fire is on combustible soils, it is safer and more practical to use a stove.

Wire grate

Fire irons

Adding wood to the fire ————————————————————

Environmental fireplaces

It is more difficult to practice the no-trace camping ethic with the Campfire tent because the fireplace leaves a permanent scar on the ground. For a while, I rationalized this by arguing that the fireplaces I built were better and more practical than the existing ones, and that when I left, there were never any half-burned logs, bits of tinfoil, or melted plastic lying around. But the heavy traffic on many wilderness rivers is having an impact which can't be rationalized away. Now I carry a sheet of aluminum to put on the ground before I build the fireplace. A layer of sand, gravel or stones on the aluminum insulates the ground cover from the heat.

Recently I have made a portable environmental fireplace that works very well. It folds flat and is carried in a bag with reinforced corners so it doesn't cut the packsack. It can be assembled or taken apart in two minutes. It is true that it's one more thing to carry, but 4 to 8 lb. (2 to 3.5 kg) extra weight is not excessive when travelling by canoe.

The environmental fireplace brings a whole new adaptability to the Campfire tent. When there is an extreme change of weather, I pick up the fireplace and move it to the other side of the tent so the smoke blows away from the front. Another advantage is the fireplace's fuel efficiency. The heat is contained on three sides and is deflected upward under the pot where it's needed. It also reflects heat into the tent efficiently. The portable fireplace is suitable for cooking for two people. For more than two, you might want to buy a larger fireplace.

The intense heat of the fire causes light sheet metal to buckle and warp. For this reason the fireplace is equipped with a double bottom. Only the top level warps. If you decide to go light, without the upper level, you should cover the bottom with 1 in. (2.5 cm) of wet sand or gravel. The alternative is not to worry about it, let it warp and have a wobbly fireplace.

The environmental fireplace can be easily constructed by following the accompanying plans, or a manufactured fireplace can be purchased from Horizons Unlimited, Box 1110, La Ronge, Saskatchewan, S0J 1L0.

Environmental fireplace

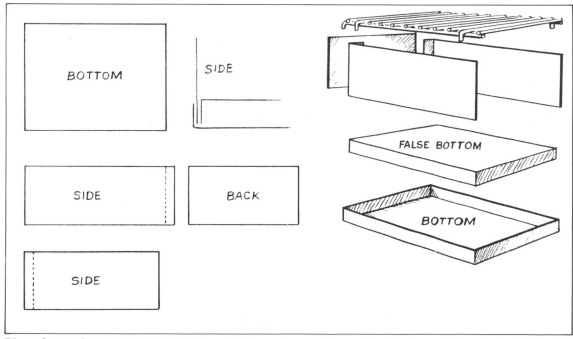

Plans for environmental fireplace

45

Wood stoves

The wood stove is a simple but efficient device. It radiates heat, boils water, cooks food and sends the smoke up the chimney. The smoke escaping up the chimney pulls fresh air into the tent, which is quickly heated by radiant heat from the stove. A stove-heated tent feels dry and warm.

The amount of wood consumed and heat given off can be controlled in various ways. The size of the air intake at the front of the stove controls the rate of burn by controlling the amount of oxygen entering the stove. You can also close a damper, a round piece of metal on a swivel inside the pipe, which cuts the draft and slows the rate of burn. A well-designed stove has a baffle which causes the flames to come forward and lick the top of the stove before going up the chimney. This puts the maximum heat under your pot where it's needed. The baffle also enables the whole stove to put out more heat. Unfortunately, even commercially-made trail stoves seldom have baffles. A few sophisticated models have one and an air intake at the back as well.

Constructing a wood stove

Film can stove   I made my first wood stove with film cans (illustration 1 A and B) for ends and thin sheet metal for the barrel (C). One film can is hinged to make a door (D). A hole (E) is cut in the top of the barrel and a cover (F) is bolted in place for a lid. I hammered the top flat so the pot wouldn't fall off. The chimney coupling is made by cutting flaps and bending them up (G). Rivet a ring (H) to the flaps to receive the stove pipe (I). A damper can be installed in the pipe. Cut a hole in the door (J) for an air intake and bolt the swinging door in place. You can use either small bolts or steel (not aluminum) pop rivets to hold everything together. Eyebolts (K) are used for feet. If the stove is used on snow, a couple of sticks threaded through the bolts keep it from melting down into the snow. An insulating ring (L) prevents the stove pipe, which gets very hot, from burning the tent roof or the polyethylene front closure of the Campfire tent. In commercially-made tents, the ring is usually made of asbestos. For a polyethylene closure, I use two small film cans bolted on either side of the material. Duct tape must be applied to the polyethylene around the hole to keep it from melting.

Sheet metal wood stove   A more sophisticated small trail stove can be cut from sheet metal and pop riveted together (photograph 2). It is a good idea to use a non-galvanized metal. If galvanized steel is used for the stove, it must be fired up and burned at cherry-red temperatures outside the tent before use. This will burn off the galvanizing—the fumes are poisonous.

Manufactured stove

Good commercially-made stoves are hard to find, but I recently hit the mother lode of wood stoves at Campers Village, 10265-107 Street, Edmonton, Alberta T5J 1K1. They are also at 807-34 Avenue, S.E., Calgary, Alberta T2G 4Y9. They have every size of folding and non-folding stove. An oven is available with the two-, three- and four-pot hole sizes. Because I haul my gear in the winter on a toboggan or sleigh, I bought the folding, single-pot hole size with four lengths of pipe. This stove measures about 11 by 12 by 20 in. (28 by 30 by 51 cm); it collapses to 1½ in. (4 cm) for packing and weighs 10 lb. (4.5 kg). I was upset to find the pipe couldn't be taken apart for folding, but by bending it along the joint with a screwdriver (photograph 3) I can now nest it for packing.

Another excellent wood stove is designed by Craig MacDonald, an expert on winter travel and camping. His stove is the non-folding type, but designed so that all the pipes will fit inside. Although it doesn't have a hole for the pot, you can boil water by inverting a larger pail over it to concentrate the heat. Craig claims you can get a better drawing fire without extra openings. For information, write to Craig MacDonald, Frost Centre, Dorset, Ontario P0A 1E0.

In the United States, the North Woods Arts Center carries sheet metal portable wood stoves in addition to a wide variety of hard-to-find winter and summer equipment. Contact the center at RFD #3 Box 87A, Dover-Foxcroft, Maine 04426.

The first time you fire up your stove you will be shocked by the way it buckles and bends out of shape. This is unavoidable in light trail stoves. The bottom won't warp if you cover it with sand or an inert material. But where are you going to find sand in the middle of winter? You just have to get used to a stove that looks as if a truck ran over it.

1 Film can homemade stove

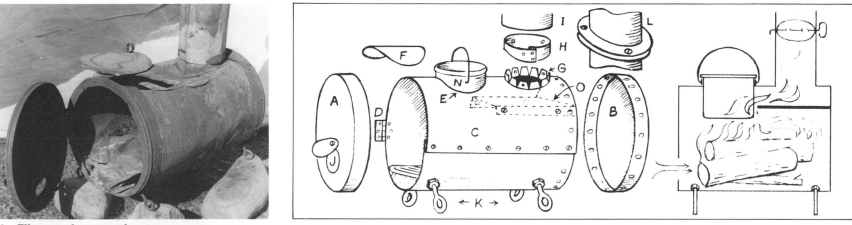

2 Sheet metal homemade stove

PIPE
METAL
COTTON

METAL
DUCT TAPE
PLASTIC

BOLT

← BOLT LEG ↗

3 Commercial folding stove

Camp stoves

As the traffic grows on the more popular rivers, and deadwood becomes more and more scarce, the open camp fire may have to be sacrificed. In mountain country above the tree line, open fires can severely damage the ground cover and deplete the supply of deadwood. As much as I love the open camp fire for light, heat and cooking, the liquid or gas stove is a necessity in many situations.

I bought the Optimus 111 many years ago for canoeing, and the Optimus 8R and the Svea 123 R for backpacking. There are many other superbly designed stoves from which the camper can choose. Each one has its advantages and disadvantages. The three points to consider in buying a stove are fuel, size or weight, and design.

Fuel

There are four common types of fuel: white gas, kerosene, alcohol and propane or butane.

White gas   Also known as naphtha or camp fuel. Heat output is very high. Maximum heat output can be obtained with pump-pressurized stoves. With a very low flash point, white gas is the most volatile of stove fuels. Fumes can be ignited by an open flame, causing an explosion. It works better than other fuels at low temperatures; therefore, stoves using it are best for winter. All types of stoves should be allowed to cool before refilling, but especially white gas stoves. Use a funnel with a felt filter to strain out impurities. Available anywhere in North America.

Kerosene or coal oil   Puts out a lot of heat and is one of the cheapest fuels. It has a high flash point, which means it doesn't give off volatile fumes at average temperatures. In fact, it won't burn by itself, and has to be in a wick or generator to burn, so it is a very safe fuel to use. Good for winter use. Requires more preheating to ignite the stove than white gas, is smoky when first lit and has an offensive smell. Because it doesn't evaporate quickly, the smell lingers if spilled on clothing or tent. Available worldwide.

Methanol or wood alcohol   Produces much less heat for its weight than other fuels, but is the easiest fuel to ignite. No preheating required. Alcohol stoves are the ultimate in simplicity. There's nothing to break. Not suitable for large-group cooking. Will burn if spilled, but won't explode. A safe fuel. Works poorly at cold temperatures. Available worldwide.

Propane or butane   Heat output good in summer weather. Poor at cold temperatures. Simple to use; no pumping or priming required. Performance better at high altitudes. Container is pressurized and can be dangerous if you're not careful when changing tanks. Most expensive fuel. Available most places worldwide.

Types of stoves

Stoves can be grouped in three categories based on the size of the party and type of trip. All of these stoves are available in both Canada and the United States.

Base camp stoves

Coleman stove and Optimus 00   For base camp cooking, weight is not a factor, so you can enjoy the luxury of a two-burner Coleman stove or an Optimus 00. They both put out a lot of heat quickly. The Coleman two-burner stove operates on white gas and is self-contained in a sturdy metal case. The Optimus 00 operates on kerosene. It's a good stove for a group of more than four. Both stoves are very stable. Both have good simmer control.

Coleman double burner

Optimus 00

Medium-size stoves for canoe or toboggan

Optimus 111   When I bought my first stove I made the right choice with the Optimus 111. Although it's a bit heavy for backpacking, it's a rugged piece of machinery, fast for boiling water, simple to operate, has good stability and requires only basic maintenance. Unfortunately, it sounds like a Boeing 747 on takeoff. Mine operates on white gas. The pressurizing pump is built in. Priming paste is recommended for priming the stove before starting it (see page 51). This is true of all white gas and kerosene stoves. (With kerosene the stove must be primed longer or it will soot up badly.) Simmer control is very good. The Optimus 111 has been redesigned recently with an adapter to burn either white gas, kerosene or alcohol (denatured spirits). This stove is one of the most expensive.

Coleman Peak 1   When I was first introduced to this stove, I couldn't believe how such a quiet stove could put out so much heat. The silence was beautiful. The Peak 1 burns white gas and can be adapted to kerosene. I prefer white gas, but the kerosene is much safer around children. Simmer control is good. One disadvantage of the Peak 1 is that it doesn't come in a metal container for protection. However, you can purchase a container separately that can also be used as two pots for cooking. The new Peak 1 model has an aluminum tank, which makes this model much lighter than the original.

Ultra-light backpacking stoves

Optimus 8R   This stove is the small, lighter version of the Optimus 111. It has the same characteristics but doesn't have the built-in pressurizing pump. The Optimus Mini Pump is recommended for maximum performance. Like its big brother, it's contained in a rugged metal case. Simmer control is good. All Optimus stoves are supplied with a needle for cleaning the generator and a small wrench for tightening nuts to prevent leakage of fuel. The new model also has the adapter for burning kerosene or alcohol.

Optimus 8R

Coleman Peak 1

Types of stoves . . .

Svea 123 R   A popular backpacking stove throughout the world, the Svea 123 R is very simple to operate, requiring no cleaning or pressurizing. The lower part of the container serves as a windscreen and the upper part is used as a cooking pot for one person. To cook for more than one requires a pot set. Operates only on white gas.

Trangia stove   The Trangia stove system is the ultimate in simplicity and convenience. It is light and self-contained. The stove consists of a small container for the alcohol with a lid to use for snuffing out the fire. The set includes two pots, a lid frying pan, an efficient wind-screen and a stove base that provides stability. The bad news about the Trangia, and alcohol stoves in general, is the lack of simmer control; this limits you to very basic cooking.

The Bleuet S200S, the MSR Whisperlite and the MSR X-GK   These stoves operate on pressurized gas cylinders. They are easy to light, require no priming and are simple to operate. Simmer control is good. I haven't used these stoves in the field because they don't work well in the cold. I would rather own a stove that blasts out the heat anywhere, anytime and in all conditions. My son, Paul, on the other hand, has used them and prefers the MSR Whisperlite because it's so simple to operate. There is no filling and spilling of liquids. When you run out of fuel, you simply change cylinders.

Trangia stove ————————

MSR Whisperlite ————————

Svea 123 R ————————

Sigg Tourist Cookset

If your pots are to be used only on the stove, the Sigg Tourist Cookset or the Trangia cook set are excellent. The Sigg set comes in aluminum or stainless steel. For backpacking, I would suggest aluminum and a stove that nests inside. For solo backpacking, use a stove with a container that can serve as a cooking pot.

Sigg Tourist Cookset ──────────

Cooking pots

I use the same nesting pot set on my stove as I use over a camp fire. When I go solo or with one other person, I take small nesting pots plus a separate frying pan. The lid that doubles as a frying pan doesn't work very well.

Washing the outside of pots is nothing more than a make-work project. The outsides of my pots haven't been washed in ten years, which is about the life expectancy of heavily-used pots. They probably lose a little efficiency in transmitting heat, but I haven't noticed. I use a pot bag for carrying them. A small piece of waxed paper or foil inside each pot helps keep the inside clean when they are nested for carrying.

Cooking pots ──────────

Priming

Kerosene stoves and some white gas stoves (not the Coleman) must be primed before starting. Alcohol can be used, but the safest primer is priming paste. You put a little paste in the bowl and light it to heat the vaporizing tube. Wait a minute or so, then open the valve and your stove will ignite. If you are without the paste, pump up the pressure a bit, open the valve just enough to allow some gas to run down the stem, close the valve and then light the stove. Don't open the valve again until the flame is almost out. Then open the valve a little and the stove will flame and begin to roar. If the flame goes too high, turn off the valve until the flame dies and then open it again. It takes some practice, so do it away from the tent. Never leave the valve open while lighting the stove; too much gas will escape and you'll have an inferno.

Points to remember

- White gas should be carried in special aluminum fuel bottles which are strong and leakproof. A pouring spout is useful.
- A funnel with a felt filter avoids fuel spillage and removes dirt and water.
- Most white gas stoves require periodic cleaning and tightening of nuts.
- Some stoves have loose burner plates which can get lost, so carry a spare.
- Windscreens add to the efficiency of a stove, but be careful to allow complete circulation of air or the tank could overheat and explode.
- Stoves should be cool to the touch before refilling and should be filled outdoors. Wipe clean before lighting.
- Cooking in a tent is not recommended because of the danger of carbon monoxide poisoning and of burning down the tent.
- A well-designed tent has an outer vestibule that can be used for cooking. If your tent doesn't have a vestibule, you might be able to design one and add it to your fly.

Camp tools

Splitting with safety log in place ————————

Axe

We have all enjoyed films or stories about the hero who goes off into the forest with a packsack on his back and an axe in his hand and hacks and hews himself a cabin out of the wilderness. Amazingly, a few people still do this, but it is not an everyday occurrence. Now that it is no longer necessary, or even desirable, to cut tent poles, the role of the axe has diminished. Today its primary purpose is for splitting wood and driving in tent pegs.

Some of the latest books claim that you can cut all the firewood you need with a saw, and that if you have an older tent, you can hammer your stakes in with a rock or hatchet. I don't agree for several reasons. I enjoy handling an axe and working with it. I find it comforting to know that I could carve a paddle if I ever lost mine in an upset. And I like cooking over a small fire and a small fire has to be fed with fine kindling. Splitting wood with an axe allows you to get at the dry inside wood in a log when everything is wet. People who don't split their firewood tend to leave a mess of half-burned, oversized logs in the fire pit for the next camper to clean up.

The down side of carrying an axe is that chopping wood is one of the most dangerous things you can do on a canoe trip. Axe injuries are almost always serious. I don't believe in trying to teach someone to use an axe on a trip: the place to learn is at home. Apart from one or two friends, I don't even like anyone using my axe. In the wilderness you rarely have the luxury of a splitting block. People who pick up your axe and start splitting on a rock invariably split through a log and hit the rock. It can take hours of filing to eliminate the nick. A dull axe is dangerous because it is more likely to glance off the wood.

For a wilderness axe, I like a 2½ lb. (1 kg) head on a full-length 28 in. (70 cm) handle. It should be a cutting axe, not a splitting axe. Splitting axes are only useful for very large logs. A cutting axe is more versatile and is best for fine kindling. A good leather axe sheath is essential. It should be lined with a piece of tin or aluminum to prevent the blade from cutting through the leather. For sharpening, carry an axe file and a whetstone.

Splitting — cautious method   The log that you want to split won't stand on a round log lying on the ground. The trick is to hold the blade in contact with the end of the log (photograph 1). Bring the two down together onto the log on the ground, removing your grip on the log to be split as it makes contact. The blade will sink deeply enough for the axe to grip it. Now you

can grip the axe handle with both hands and bring the butt of the log down onto the round log. Repeat until the log splits.

Splitting — back of axe method   A neat trick is to turn the axe over so the log is up and bring the back of the axe down onto the chopping log (photograph 2). This is an efficient method for splitting troublesome logs with knots.

Splitting — most effective but dangerous method   Another way to split, when there is no chopping log, is very efficient but potentially dangerous (photograph 3). A safety log is placed immediately in front of the feet, (A). A second log, for chopping on, is positioned just beyond the first one and parallel to it, (B). Cut a notch, (C), in this log, then place the log, (D), to be split in the notch. The end of the log must not extend toward you beyond the notch. Hit the log on the end, (E), and it will split easily unless it's full of knots. Because your target is a round log it takes some skill to hit it just right. Do not hit the log to be split on your side of the chopping log, (F), or it will fly up and possibly hit you in the face. Be sure no one is standing near because the axe can glance off your round target.

Short-handled axes are particularly dangerous because, if you miss or glance off the log, the axe might end up in your foot or leg. The full-length axe will hit the ground if your stance is correct. Either way, it is a good idea to place a safety log between you and the log you are chopping on.

Splitting — two hatchet method   Many people prefer the hatchet for splitting wood because of the light weight. However, the lack of weight and leverage makes it very inefficient for splitting unless you use the blade as a wedge (photograph 4). Gently bury the blade into the end of the log and hammer it through with a second hatchet or a log until it splits. This method is the safest method for splitting logs.

Splitting — belt knife method   Small logs can be split by hammering your belt knife through the log with a second log (photograph 5).

1   Splitting, cautious method —————————————————————————

2   Back of the axe method —————————————————————————

3   Most effective but potentially dangerous method ——————————————————

4   Splitting, two hatchet method ————————————————————— **5   Splitting with belt knife** ————

Camp tools. . .

Saw

A long time ago I came upon a campsite where the previous camper had left a nice supply of firewood. The wood had been cut with a saw and I wondered why anybody would go to the trouble of carrying one, since an axe can do anything a saw can do, as well as splitting and hammering in tent pegs. Then, one day, a friend brought a saw along. I tried it and have never gone anywhere without one since. On most trips I carry both.

The fold-up saw is easy to pack. The non-folding saw has a longer cutting stroke. For a blade guard, cut a slit in a piece of 1 by 2 in. (2.5 by 5 cm) wood and secure in place.

Folding and non-folding saws ⸻

Sawing driftwood, Lake Superior ⸻

Knives

The sheath knife is a must for canoeing in rapids. Fold-up knives (see Swiss army knife, page 133) are not adequate because you might have only one hand free for cutting your ropes loose, and you don't have time to go groping around for a pocketknife (see Emergency Gear, page 134). I line my sheath with a piece of tin or aluminum. The rivets hold it flat along one edge, which creates friction on the blade so it can't fall out. In 30 years my knife has never fallen out of the sheath.

Sheath knife and Swiss Army knife ⸻

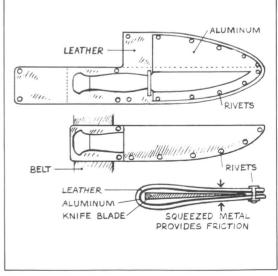

Plans for sheath ⸻

Flashlights

It's the middle of the night and I have to get up. I reach for the flashlight, switch it on, climb out of my sleeping bag and reach for my shoes, but the flashlight goes out. I jiggle it. Nothing happens. I fiddle with the switch. The light comes on and I find one shoe just as it goes out again. I jiggle it and it goes on and off but not long enough to find the other shoe. I stop jiggling it and the light comes on. Moving very gingerly so as not to jar the flashlight, I find the other shoe. As I put the flashlight down to put on the shoes, it goes out. I put them on in the dark, find the zipper to the mosquito netting and climb out of the tent closing the zipper behind me.

I have another go at getting the flashlight to work. It's pitch black and the outdoor toilet provided by the parks is along a narrow, twisting trail. I try to keep the light on by jiggling it. It stays on only if I jiggle it. I stumble along the trail as best I can. As I near the biffy, the light suddenly goes dim. It's nearly impossible to see where I'm going. Then it goes out and won't go on anymore.

On the way back to the tent the flashlight with vigorous shaking, banging and flicking of the switch, comes on from time to time. Finally, I belt it hard and the light never comes on again. I know it isn't going to shine again: I've broken the filament. I bend down, pull the axe out of the chopping log, and with the back of the axe, I pound the flashlight out as thin as a piece of paper. All the inner frustration and pent-up fury drains from my body. Joyce and the children ask me sleepily, "What's going on?" I explain that I'm fixing the flashlight! I drop it into the garbage bag and return to my sleeping bag.

For the past few years I've been carrying a foolproof candle lantern. Just recently I saw a guy with a flashlight that had no switch. He showed me how to tighten the lens to turn it on and loosen it to turn it off. Absolutely brilliant! Space age technology finally came through with a bomb-proof flashlight. For wilderness trips, buy the lithium batteries. They are expensive but last many times longer than ordinary batteries. One of the joys of canoeing in the Arctic in summer: you can leave the flashlight at home!

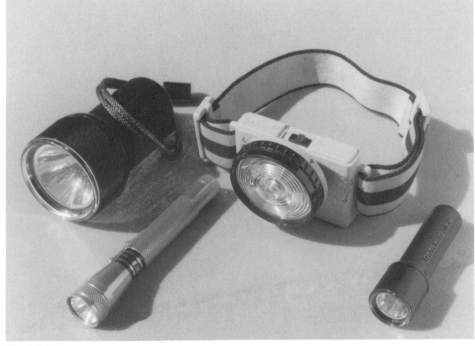

Flashlights

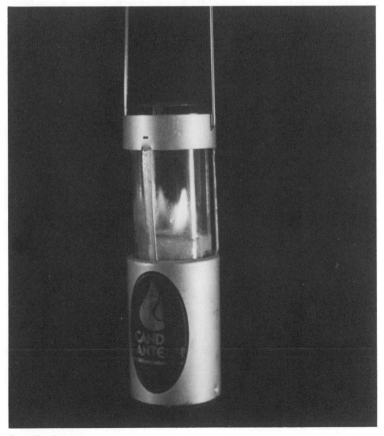

Candle lantern

A meal at the mouth of First Canyon, Mountain River

5 COOKING IN THE WILD

The kind of food you take on a canoe trip depends on the length of the trip, the number of portages and most importantly, the reason for taking the trip. In my early years of canoe tripping, I was fanatical about weight. Everything I took to eat was dehydrated or had a low water content. I've never met anybody who prefers dehydrated to fresh food, but dehydrated foods make possible long, arduous trips into the wilderness.

Some wilderness travellers delight in cooking good food and make an art out of it. Others place a low priority on food and will eat anything as long as it keeps them going. I'm somewhere between the two extremes, maybe leaning toward the latter. When I was involved in filmmaking, and we had all the film and camera gear to lug around, carrying fresh food was out of the question. Wilderness filming and painting are demanding work and at the end of a long day, usually after dark, what I eat isn't all that important as long as there is a lot of it. Fortunately, the people I worked with felt the same way. We would film from sunrise to sunset when the weather was good. Then on the cloudy days we would sit in camp and fret about the fact that we couldn't film.

In recent years we've been doing more travelling with friends, and it's been interesting to see what other people eat. Some people like to stop early and enjoy a leisurely evening of cooking and eating. Others like to cover long distances, perhaps matching themselves against the almost unbelievable standard set by the voyageurs and early explorers. Their choice is usually simple fare, but lots of it. I've also been influenced by my son Paul, who while guiding for the past several years, has invented some interesting menus. Many of his meals are baked in the reflector oven, Coleman oven or Dutch oven. He carries some fresh food, which goes a long way toward enlivening the low-water-content foods. Casseroles, pies, cookies and cakes are standard fare. The point is, you can eat as well on a wilderness trip as you can at home, if you want to take the time to prepare it and don't mind the weight of a few fresh foods.

Planning menus and packing food

In my early days, roaming around in my canoe by myself, I used to take a bag of this and a sack of that and just guess at the amounts. Then, one day, I packed that way for a trip with my family plus two friends. When the food was loaded onto the table at home, it seemed like a ridiculous amount for two weeks for six people, so I started eliminating things until it looked about right. Near the end of the trip, with three days to go, we were windbound and ran out of food. We spent most of our remaining time looking for edible plants, berries, frogs, fish and anything else we could eat. That about did it for me with food packing! My wife, Joyce, took over and has done all the packing ever since. She enjoys figuring out menus and packing the food as individual meals. Following this method, you won't run short of meals, but you may run out of such things as jam, butter, and sugar if the weekly allotment isn't rationed. This system is an absolute must for groups or commercially-run operations.

The factors that must be taken into consideration when planning menus and packing food are:

1. Length of trip.
2. Number of portages.
3. Lake or river travel. Whitewater or flat water.
4. Mode of access to the beginning of the trip; that is, plane, car, or other means.
5. Reason for the trip. Is it a vacation or a working trip? Or a little of both?
6. The time allowed for leisure. Will you be up and on the water early and paddle late? Or have you allowed for a slow pace?

The trick is to match your menu to the trip you have planned. Six hours a day of paddling is a leisurely pace, which allows plenty of time for cooking and camp chores.

On some trips, the best scenery and hiking are at the fly-in point. Spending a few days there enables you to include a supply of fresh and heavier foods to be used before the downriver run. It's quite common to carry a two- or three-day supply of fresh food before getting into the dehydrated stuff.

I know of canoeists who have travelled on remote and difficult rivers with fresh meat and vegetables for the entire trip. They put one cardboard box inside another with insulation between them. They load the inner box with dry ice and meat and, after ten days, the meat is still frozen solid. In fact, the dry ice outlasts the meat. That's what I call ingenuity. While I would be very happy to enjoy their meals, I am not willing to carry the extra weight or go to the trouble.

On river trips, in particular, you must remember that it is not only the weight on the portages that you must consider, but also the difficulty of navigating an overloaded canoe through rapids. A loaded canoe is much more sluggish and more easily damaged than an empty canoe.

Purifying water for drinking and cooking

I've always lived by the rule, ''Never paddle on anything you can't drink''; however, this is becoming increasingly difficult. In the past, I've had to resort to boiling my drinking water or adding a few drops of bleach. Today there are numerous water disinfectants available, such as Micropur, Polar Pure and Potable Aqua.

One of the best methods of purifying water is by filtration. There are several filtration systems to choose from. The Katadyn Pocket Filter is probably the best one.

Types of food

Low-water-content foods

Removing water from food reduces weight and bulk, but it also reduces the food value and taste. Although the flavor of dehydrated food has improved over the years, it still doesn't equal fresh food and it's very expensive. Another drawback is that it is full of preservatives. Fortunately, many of the foods we use every day have a low water content. Examples are flour, rice, beans, raisins and nuts. There are also inexpensive, dehydrated foods available at the supermarket such as powdered milk, instant potatoes and soup mixes.

Dehydrated and freeze-dried packaged meals

For outdoor living there is a bewildering array of dehydrated and freeze-dried packaged meals on the market. The amount of preparation varies with the type.

1. The simplest type consists of a plastic pouch of freeze-dried food to which you add boiling water and stir. This is the most energy efficient method and is used for arduous or high-altitude hiking and climbing trips where you carry your stove and fuel on your back.

2. Another type is a packaged freeze-dried meal which requires from five to twenty minutes of boiling.

3. Some packaged dehydrated and freeze-dried meals require pre-soaking for five to fifteen minutes before boiling or they won't fully rehydrate.

4. Another method is to use individual freeze-dried foods such as peas, carrots and ground beef in combination with foods such as instant potatoes, rice, noodles, sauces and so on. This method requires more expertise in preparation, and more time in packing, but is less costly. We have always preferred this method for our family trips.

5. Dehydrated or freeze-dried foods can be supplemented with fresh foods such as cabbage, onions, carrots and fresh eggs. We add a few of these high-water-content foods if there isn't too much portaging.

Vegetarian, preservative-free meals

Meat is the single most expensive constituent in freeze-dried foods. It doesn't dehydrate well and is laced with preservatives. Harvest Foodworks (40 Hillcrest Drive, Toronto, Ontario M6G 2E3) has a wide range of tasty, reasonably priced freeze-dried meatless meals without preservatives or additives. The spices and sauces are packaged separately, so the meals can be prepared to individual taste and the servings are very generous. Bannock mix, bread mix, pancake mix and omelette mix are also available. The omelette is the best-tasting powdered egg mix I've tried yet.

Meatless, additive-free meals ———————

Common waterless foods ———————

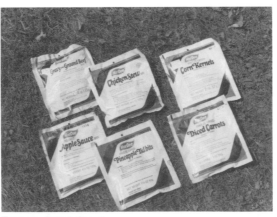

Freeze-dried foods ———————

Meat

If you are cooking from staples as opposed to packaged meals, meat is always the biggest problem. The most common method of preservation without refrigeration is the can. Most canoeists try to avoid cans and bottles and many parks don't allow them. For these trips, beef jerky, dry salami, vacuum-packed smoked bacon, and freeze-dried meat are used. When cans are allowed, tinned meats such as ham, corned beef, chicken, and tuna and sardines are popular. The best solution to the meat problem is to include one fishing fanatic in the crew.

Vacuum-packed bacon and salami ————

Freeze-dried and canned meat ————

Meat substitutes

Couscous, falafel, bulgur and beans such as soya and lentils can be used instead of meat. Try the recipes out at home before your trip so you can package them correctly.

Fresh vegetables, fruit and eggs

Potatoes, cabbage, carrots, onions, turnips, apples, oranges and eggs travel well. Packages of vegetables and fruit should be opened to the air and kept in the shade when in camp. If handled with care, they will last two to three weeks. Eggs can be placed in flour or pancake mix inside a hard container.

Heat-and-eat packaged meals

This type of packaged meal comes in a soft container and is available in the supermarkets. You place the pouch in boiling water and eat out of it. It is simple but, because of the water content, it is almost as heavy as canned food. It also tastes exactly like canned food.

How good are these packaged meals? There was a time when I would have said they were not very good. But now some of them are excellent. However, serving sizes are almost always underestimated and they can be quite expensive. If you are on a holiday and want to live it up a bit, that's fine, but for trips to remote places, where the transportation costs are expensive, supplementing dehydrated foods with fresh foods will help to keep the costs down.

Butter

I carry canned butter when available, otherwise margarine, because it is more resistant to going rancid than packaged butter.

Bread

Fresh rye and pumpernickel keep well for the first week. Then bannock (see page 62) replaces the bread. It is pre-mixed and measured at home.

Cakes and cookies

A fruitcake is a wonderful treat that will keep a long time. Cake and cookies usually last the first week, then can be made over the fire using cake and cookie mixes.

Cereals

Homemade or commercial granola is ideal for cold cereal. It can also be used for some dessert toppings. My cereal choice is rolled oats and Red River cereal.

Desserts

Many of the packaged desserts that you use at home are ideal for outdoor cooking. Dried fruit can be eaten raw or stewed.

Desserts ————

Group trip menu

When we canoe as a family or with friends on a holiday, we spend more time on meal preparation because that's half the fun. If there isn't too much portaging, we might carry a few fresh vegetables and fruit, as well as the no-water-content foods. Since the evening meal is my favorite, I sometimes make a lot and serve the surplus the next day for lunch. If the weather is dreary, I build a fire, add the leftovers to soup and call it stew.

The following is our basic menu plan. It bears little resemblance to the casseroles, beef stroganoff, quiches, fondus, and exotic desserts that commercial outfitters and some of my friends serve.

BREAKFAST

SUN.	MON.	TUES.	WED.	THURS.	FRI.	SAT.
bacon	granola	pancakes	hot cereal	granola	hot cereal	granola
eggs	bread	bacon	bread/bannock	bread/bannock	bread/bannock	eggs
bread	honey/jam	syrup	honey/jam	honey/jam	honey/jam	bacon
honey/jam	coffee/tea	coffee/tea	coffee/tea	coffee/tea	coffee/tea	bread/bannock
coffee/tea	juice/cocoa	juice/cocoa	juice/cocoa	juice/cocoa	juice/cocoa	juice/cocoa
juice/cocoa						coffee/tea

LUNCH

SUN.	MON.	TUES.	WED.	THURS.	FRI.	SAT.
tuna sandwiches	soup	peanut butter and	soup	cheese	tuna sandwiches	peanut butter and
oranges/dried fruit	cheese	jam sandwiches	sardines	peanut butter and	cookies	jam sandwiches
drink	bread	cheese	bread/bannock	jam sandwiches	drink	cheese
	cookies	dried fruit	cookies	dried fruit		bannock
	drink	drink	drink	drink		dried fruit
						drink

DINNER

SUN.	MON.	TUES.	WED.	THURS.	FRI.	SAT.
canned ham	chili	spaghetti with	canned corned	canned turkey	chicken curry	beef stew
scalloped potatoes	mashed potatoes	meat sauce	beef	mashed potatoes	rice	hash brown
corn	peas	fruitcake	hash brown	sour cream mix	apple crisp	potatoes
applesauce	pudding/nuts	tea	potatoes	green beans	tea	no-bake
tea	tea		peas	fruitcake		cheesecake
			snack cake	tea		tea
			tea			honey/jam
						coffee/tea
						juice/cocoa

Paul's cooking tips

Here are a few kitchen tips that Paul has divulged to me:

- Presentation can make a ho-hum meal fantastic. When cooking main dishes, be innovative: orange fruit crystals on fried canned ham give it zip; Worcestershire sauce on fried rice or vegetables gives a nice aroma. A little nutmeg in oatmeal makes it more palatable, and anything added to dried eggs helps. Try spices, bacon bits, canned or dried mushrooms, dried green pepper and Tabasco with them.
- Add water slowly to dry mixes. Never the other way around! Did you ever try to strain the excess water out of soupy cheesecake? Disregard the instructions for liquid amounts in the recipe. The manufacturers didn't take into account the amount of rain that would fall into the mix and the fact that your spoon doesn't have a high-speed setting.
- A wire whisk for mixing makes a big difference in keeping the frustration level to a minimum.
- Take a food repair kit. (I didn't know what it was either until Paul explained that it's a spice bag. He believes it's the camp cook's most important asset. Disillusionment set in when I found out he adds spices by colors, rather than flavors!)
- It's a good idea to bring a bag of white flour as a back-up. It can be used to make a fish batter, a sauce, a crust or bread.
- Do not rely on fish as a food supplement.
- One last thought: it's rare to have people complain about eating seconds, but watch their patience disappear when there isn't enough for firsts!

Recipe ideas

Chicken pot pie Dehydrated chicken and vegetables can be made into a tasty pot pie if topped with biscuit dough and baked. Place coals on an inverted lid in order to cook the crust to a golden brown.

Chicken pot pie ————————————

Ham and pineapple dinner A canned food dinner might consist of canned ham cooked in pineapple juice and served with rice and vegetables.

Ham and pineapple dinner ————————

Quiche Mix dried eggs with water and add sliced carrots, onion, celery and chopped walnuts. Add nutmeg. Put the egg mixture on the bottom of the pan and then spread Tea Bisk dough on top. Don't worry if the dough seems to sink. Cook until the quiche is set but still moist.

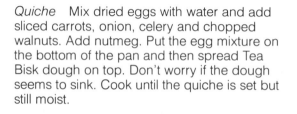

Quiche ————————————

Dumplings Regardless of the mix you use, divide the dough into golf-ball-size pieces. The dough should be sticky enough to stay together, but not gooey. The soup or fruit syrup should be boiling before putting the dumplings in to cook. Cook for a few minutes and then start taste-testing.

Recipe ideas. . .

Bannock Using this basic bannock recipe, which serves six, you can turn out a variety of filling breads.

3 cups (750 mL) white flour
2 cups (500 mL) whole wheat flour
½ cup (125 mL) bran
½ cup (125 mL) wheat germ
2 tbsp. (25 mL) baking powder
1 tsp. (5 mL) salt
⅔ cup (150 mL) shortening
⅔ cup (150 mL) milk powder

Combine all ingredients and add enough water to make a dough. Place the dough in the frying pan on the grill over coals, not an open flame or it will burn. As the dough rises and becomes firm, place the pan beside the fire. Tilt the pan toward the fire, gradually increasing the angle. If the dough flows to one side, you are rushing the process. When the pan is standing on edge, test the bannock with a splinter to see if it is cooked through. It helps to hold the heat around the pan if you place some rocks beside it.

Fry bread Use the basic bannock recipe and cook as pancakes in oil or bacon fat.

Fruit bread To the basic bannock recipe add chopped, dried apples or apricots.

Sweet fruit bread To the basic bannock recipe add diced candied fruit, brown sugar and cinnamon for a sweet dessert-style bread. Just before pouring the batter into the pan, add cinnamon for a swirled effect.

Pancakes Paul uses a pancake mix that usually requires some dried eggs. The key to making great pancakes is the additions that you can scrounge up. He's had success with these: pineapple, raisins, blueberries and fresh or freeze-dried diced apples. Syrup can be made from brown sugar and hot water, but to avoid a sugar shortage, bring syrup. Although the cheaper brands are in a plastic bottle already, be sure to tape the lid before packing.

Cake Use the basic snack cake or layer cake mix. These both produce light, fluffy cakes. The fun begins when you start adding your personal touches. Make two cakes and put canned mandarin oranges between the layers, smother with chocolate icing (from a mix) and top with cake sparkles. For a pineapple upside-down cake, put canned pineapple slices in the pan and then pour the cake mix over them. This also helps to keep the bottom of the cake from burning.

Cake

Pancakes

Bannock

62

Brownies   Brownies from a mix cook faster than cakes and also seem to be more prone to burning.

Cookies   The easiest way to make delicious cookies is from a mix. They usually require some dried egg. Chocolate chip seems to be the favorite. Remember to keep the dough sticky as it will spread as it cooks. Paul's "cookies" always turn into a cake, which he then cuts up.

Cookies ————————————

Pies   Pies are always a camp favorite. They can be made with fresh berries or dried fruit such as apples, apricots, raisins or even banana chips. Pudding mixes can also be used.

Cheesecake   Cheesecake is made from a mix, then topped with anything you can find.

Estimating food quantities is difficult although Carol Hodgins has attempted it in her *Wanapitei Canoe Trippers' Cookbook*. She also lists many more recipes than I am able to here.

Pies ————————————

Blueberry cheesecake ————————————

Snacks and treats

Gorp (granola, raisins, peanuts), CPR (raisins, peanuts), scrog (anything goes) — whatever its name, it's the equivalent to the voyageur's pipe tobacco. Every hour the voyageurs would stop for a pipe rest. The average canoeist doesn't smoke now, but the ritual of stopping and diving into a bag for a handful of gorp is fun to look forward to. This pleasant interval provides a rest, a chance to refuel and time to look around.

The combinations of ingredients that can go into gorp are endless. There is the basic or inexpensive stuff made up of raisins and peanuts, and the more exotic and expensive, which might include such luxuries as candied pineapple, apricots, cashews, almonds, Smarties, coconut and banana chips. (In hot weather avoid the chocolate chips.) You can tell a great deal about a canoeist by the kind of gorp he or she carries.

There is something you should know about gorp if you're paddling with others. You have to watch out for high-grading. High-grading is the despicable practice of removing only the exotic stuff when reaching for a handful of gorp. There are several ways to detect a high-grader. One way is to watch how long the hand stays in the bag. Another way is to use transparent plastic bags. Of course, the hard-core high-grader will take advantage of this to spot the good stuff and go straight for it, but most aren't that blatant. Watch their eyes. If they are clever at it, they glance at the bag, then turn away. What they are doing is memorizing the layout. I know people who can high-grade the candied pineapple out of a bag in one or two dips. The best way to control high-grading is to pretend you're being polite, grab the bag and give it a good shake as you hold it out. (But don't let go!) Then watch the pained expression as he or she comes up with just a handful of peanuts and raisins. I know canoeists who have tried to solve the whole high-grading problem by making their gorp with only choice items, but that's no fun at all.

Food box or wanigan

Have you ever noticed that if you go digging for the jam container, it's always at the bottom of the pack? And if there are several packs, it's always in the last one? The same applies to honey, butter, coffee or whatever. The way to combat this miserable tendency is to use a food box or ''wanigan'' that holds all the utensils, bowls, cups and food that you need at every meal. An added plus is that the lid becomes a countertop.

My first food box was made of wood and was large and very heavy because it held too much. The wanigan I have now is an old tin bread box 16 by 20 by 18 in. (40 by 50 by 45 cm) deep, which is an ideal size for one to four people. It's not very strong, but I've taken care of it. It carries small, hard plastic containers of milk, sugar, coffee, tea and so on, which are refilled from larger plastic bags as required. As the jars of honey, peanut butter, jam or whatever run out, they are replaced with full ones. My food box fits nicely into the top of one of the canvas food packs. If you carry your food box outside your pack, and are paddling large, windswept lakes or difficult rapids, your food box should be waterproof.

On long trips with four or more people, the plastic food barrel makes an excellent food box. It is waterproof and virtually dent-proof. Round trays, holding various items such as spices, can be made to drop inside. You can also make an apron to hold utensils that can be hung around the barrel for easy access. The lid can be used as a cutting board or serving tray. I carry my pots in a separate pot bag, but many people carry the pots, fold-up ovens and anything else related to cooking in the food box. Your cups and bowls must be nested or you'll never fit them all in.

In my travels I have come across people who make a hobby of designing and making their camp equipment. We found the Rolls-Royce of food boxes on the Mountain River. We pulled into an eddy beside a group's camp to say hello. I saw this exotic-looking kitchen laid out and was invited over for a closer look. The wanigan was made of

aluminum and had compartments and trays within trays that folded out to display everything. The possibilities are limited only by imagination and skill.

The following is a list of articles that I carry in my food box: cups, bowls, spoons, spatula, flipper, can opener, salt, pepper, sugar, milk, cinnamon, other spices, butter, peanut butter, oil, jam, honey, tea, coffee, cocoa, wash cloth, small tea towel, scouring pad, matches and cutting knife. The trick is to use containers of a size that allow you to include all these items in your box. Beware of waterproof containers that aren't. There's nothing more frustrating than finding that the honey or jam has leaked all over everything else. Fill them with water beforehand and squeeze them hard to see if they leak.

Table

When I am travelling alone or with one other person, the lid of the food box serves as a table, but with a larger group, we use an overturned canoe. Make sure that you support both gunwales with a log or rock, otherwise if someone leans or sits on one side, you could be in for some adversity.

Bowls and cups

If you put your main course on a plate while you eat your soup, it's only a matter of time until someone steps or sits in it. It also gets cold quickly. A bowl can do anything a plate can do. Food doesn't spill off it and you can't eat soup off a plate! If someone shows up with a dinky little tin cup straight out of a cooking pot set, you know that the first time he reaches out with his tin cup and you pour that hot tea into it, you're going to see a lot of action as he runs around looking for a flat spot to put it down on. Metal plates present the same problem. When you buy a nesting cooking pot set, the first thing to do is to throw away the tin cups and plates and replace them with nesting plastic cups and bowls. I like the double-thickness cups for insulation. I cut the handles off so they will nest. When I need an extra cup for company, I can separate the inner and outer to make two cups.

Food box or wanigan ————————

Plastic barrel wanigan ————————

High-tech, state of the art wanigan

Contents of food box

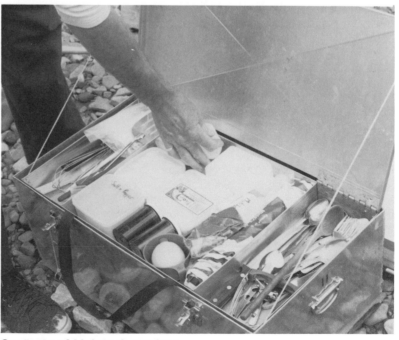

Contents of high-tech wanigan

65

Cooking methods

Boiling and frying are the fastest and easiest cooking techniques, but on a holiday trip there should be time for the leisurely preparation of meals. One of the greatest assets to any trip is a person who enjoys baking. The rest of the party will be glad to fill the roles of hewers of wood, haulers of water and washers of dishes!

Fires for cooking

For a cooking fire, keep the fire concentrated under the pots. It's much easier to cook with small sticks and split kindling than logs. Logs take too long to catch, and burn too hot when they do get going. If your fire gets too hot, just pull out some sticks and snuff them out until they are needed. Half the art of camp fire cooking is controlling your fire the same way you would your kitchen range at home.

The most important thing about a cooking fire is the height of the grill: 5 to 7 in. (12 to 18 cm) is average. If it's too low, you can't get enough wood under it. If it's too high, you need too big a fire to heat the pots. You will fry yourself as well as the food, and waste a lot of wood which, in well-travelled areas, is hard to come by.

Boiling

When you don't want to spend much time cooking on a trip, boiling is a good method to use. Preparations consist of boiling water then dumping in packages of freeze-dried stew or whatever. Dried or reconstituted freeze-dried fruit can finish off the meal.

If you have a wood stove and it doesn't have a hole for the pot, it is difficult to transfer enough heat to the pot to boil water. Inverting another pot over it will get the water boiling more quickly. You can also make a hole of pot-size so your pot fits into the stove. Water will boil almost instantly.

Pressure cooker

The pressure cooker is heavier than a normal pot, but is the fastest and most efficient method of cooking. It can be used over an open fire or stove.

Frying

The frying pan instantly brings to mind images of trappers, prospectors and the outdoors in general. There is something wonderful about the aroma of frying bacon and the sound of eggs sizzling in the pan. On the more remote trips, powdered eggs might have to suffice. Frying is the usual method of cooking fish. Just make sure the person doing the fishing catches the right size for the frying pan.

Baking over an open fire

A very tasty bannock can be prepared in the frying pan (see recipe, page 62). Hot bannock with butter is pure heaven. When you bake, it is a good idea to do enough for lunch, a snack at night and breakfast the next day.

Reflector oven

The fold-up reflector oven is a more efficient method of baking than the frying pan. Cakes, cookies, casseroles, quiche, meat and dishes like scalloped potatoes can be prepared to perfection. A primitive but adequate reflector oven can be fashioned from aluminum foil. With care it can be reused many times.

Coleman oven

The Coleman oven is heavier but more efficient than the reflector oven. It even has a built-in thermometer. The oven is placed on the grill over the fire. The fire is fed as required to hold the thermometer at the desired temperature. Placing rocks in the corners of the oven helps to give an even heat.

Dutch oven

The Dutch oven is the heaviest but most versatile cooking device of all. The oven is placed over a low fire with coals placed on the lid to give an even heat, or else it is placed on the ground with coals piled around it and on top. It takes a while to become proficient at cooking without burning.

Dough on a stick

Children enjoy cooking by winding dough around a stick and holding it over the fire. You can even cook by simply placing food on a hot rock beside the fire. We take our pots and frying pans for granted; the native peoples boiled water by placing hot rocks into a birchbark container of water.

Aluminum foil

Delicious meals can be baked in foil. This is another standard method for baking fish. A large fire is built and allowed to burn down to coals. The foil-wrapped fish is placed in the coals and some coals are pulled over the foil. Potatoes and other vegetables can also be cooked by baking in tinfoil. Use heavyweight foil or double wrapping to avoid burning.

Baking over a stove

The usual method of cooking over a fuel stove is by boiling, stewing, frying or the pressure cooker, but you can also bake quite efficiently. You must not allow the flame to come in contact with the baking pot. Take your largest pot and place several stones on the bottom. Now place the baking pot inside the larger pot on top of the stones. Cover the large pot to create the oven effect. It takes some practice to cook without burning. Another trick is to carry a tube pan: you can't end up with an uncooked middle to your cake because there is no middle.

Frying

Reflector oven

Dough on a stick

Coleman oven

Baking over open fire

6 BOOTS TO BAGS Clothing

Whenever I observe animals or birds in their natural habitat I am envious of their freedom of movement. Whether clothed in fur or feathers, they seem to be oblivious to the elements. I'm not suggesting that I want to trade places with them. There are advantages to being human, but body covering sure isn't one of them. No one set of clothes or sleeping gear is adequate for all conditions. This is particularly true when we are engaged in outdoor activities.

There was a time when most people had two sets of clothing: good clothes and old clothes. The good stuff you wore in the city; the old stuff you wore camping. But not anymore.

Now there are clothes for spring, fall and summer canoeing, hot dog canoeing, hiking, cross-country skiing, telemark skiing, mountain climbing—the list goes on and on and the prices go up and up. Manufacturing outdoor equipment and clothing has grown into a multi-million-dollar industry. Much of the new, high-tech outdoor clothing is expensive, but it looks so good you can wear it anywhere. You kind of hate to get it dirty though. Fortunately it's tough. One manufacturer of outdoor clothing, Tilley Endurables, includes these instructions on caring for their clothing: "Give 'em hell."

How much and what kind of clothing you need depends on the range of conditions you will be canoeing in. If you intend to canoe and camp only in summer, old clothes will do fine. I have a friend who buys all his camping clothes in the spring at a second-hand store and throws them away in the fall. For protection against the scorching sun and bug bites, there is nothing more comfortable and cool than an old light-colored dress shirt. Just stitch up the front, put Velcro fasteners on the cuffs and add a hood so that the blackflies can't get in. On the other hand, if you are a whitewater paddler and begin when the ice goes out, you need the high-tech stuff.

Dressed with full protection against cold air, cold water, big rapids, Hood River, NWT ————

Styles and fads

Styles and fads can get us into some uncomfortable outfits. Jeans are a good example, especially the tight-fitting style. They are too hot in warm weather and too cold for cold weather. Because most blue jeans are designed to be tight in all the wrong places, they don't allow heat and moisture to escape. If you get them wet in cold weather, it's like being encased in a suit of icy armor. They take forever to dry and create a refrigeration effect in the process. When wet, they also bind on the thighs. Cowboys didn't have these problems because they spent most of their time on their horses, and horses are a lot warmer to sit on than the seat of a canoe.

Another material that belongs in the cowboy era is leather. If you are riding a horse or a motorcycle, it does cut the wind. But walk a couple of hundred yards at a brisk rate and you work up a sweat. And in rain, leather turns into a soppy, spongy mess. Leather is hot when it's hot and cold when it's cold.

Traditional fabrics

Barely ten years ago the list of materials I knew would have consisted of wool, cotton, down, nylon and some kind of rubber raincoat. Cotton is a comfortable material for warm weather, but very uncomfortable for wet, cold weather and strenuous activity. It holds the moisture right next to the skin. Wool is noted for its insulating quality even when wet. It also allows moisture to escape from the body. In winter, a cross country skier's wool sweater will be white from moisture that has escaped and then frozen on the outside. Wool fibers absorb moisture and require a source of warmth to dry thoroughly. For this reason, wool is losing in the popularity contest to the superior synthetics.

Synthetic materials

Synthetic materials have completely changed canoeing and camping techniques. Gore-Tex, polytetrafluoroethylene, polyurethane, neoprene, SealCoat, Hypalon, latex, Capilene, polyester, pile, nylon, Hollofil 808, Synchilla, Polar Plus, Dacron: they sound like ingredients for a spray to combat spruce budworm, but they are just part of the new wave of materials to combat cold, wet and perspiration buildup in the new high-tech clothes for outdoor activities. High-tech equipment and clothing have enabled us to go places canoes were never meant to go, and in weather conditions and water temperatures that would have been suicidal in just "old clothes."

Ever since I climbed out of woolen undergarments and into polypropylene, I have been wondering why it works so well. Even after an accidental swim, I find I'm soon warm without the wet feeling that wet wool would give. The fibers in the new synthetics absorb little moisture and have proven more capable of "wicking" moisture away from the body than wool. You can whirl a wet synthetic garment around your head and the moisture will be forced to the outer extremities where it can be wrung out. The garment will feel dry when it is put back on because body heat pushes the moisture away from the skin and into the outer layer. Polypropylene, also known as "poly-pro," comes in a great variety of fabrics. Some of the knits are amazingly soft and comfortable. One of the recent arrivals is called Synchilla. Pile is a very thick, warm version of polypropylene. Nylon or polyester pile could be described as a rug made up of long fibers held together by a backing. It is warm but not windproof. Pile garments under a windproof, waterproof or breathable outer garment are just about the warmest thing you can wear, wet or dry. One disadvantage of the synthetics is that when they have been worn for a while they smell very bad. The manufacturers are aware of the problem and are working on it.

I haven't completely forsaken wool, because I do tend to be a bit of a traditionalist with my cotton tent, down bags, canvas packsacks and Prospector canoe. But I am sold on the synthetics for the extreme conditions in the North and for early spring and late fall. I am also convinced that waterproof paddling jackets, wet suits and neoprene socks and gloves are the way to go for cold-weather canoeing.

There are a few things about the high-tech stuff that I'm not completely comfortable with, though. Take colors for example. The designers of high-tech clothes apparently assume that you are going to get lost and that the bright colors, racing stripes and multi-colored shoulder panels will make it easy to find you. Some of the canoeists and kayakers I've seen recently look like they've stepped out of a spaceship or a race car. Not long ago, I was involved with the filming of a voyageur scene. The canoe was a 40 ft. (12 m) birchbark canoe from the Kanawa Canoe Museum near Dorset, Ontario. The paddlers were all decked out in authentic costumes. The colors were faded and very subtle. I looked up into the forest at the procession struggling over the portage and was struck by the beautiful harmony of the colors. And when they paddled that canoe you couldn't help but feel that they belonged there. Those old costumes seemed to me to be far more appropriate than the new.

It is frustrating to buy an expensive piece of clothing only to discover that it doesn't do what it is supposed to do. Here are some ideas to help you choose wisely.

Zippers

Zippers are a big part of outdoor clothing now. They enable you to open up your clothing to allow heat and moisture to escape. Badly-installed zippers are an abomination. Make sure that the zipper is installed in stiff material so that no soft flaps can get jammed in it. Zippers under the arms of jackets for air circulation are a good idea but I wouldn't miss them. When I get too hot I just peel off a layer of clothing. However, zippers on pant legs are a marvellous asset as they make it possible to remove overpants without taking off your footwear. Plastic zippers have some advantages over metal ones. They are less likely to jam. If they wear and begin to come apart, a gentle squeeze will close the zipper until you have a chance to replace it.

Clothing . . .

Layering

To outfit yourself for strenuous activity in adverse weather conditions, it's important to understand how the body works. When we move, we generate heat, then perspire to cool off. When we perspire too much, our clothes get wet and lose their insulating quality, so we get cold. This is particularly true if extreme activity is followed by inactivity. The moisture evaporates, creating a refrigeration effect. In extreme conditions this can lead to hypothermia (the lowering of the core temperature of the body). It's more complicated than that, but the point is to wear layers of clothing that can be put on or taken off to stay comfortable and dry.

If it's windy, a breathable windproof garment is worn over the insulating layers. A good breathable material will cut the wind, but at the same time allow most of the moisture to escape. In difficult or dangerous situations, the objective is to lose as little heat and moisture as possible. In warm and dry conditions, with an unlimited water supply and ample food, excessive perspiration is not a problem as long as you drink enough to prevent dehydration.

When the weather turns bad, there isn't much you can do to avoid discomfort if you have brought the wrong clothes. A wet piece of clothing stays wet until the weather clears. However, it is always possible to be wet and warm if you've got the right clothes. When the rain stops or when you drag yourself out of the river, it's amazing how fast your wet clothes will dry out while you're wearing them, once you have removed your waterproof outer clothing. If the air is cold and you become chilled, simply put on extra layers or change into dry clothes. And you must eat enough to feed the inner fire or your reserves will be quickly depleted.

Understanding this fine balance is particularly important when it is not possible to make an open fire. If you've got all your clothes on, and they are all wet, and you begin to shiver, your last resort is your sleeping bag. Being wet and cold will kill you if you remain that way too long.

It is particularly important to pack the right clothes when family camping or guiding children's trips. It's the responsibility of the person in charge to see that everyone has the right kind and amount of clothing. You should be aware, though, that too much clothing is almost as bad as not enough. You can let children bring everything they own and, if the weather turns wet, it will all be soaking wet in the bottom of their packs long before the trip is over. The trick is to carry just enough clothes and to make sure the group isn't wearing its last remaining dry clothes in a situation in which they are likely to get wet.

Cool and comfortable old clothes ———

Tough, superbly designed outdoor clothing ———

Cold weather clothes for flat water ———

Rainwear

Fortunes are made and lost by clothes manufacturers trying to create the perfect garment to keep you warm and dry in the rain. For city wear, they have met with considerable success. For outdoor use, where the activity range is extreme, nothing seems to be totally successful. Some manufacturers claim that their miracle materials allow perspiration to escape while preventing water from getting in. During strenuous activities the body gives up amazing quantities of water. It is unlikely that unlimited amounts of water vapor can escape while keeping the water droplets from getting in.

I wish I could be more enthusiastic about the new high-tech breathable rainwear. Just about everybody who has this kind of rainwear says it's great in cold conditions, but for paddling all day in the rain, or portaging sodden, muddy packs, reactions are mixed. Very expensive high-tech materials are often too fragile for rough outdoor wear. Paul's ''absolutely non-sweating waterproof'' rain gear kept the water out for almost a month before it started leaking like a sieve. A leaky raincoat, cold feet, cold hands and cold rain running down your face because of a badly designed hood rate up at the top of the adversity scale. It's tough to hear any part of the song in these conditions.

I prefer to go with a totally waterproof fabric and cope with moisture buildup from perspiration by wearing something (Synchilla, polypro, pile or fleece, for example) that retains the air pockets even when wet, since these minute pockets of air provide insulation. I never hesitate to adopt a new material if it proves to be better than what I'm using and I can afford it. I have learned to be cautious, though, because several of the wonder materials only work when new and clean, and you know how it is, somebody drops your pack in the mud and what are you supposed to do?

Other materials are only waterproof until the coating begins to peel off. When they are stitched together, the needle punches holes in the material, so all the seams have to be treated or taped. In time, seam sealer wears off or cracks. Natural materials such as cotton don't have this problem, because the fibers swell and close the holes naturally. A few years ago I thought I had found the solution to this problem. I discovered a rain suit made from a tightly-woven cotton that was heavily impregnated with wax. As the wax wore away it was retreated with more wax. At last the perfect solution! I bought the jacket and pants and headed off. It seemed to work. Any time the rain got through, I dried the material and slathered on more wax. I still got wet, though. Then I thought that it must be perspiration condensing on the inside. To test my theory I put on the outfit and went out in a rainstorm. I was soon soaking wet. It finally dawned on me that a great idea was not working. Paul has come to the same conclusion and we've all gone back to the totally waterproof coated nylon. When the coating breaks down, we chuck it.

Another way in which raincoat manufacturers try to deal with moisture buildup is through design. This is the method I prefer. They use a waterproof material, but make the shoulders a separate flap of material that comes down the front and back. This flap protects a loosely-woven screen that is stitched into the coat. Since warm air rises, moisture is carried up and out through the vents. Most raincoats have hoods; however, a loose collar that allows moisture to escape and a Tilley brim hat or a sou'wester rain hat, which is an oilskin hat with lined ear flaps (see page 73), do a better job. If you do use a hooded raincoat, the hood should have a small peak to shed the water from the face.

Totally waterproof or breathable fabric rainwear

Clothing . . .

Wet suits and dry suits

To lose your canoe and gear on a wilderness river trip would be a disaster. In an upset, you must stay with your canoe to work it to shore. If the water is very cold, you have to think of the effect it will have on you. For this reason, in anything more than Class 2 rapids, you should wear protective clothing. Unfortunately, on hot, sunny days, protective clothing can be very uncomfortable. Wearing it while travelling in cool weather is more comfortable. Some protective clothing can be more easily removed than others; usually when you put on a wet suit you keep it on all day.

The wet suit is an amazing invention. It protects you from frigid water for a long time if you remain active. (If you are inactive, you will soon begin to feel the cold.) I find my legs get cold but my upper body can get very warm while paddling. Wet suits of necessity fit tightly, so they restrict movement and can cut off circulation in the lower legs when the wearer kneels for any length of time.

Dry suits are the warmest outfits for cold water conditions. They are loose and roomy, allowing you to wear warm underwear next to the skin. The waterproof outer layer fits tightly around the neck, wrists, waist and legs to keep out the cold water. These suits are great for arctic conditions. In frigid water, a wet suit will keep you alive for a while; a dry suit will keep you alive a lot longer.

Two of my friends, Mike Beedell and Jeff MacInnis, were sailing a Hobie-Cat catamaran through the Northwest Passage. The boat was very fast and light, but wet to sail. And there was always a chance of upsetting or falling into the deadly cold water. For this expedition they had to wear dry suits at all times. Because of their inactivity on board, they couldn't generate enough internal heat to keep the cold from seeping through their suits. Whenever they landed and were able to run around on shore, they could generate enough heat to get warm, but too much activity would cause them to perspire and dampen their inner clothing, thus leading to even more chilling. They told me they have never been

more cold or miserable in their lives.

Unfortunately wet suits and dry suits don't keep you as warm and comfortable as normal clothing when you are out of the water in very cold conditions.

Loose-fitting waterproof paddling jackets and pants over pile clothing are much more comfortable than a wet suit and much less

expensive. This arrangement is adequate for reasonable whitewater conditions, when a wipeout is unlikely. You vary the weight of the underwear depending on the air temperature. If you tuck the legs securely into wet-suit socks and tighten the pants and jacket at the waist, wrists and neck, the protective effect is enhanced.

Clothing for cold whitewater canoeing

Hats

For years, I never wore a hat except for a tuque in cold weather, and a rain hat in wet weather. Then I began hearing about all the holes we're punching in the ozone layer. It seems that the sun we once worshipped has become our enemy, and we have to cover up to avoid skin cancer.

Old hat

Many people get their hats from the second-hand stores. You can find some real gems. You, too, can look like you've just robbed a train.

Old hats have character

Hood

A good idea for cold weather, a hood keeps the draft off your neck. However, a hood on a raincoat holds perspiration in. Water also runs down your nose unless the hood has an ample peak.

Hooded raincoat and sou'wester

Helmet

A helmet is a must for playing around in big whitewater in canoes or kayaks. Surfing upstream on a wave and sitting broadside in a hole puts you in a vulnerable position: you can get clunked by your rolling canoe or a rock.

Helmet

HFD

All favorite canoeing hats should be equipped with an HFD (hat floatation device). An HFD consists of a piece of Ensolite glued with contact cement into the crown of the hat.

Peaked hat

About the only place you'd catch Paul without a peaked baseball hat is in bed, and he doesn't even play baseball. He's collected them from all over. A real collector trades, barters, steals, cajoles and pleads for them, but never buys them. However, the peak tends to catch gusts of wind which can often snatch the hat into the water.

Rain hats

The sou'wester is one of those great inventions of man that has gone the way of the dodo. Mine was a gift and I wouldn't trade it for the crown jewels. In cold weather it keeps the cold off the back of the neck and ears, yet allows moisture to escape up under the collar. Totally waterproof and very comfortable, it protects the face and neck from drips and has a warm lining and ear flaps.

Brim hat

A hat with a brim keeps the sun out of your eyes and cuts the glare from a bright hazy sky, but it doesn't do much about the reflection off the water. Fancy brim hats don't stay that way for long if you use the tumpline over them or stuff them in a pack when not needed. If it's too good for this kind of abuse, then it's not suitable for canoeing.

The Tilley Endurable hat has a great reputation. It comes in four styles with a virtually unlimited guarantee. You can scrunch it, roll it, sit on it, wash it and it still looks good and is comfortable. It has a double strap system so it can't blow off, but you've got to use both straps. I should warn you, however, that Tilley hats can be dangerous. Once a group of us was drifting down the Mackenzie River in a sail-rigged trimaran of canoes. I was swimming in the frigid water to get a shot of the rig, when Louise Schaber's Tilley hat blew off because both straps weren't in place. The crew immediately began a desperate search to recover it. Meanwhile, I was perishing from the cold, but my frantic pleas fell on deaf ears. There was no way they were going to give up the search until all hope was gone. When they finally paddled over and pulled me from the water, I felt like I was slipping into the final stages of hypothermia! Alex Tilley has since built floatation into all his hats. Anyone with an older Tilley can do the same, gluing a piece of thin Ensolite inside the crown.

Tilley brim hat

Footwear

Hiking, a welcome diversion on any canoe trip, Mountain River

The most sadly neglected bit of the canoe camper's anatomy is the feet. They are usually too hot, too wet or too cold. The ideal footwear has to be warm in cold weather, dry in wet weather, non-slipping for wet rocks and light in case of an upset. Sadly, this combination is impossible to achieve in any one type of footwear.

Running shoes

High or low running shoes are the standard footwear for summer canoeing (A and B). Nylon shoes dry much faster than canvas. However, running shoes are too cold for cold weather and cold water, and get wet too easily.

Moccasins

I have a combination that solves most of the problems. Again I learned about this footwear from Calvin Rutstrum's book *The Way of the Wilderness*, and he learned about it while travelling with Indians in the North. The footwear consists of moccasin rubbers over smoke-tanned moosehide moccasins (C and D). It's the only kind of footwear that has kept my feet dry, warm and comfortable in all weather and canoeing conditions, excluding upsets or having to jump overboard when landing. My toes bend easily when I kneel in the canoe without cutting off circulation. (I wear an inner felt sole to cushion my foot.) It's true that there is no ankle support, but I've worn them for years and have never twisted my ankle. Another thing I like about the moccasins and rubbers is that the rubbers can be kicked off before you enter the tent, which helps keep the floor clean. You can also take them off if you are paddling a dry canoe and slip them on for the portage.

For bad weather, I carry a light pair of rubber overshoes that fit snugly over the moccasins (E). I prefer buckles to zippers, but they are difficult to find. This combination is perfect for portaging the muskeg country in the far north. It also keeps your feet dry in any downpour if you let your rain pants hang over them. With wool socks I can enjoy warm, dry feet in temperatures well below freezing.

A compromise that might appeal to you is to buy a pair of moccasin rubbers to fit over your favorite runners (F). You can also do the same with the overshoes. In cold weather the moccasins are warmer because you can add socks. And for the warmest and driest feet, you can put several pairs of socks in your overshoes with or without the moccasins.

Boots

Leather boots are not very suitable for canoeing. They cannot be dried over a fire without damaging the leather and, if they have been waterproofed and get damp inside, they are difficult to dry. Hard or stiff-soled boots are also a poor choice. When you kneel to paddle, you must be able to bend your toes to grip the bottom of the canoe. One last disadvantage: stiff-soled boots are very difficult to get out from under the seat and, in an upset, your feet could get caught.

Rubber boots are another bad idea for canoeing. The open tops act like giant scoops on your feet when you try to swim. Jettisoning your boots on a wilderness trip is unthinkable. The overshoes mentioned earlier are tight, light and easy to store.

The famous L.L. Bean boot (G) is a dependable piece of footwear. The toes are soft and bend easily when you kneel in the canoe. The bottom part is rubber and the upper is leather. There is no lining, so they can be wiped out if you get them wet in an upset. Your feet will perspire because of the rubber, but the inner sole is easily removed for drying. I prefer the 6 in. (15 cm) top.

Neoprene booties and thongs

When canoeing rock-studded rapids in cold water, you must have protective clothing and footwear. I have been using extra-thick neoprene booties inside a moccasin rubber (H). Most of the people I canoe with use a neoprene sock inside runners or light canvas boots (I). The neoprene sock has revolutionized canoeing. In neoprene your feet may be wet, but they're almost always warm. For canoeing, wet-and-warm sure beats wet-and-cold. The latest thing is a neoprene boot with a heavy sole and laces

Never try to make do with only one pair of boots or shoes: you will spend most of every evening trying to dry them before the fire. Chances are, they will either melt or burn before the trip is over. I carry two pairs of moccasins, so if I get one pair wet I still have a dry pair. The wet ones dry quite fast on a pack in the sun or over a fire.

Drying neoprene socks or booties is a total waste of effort. No matter how cold and wet they are in the morning, they get warm from your body heat as soon as you put them on. I remember a morning when I had to dig around under inches of fresh snow to find them. I inadvertently spilled some hot coffee into them before I put them on and it warmed them up beautifully.

For summer wear around camp, some people like the comfort and airiness of neoprene thongs.

Hiking boots

Heavy hiking boots have long been considered essential to prevent twisted ankles on hiking trips. This attitude is slowly changing as hikers and climbers take to the heights in lighter footwear. I'm talking about hiking and rock scrambling, not the heavy duty stuff like scaling vertical walls and overhangs. That's a little out of my league.

On my mountain canoe trips, I climb with nylon-topped shoes. The shallow treads cause less damage to the fragile alpine meadows. Blisters are also less likely to occur with this kind of footwear. Blisters are the curse of hikers, and are much more common with the heavier boot. When walking up steep slopes, the foot is placed flat on the surface, not dug into the hill. Walking flat in this manner is actually less tiring, as well as being less damaging to the terrain.

Leather-reinforced nylon shoes or boots are great for any combination of conditions. Buy them large enough to be worn with heavy wool socks. This arrangement is very comfortable and suitable for your average fine-weather lake expedition, easy river travel and for hiking.

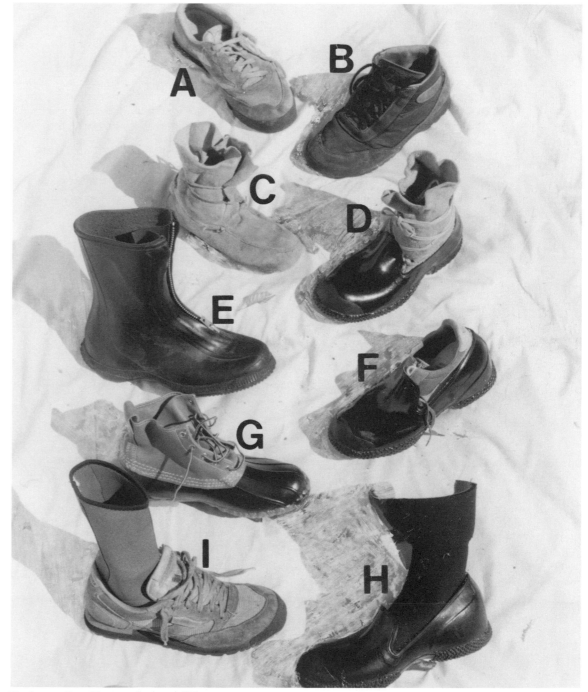

Footwear for all canoeing conditions

Gloves and mitts

Leather (A)
For canoeing or kayaking in the summer, most people allow their hands to toughen up naturally. You might want a pair of light leather gloves for bringing in firewood, preventing blisters while paddling or protection from bugs. I've heard of people who wear cycling gloves to avoid blisters and provide warmth.

For early spring or late fall, it's difficult to find suitable gloves for paddling. Gloves that are both waterproof and warm are bulky, and it's hard to get a feel for the paddle, especially in whitewater, when you need to perform a number of maneuvers. In anything other than flat water, it's impossible to keep the lower hand dry. And since most people occasionally change sides, that means both hands get wet. In cool-water, cool-air conditions you can use ordinary leather gloves; your hands will be wet but warm.

Leather palm, neoprene-backed gloves (B)
The leather palms give you a feel for the paddle while the neoprene backs keep your hands warm.

Neoprene gloves (C)
The full neoprene gloves are much warmer than the first two examples, but they are bulky, and it's hard to get a feel for the paddle.

Cordura or nylon shell with wool or polypro liner (D)
For winter canoeing, I use wool mitts with a nylon or Cordura cover, and keep them dry at all costs. I don't run rapids or paddle in large waves in winter. To upset in sub-zero air and freezing water temperatures is almost certain death, unless you are dressed in a survival suit.

Pogies (E)
The nylon or neoprene pogie is a recent invention for kayakers and canoeists. It attaches to the paddle with Velcro. You slip your hand inside the pogie and grip the paddle directly, so you have full control. Your hands will be wet, but they are protected from the chilling effect of the wind. However, when paddling a canoe in rapids, it's difficult to change hands quickly.

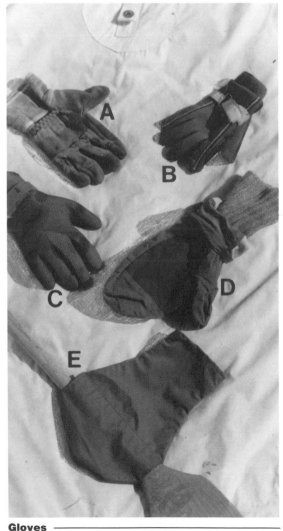

Gloves

Knee pads

Knee pads are a must for running rapids if you are paddling a canoe that doesn't have foam pads or knee blocks cemented in place. There is an endless array of them on the market. They tend to stretch with time, and then constantly slip down. On the other hand, if they are too tight, they can cut off circulation. Those designed with a hole behind the knee tend to be more comfortable. Some paddling pants have the pads sewn right into the knees.

Knee pads

Clothes checklist

Summer clothing (warm water)
- Sun hat
- Rain hat or hood on raincoat
- Windproof jacket
- Raincoat jacket
- Heavy shirt or sweater
- Medium-weight shirt or sweater
- Light cotton long-sleeved shirt
- Light cotton T-shirt
- Windproof pants
- Rain pants
- Warm polypro or wool pants
- Light cotton or nylon pants
- Shorts
- Bathing suit
- Underwear
- Belt or suspenders
- Two pairs wool or polypro socks
- Two pairs cotton socks
- Two pairs light, non-waterproof footwear
- Rubbers to go over footwear
- Bandana
- Gloves, if desired
- Bug jacket and/or head net

Spring or fall clothing (cold weather and/or cold water)
Add these clothes to the above list:
- Wet suit or dry suit, either one-piece or two-piece
- If no wet suit or dry suit, wear rain pants over heavy polypro underwear
- Waterproof paddling jacket over polypro underwear
- For maximum protection in extreme conditions, wear dry suit over wet suit
- Neoprene socks inside oversized running shoes, or neoprene boots, or moccasin rubbers over heavy neoprene socks
- Rubber or neoprene gloves
- Windproof over-mitts with wool or polypro liners for flat water paddling and around camp
- Tuque or hat with ear flaps
- Buckle overshoes for dry feet around camp

All the clothes you'll ever need

Sleeping bags

If you spend a lot of time outdoors and travel very far afield, a certain amount of adversity is unavoidable. I've been on trips when it never rained and the wind was with us nearly every day. I've also been on trips when I never saw the sun, it rained every day, the wind was always against us, the rapids were unrunnable, the portages indescribable and the bugs merciless. Climbing into a bug-free, bone-dry tent and rolling into a warm sleeping bag was pure heaven!

Any successful outdoor venture begins with a warm, dry sleeping bag. There is no such thing as the perfect sleeping bag. Even in the middle of summer, temperatures can range so widely that one night you're too hot and the next you're freezing. In spring and fall, the temperatures are even less predictable. There are people who sleep comfortably in winter bags in any temperature: they amaze me. Being too hot is as much a problem for me as being too cold.

The first decision to make when choosing a bag is whether to buy a down or a synthetic one. Despite all the amazing advances in creating light, warm synthetics, technology has not yet put ducks and geese out of business. But they are definitely in trouble. The synthetics are almost as good and much cheaper than duck and goose down and, for most campers, they are adequate.

Looking out at a Superior sunrise ————

Down
ADVANTAGES   No other material is lighter, warmer or will roll up smaller than high-quality down. And there is no other material that is so durable when cared for properly. My down bags are 25 years old and still work just fine.
DISADVANTAGES   First, down is expensive. I've heard that genuine eiderdown can cost $400 a pound (about $880 per kg). Fortunately duck and goose down are cheaper. Second, down will work its way out of most materials unless they are very tightly woven. Third, down mats when wet, thus losing its insulating quality. Because it is difficult to dry, this can be dangerous on an arduous trip. Anyone who uses down must be proficient in keeping things dry.

Synthetics
ADVANTAGES   The high-quality synthetics are considerably cheaper than down. The bag construction can be less complicated because synthetics are easier to hold in place. They retain their loft even when wet. A wet synthetic bag is warmer than a wet down bag. Synthetics are easier to wash than down bags, much easier to dry out and less allergenic than down.
DISADVANTAGES   Unlike ducks and geese, which have been using the same down for who knows how long, synthetics change from year to year. A state-of-the-art bag one year is old-fashioned the next. Synthetic sleeping bag fillers are excellent, but fall short of down in warmth, lightness and compactibility. In two bags of equal warmth, the down packs smaller and weighs less.

Down bag construction
In a well-made bag the insulation is distributed evenly so there are no thin spots. In one design (illustration 1 A) the upper and lower coverings are sewn together. Wherever the coverings touch, there is little or no insulation. These bags have the simplest construction and are therefore the cheapest. They are fine for summer conditions.

In another design (illustration 1 B) the inner and outer coverings are separated by a baffle. This makes an even thickness and therefore a better bag. When you inspect a bag, you can feel the difference easily by pulling the outer and inner coverings apart. Because these bags are more difficult to make, they are more expensive. This is the type of bag that is needed for adverse conditions.

In a third design (illustration 1 C) a reasonably even thickness is achieved by offsetting two bags sewn through. This construction is not as common as it used to be.

Bag shapes
For canoeing, I prefer the comfort of the roomy rectangular bag. For backpacking, the mummy bag (photograph 5) is preferable because it's more compact. It is also warmer because there is less air space for your body to keep warm. For cold weather, a lined hood keeps your head warm and keeps the draft from your neck and back. If you are using hoodless summer bags nested (see below), just wear a tuque or buy a separate hood that comes down over your shoulders. A sleeping bag must have a zipper all around for ventilation when the temperature rises. I have two identical bags that can be zippered together to make a double bag when Joyce and I go on a trip.

The ideal sleeping bag
This exists only for people who can crawl into a warm bag and sleep comfortably regardless of the air temperature. For those of us who are generally either too hot or too cold, this is impossible. Fortunately there are a number of solutions. You can buy several sleeping bags of varying weights and hope you choose the right one when you head out. Or you can try my solution, which came about inadvertently. I bought the lightest summer down bag. It was the least expensive sewn-through construction but was adequate with a cotton liner. As I began to extend my camping into fall, I needed a warmer bag. Again I didn't want to spend a lot of money for a big bag, so I bought another light down bag. By nesting the

two together, I now had a bag suitable for spring and fall. But more importantly, if the weather got warm I could climb into the upper layer so I had only one layer over me, and if it got colder I could climb down into the lower level. This put three layers of down bags over me and only one under me (photograph 3), but I found that with a good sleeping mat I didn't need the thickness underneath. Finally, when I started winter camping, I bought another light but oversized down bag and nested them all together. They work well because the layers are offset, which results in a relatively even thickness. In addition, the air spaces between the bags provide insulation.

By carrying three bags and a liner, I have five different options, depending on what level I climb into (illustration 2). I have used this arrangement even in the Arctic. Although my arrangement isn't as light or compact as the best arctic bag, it's not unreasonable (photograph 4). One disadvantage to layering is extra shell covering. With the three bags, I am carrying six layers of material instead of two, but they are light materials. The layering system would work with synthetics, but would make a huge, unmanageable bundle.

On summer canoe trips with Joyce, Becky and Paul, we would separate the bags, put a liner in each and head out. It is expensive to outfit a family of four with state-of-the-art down bags. If I were going to be backpacking in consistently cold, −40° weather, I would love to own the best, warmest down bag, but as it is, I wouldn't get enough use out of it.

Paul's medium-weight down bag is designed to be versatile. When the air temperature moderates, Paul shakes all the down to one side. With only a thin layer of insulation he is very comfortable. If the temperature drops suddenly, he just pounds the bag to distribute the down and feathers across the bag.

I would suggest that you beware of some of the fancy new bags with a reflective layer that is supposed to reflect your body heat back into the bag. I took one along on a trip. One night was more than enough. It had a clammy, hot feeling which I found most uncomfortable.

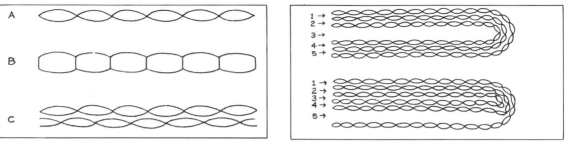

1 Sleeping bag construction

2 The layering principle

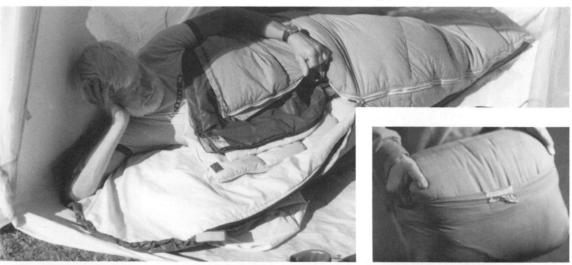

3 Three bags into one

4 Three bags rolled up

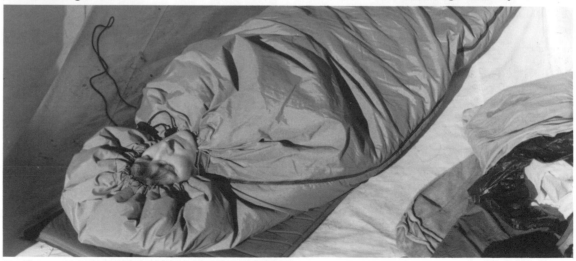

5 Mummy bags — constricting but warm and efficient

79

Sleeping mats

I've tried them all. I've gone from the big tube air mattresses to waffle foam, to Ensolite and the sophisticated Therm-a-Rest. Nothing's perfect, but some materials are more imperfect than others. Take the air mattress for example. It gives you the greatest protection from rough terrain. But I agree with whoever said there is no such thing as an air mattress. An air mattress is an ingenious invention that has air in it as long as you don't lie on it.

Tube-type air mattress (A)
Comfortable if not overly inflated, this type of air mattress dries quickly when wet. It is great for rough, rocky ground, but cold in cold weather or on snow. Although it keeps you high and dry in a damp, soggy tent, it is tough to keep full of air and a real pain to blow up and deflate. Even with a hand pump, blowing one up is a laborious process. It should be easy to patch, but I find the holes are always on the seams, around the valve, or in other impossible places. They are somewhat heavy.

Waffle foam mattress (B)
This open-cell mattress has fallen out of favor in recent years. Although it is still the most comfortable mattress on rough ground, and warm in all weather, you're in big trouble if you get it wet because it is almost impossible to dry. I used one for ten years and kept it dry by packing it properly. It can be made into a compact bundle if you fold it in half lengthwise and then kneel on it as you roll it up in a ground sheet. However it takes a while for it to regain its thickness after being unrolled. Eventually it loses its thickness when rolled tightly, and for this reason should be stored open.

Ensolite closed-cell foam pad (C)
This is amazing stuff and reasonably comfortable on flat ground. It is not comfortable on rough ground unless you carry a whole bundle of them. It is easy to dry and easiest of all to roll up.

Ridge Rest Eva Foam (D)
This is a new, high-tech version of the simple slab of Ensolite. The ridge pattern cuts down on weight, while providing the same amount of insulation and comfort.

Foam-filled air mattress, Therm-a-Rest (and its imitators) (E)
This cross between the air mattress and foam pad self-inflates part way, then you finish with a few breaths before closing the valve. It is very comfortable on all terrain, warm in winter and only slightly slower to roll up than a foam pad. Although it dries very quickly, keep it away from the camp fire or it will melt. Being an air mattress, it has the usual problem retaining air. Leaks on the flat surface are easy to fix with the repair kit (page 133) but those on the seam or around the valve, which is where they usually occur, are impossible to mend. My Therm-a-Rest seam melted when

somebody, not me, spilled bug repellent on it. Four attempts to fix it with repair kits have failed miserably. Now I am working with every conceivable kind of glue, epoxy resin, clamps, and so on. I'm too cheap to give up! Despite the problems, it is still the best choice of mattress. Just keep the bug dope away from it. They are available in three-quarter and full-length sizes.

Therm-a-Rest Camp Rest (F)
This is the deluxe model. It is wider and thicker, and thus much more comfortable. It's also much more expensive, heavy and bulky to pack. I like the standard model for compactness.

Hammock
A hammock is almost weightless and fun to have along for relaxing in after a hard day.

The hammock — fun to have along

Sleeping mats

The Indian name for this falls on the Hood River is unknown; it has never been renamed ———

There is only one thing about living in Canada that makes me sad: I will never be able to paddle all the rivers and lakes in my lifetime. When I see photographs or read descriptions of some of them, I long to see them for myself. But there is enjoyment in experiencing these places vicariously through other people's eyes.

For many years, Lake Superior was my favorite place to canoe. Then, several years ago, I saw Virginia Falls on the Nahanni River and it replaced Superior. Two years later, I saw Wilberforce Falls on the Hood River and it edged Virginia off the top of the list. And last year, I canoed on the Mountain River and it has topped them both. The Little Nahanni River took the lead for best whitewater. It was a narrow, big-volume river and I'd like to check it out again to see if it's really as good as I remember.

The Hood River flows east, parallel to the shores of the Arctic Ocean. After about 100 miles (160 km) it swings north and drops over 200 ft. (60 m) high Wilberforce Falls before emptying into Bathurst Inlet. In 1985, six of us in three canoes — Wally Schaber and I in one, Alan Whatmough and Bruce Cockburn in a second, and Gilles Couët and Gilles Lévesque in a third — began our trip on the Hood.

With its remoteness, lack of people, frigid water and cold air temperatures, the Hood is in a class by itself as a wilderness experience. I don't mind running rapids in cold-water conditions, but I feel uneasy when air temperatures are also cold. In mid-July, we were dodging ice on all the big lakes that interrupt the upper Hood. You can imagine what that did for the water temperatures downstream.

We lined or portaged rapids that were questionable. When I say "portaged," that's a bit misleading. What we really did was drag the canoes cross-country. At first I thought this was sacrilegious — you don't drag a canoe! But we did. The terrain was mostly water-soaked grass, even on the sides of the hills, and the canoes slid beautifully. When going downhill, we even left the packs in. All of us

were rapids-running enthusiasts, but no one complained when the rapids we heard in the distance turned out to be thundering waterfalls. The scenery was spectacular. Each day, we tried to time it so we could camp beside a falls or a gorge.

My idea of the perfect river is one that has a spectacular falls or canyon, or both, preferably near the end of the river, so you've got something to look forward to. And if a canyon, say two miles (3 km) long and over 200 to 250 ft. (60 to 75 m) deep, is found below the falls, with rapids that might be runnable, well that would be the river of which dreams are made. My favorite rivers have a big payoff at or near the end. The Hood River is one of those rivers. About a day's journey from the mouth, where it flows into Bathurst Inlet, the river narrows into a red sandstone canyon, then plunges 80 ft. (25 m) into a caldron of seething foam followed by yet another 100 ft. (30 m) plunge into an abyss. It's called Wilberforce Falls, one of the most spectacular sights in Canada. The total drop is more than 195 ft. (65 m). Towering spires of rock soar from the base of the second falls to high above the first. A narrow ridge provides access to the very top of the pinnacle from which you can lean out and look straight down into the depths of the canyon.

I doubt that there has ever been a canoeist who hasn't stood on the brink of a falls and fantasized what it would be like to be swept into the maelstrom below. You imagine that somehow you survive the drop and look back up at the face of the falls high above. Well, at Wilberforce, having survived the first drop, the fun would have just begun. You would find yourself in a witch's caldron that empties over a second lip, with an even longer drop, into the dark depths of the canyon. Below the two falls, the river continues down several rapids, then pauses for a moment before continuing its journey through the canyon. If by some miracle you had survived all that, you would swim to shore only to stare up at sheer 230 ft. (70 m) cliffs. They are so steep that the walls appear to come together at the top. Everything I have described is from the left shore

facing downstream. This is the portage side of the river. With no trees to obstruct the view, the falls can be enjoyed from many angles and viewpoints.

The deep vertical-walled canyon twists and turns away from the falls for almost two miles (about 3 km). We had heard that the canyon might be runnable. There is nothing in canoeing as alluring as a runnable canyon. It's like entering a tunnel into the unknown. Once you enter, there is no turning back. After we had pitched camp in the rain, I rushed off to have a look at the canyon. I had heard that there were five rapids which you approached by way of a scree slope at the base of the falls. I found the scree slope and, sure enough, it looked as though the canoes could be slid down on ropes. From the rim I could also see the first rapids. It looked easy, with a clear path right of center. The river then disappeared around a corner to the right. As I followed along the rim, I was impressed by the fact that the canyon walls maintained their full height downstream. As I proceeded I saw the second rapids. It was nothing more than a series of haystacks. No problem there, just fast water. Then rapids number three, or part of it, came into view. There was big whitewater on the right, but a black, deep-water V disappeared behind the canyon walls on the left. Further examination revealed that the V turned white as it bounced off the cliff face. That would be difficult. We would have to stay on the right side of the V, but out of the white stuff, and exit from the V before we were forced into the cliff. Below me was rapids number four. It was another series of big, beautiful haystacks. We could back ferry left to set up for number five which appeared to be very interesting. It had a huge hole on the right. That was one to steer clear of! The black V on the left terminated in haystacks. A roller-coaster ending to a great run!

From my vantage point high above the fifth rapids I could look down the remainder of the canyon as the walls diminished in height and the river widened to resume its normal course. At what appeared to be the end of the canyon there was a wide, large rapids, but it could be portaged if necessary. In the canyon, though, there would be no lining or portaging—the walls were either sheer rock or steep, crumbling rock with overhangs. As I retraced my route, going over each rapids again, I estimated the degree of difficulty and multiplied by two. Experience has taught me that rapids always look much easier from above than from water level. From above, waves appear flat and not at all forbidding. Even after mentally increasing my estimate of the difficulty, however, I figured we could manage these rapids.

Wally and the two Gilles were ecstatic with the news. Our enthusiasm was dampened only by the leaden skies and cold, steady drizzle. No one wanted to tackle a canyon in this weather. Though we would be wearing wet suits and paddling jackets, the combination of water temperatures just above freezing and the cold air temperature would increase the danger of hypothermia if we became stranded on the canyon walls. Even the descent down the scree slope into the canyon would be too dangerous in these conditions. At least that's what we told each other, but there was also a psychological factor. The black depths of that canyon just looked too intimidating. We knew it would be a lot more inviting in sparkling sunshine.

Our spirits descended into the depths of despair as the rain continued all night and into the morning. About noon, we decided to portage all the gear the 3 miles (5 km) to the end of the canyon and set up camp. We would leave the canoes at the top of the scree slope in readiness for a run. From a distance, the hillsides resembled a pastoral landscape, but in reality they made for the most difficult portaging imaginable. The ground consisted of foot-high (30 cm) tufts of grass on a watery terrain. Slogging between the tufts was hard enough, but when we attempted to walk from tuft to tuft we continually slid off them. Much to our relief, the cold and wind kept the mosquitoes at bay. At the end of the canyon a rocky outcrop provided a dry, comfortable campsite. And a spice-laden supper prepared by Bruce

helped to lift our spirits as the sky cleared in the north.

The morning dawned (actually it never got dark) to a bright, clear sky. We rushed through breakfast, put on our wet suits and set out for the head of the canyon. Alan and Bruce had decided they were quite content with the view from the top, and Alan agreed to take some pictures for us from the canyon rim. On the way to the head of the canyon we had another look at the river. We were all worried about rapids number three. We were going to have to favor the right side of the V to avoid the cliff on the left, but too far to the right would put us in a deep hole.

When I'm scouting a difficult rapids, I sometimes find it hard to control my imagination. I pictured our canoe hitting that diagonal, curling wave and rolling up on its side. I imagined us hanging there, trying to recover our balance, before hitting the ice-cold water. As I surfaced, I looked up at the towering cliffs. What point would there be in going to shore and climbing onto some outcrop? Who could help? Better to stay center stream and swim it. Maybe hang onto the throw bag so the canoe wouldn't get away. To lose the canoe hundreds of miles from help was unthinkable.

As my mind returned to the present, I asked myself the inevitable questions. Why run it? What's there to prove? Well, there was sure to be an incredible view from the bottom of the canyon, a new vista as we rounded each bend. There's the sheer thrill of running whitewater. And there was the chance to take unique photographs, although that wasn't the main reason; each of us knew we would run it anyway, camera or no camera. Although we wondered if we would be the first to run the canyon, we weren't obsessed with the idea of being first. In the end, we didn't need a reason.

Looking straight down into the canyon's depths, we assessed the difficulty of each rapids. We looked for the eddies, which would give us a chance to catch our breath and time to bail. There were very few. The river surged through the canyon, but each rapids taken on

its own looked runnable. It was when you added them all up that it began to look intimidating. Nevertheless, we felt confident that we could make our way through. The holes were avoidable. The Vs were clearly defined. The haystacks would give us a good ride.

Wally and I would be running with a spray deck. The Gilles, as usual, would run without one. What few eddies there were would be used to bail and would allow Alan a chance to take photographs from the rim. While Alan and I discussed suitable locations, Wally and the two Gilles proceeded to lower the two canoes down the scree slope.

I reached water level just at the Gilles completed their front ferry across the current to the other side of the canyon. Their skill in making the crossing was impressive. The water rushing downstream from the base of the falls was a seething mass of boils. The water in the back eddy into which we were about to be launched raced at alarming speed back toward the cataract. I decided that I didn't like it much and the tension in Wally's voice reinforced my apprehension. We would have to exit from the eddy quickly or be drawn into the rapids near the base of the falls. With the canoe facing the falls, we climbed in to move out of the eddy and begin our front ferry across the river; instead we found that we were being swept rapidly upstream toward the falls. Furious back paddling only succeeded in keeping us in the same place in relation to the shore. Finally Wally grabbed onto the rocks, climbed out and dragged the canoe with me in it away from the falls. Two more attempts to break out of the eddy failed, but on our fourth try we forced our way out and pointed our bow toward mid-stream. As we ferried across the current, the boiling water was no more fun than the back eddy. The boils pulled and grabbed the canoe as we gingerly proceeded across the river. We were definitely not having a good time. The sheer volume and turbulence of the water were very unsettling. From the canyon rim we had completely underestimated the forces at work beneath the surface.

The final drop of Wilberforce Falls ————

Looking back up the canyon toward the falls ————

Hood River expedition . . .

But now that we were committed, the idea of retreating up the scree slope never entered our minds. We all believed we could make it.

We completed the front ferry with great difficulty, landed on the ledge on the right shore, discussed strategy and then looked up at Alan on the canyon rim. He was a slim speck against the sky. The canyon was completely overwhelming. The two Gilles pushed off and ran down the side of the first rapids, eddying out just around the bend. We followed with a back ferry that seemed somewhat ineffectual. Wally's stern was sucked down in a whirlpool. He didn't like the feeling at all. This stuff was big! Bigger and more ominous than anything we had ever paddled. And this was only the first rapids, which had appeared from the rim to be the easiest.

A dark premonition came over all of us. Our enthusiasm for the carefully planned approach to each rapids was fading rapidly. All we wanted to do was to get on with it. The only way out lay ahead of us, beyond four rapids that could only be much wilder than we had imagined. Instead of multiplying the degree of difficulty by a factor of two we should have multiplied by four or five.

Wally and I pulled out of the eddy and shot by the other canoe. We were on the right side of the canyon and began our back ferry to set up for number two and number three which we wanted to run near the left shore. Number two, which had looked like nothing from the rim, would have been a wild and exhilarating ride in another time and place, but my "yahoo!" at the end was forced. I reached down under the spray skirt to get my camera out of its watertight box for a quick shot

between rapids. Above the roar of the rapids I thought I heard Wally say, "Forget the pictures." I looked up to protest just as rapids number three came into view around the corner of the canyon wall. No camera was ever returned to its box faster.

Wally was yelling, "Right, we've got to back ferry right. Give me more angle, more angle!" I gave him angle, with a little to spare. Mountainous waves appeared on the right. Large, diagonal, curling waves streamed from them. The black V lay directly ahead but terminated in huge waves against the cliff face.

We hugged the extreme right side of the V which put us into the diagonal waves coming off the haystacks. Overwhelmed by the sheer

size of everything, we hit the diagonal waves broadside. The canoe rolled up on its side and, without a pause, kept on going over.

One instant I was upright and a split second later I was hanging upside-down. I kicked against the bottom of the canoe, propelling myself down and out of the spray skirt. I struggled for the surface but there was no air, only turbulent water. It seemed a long time

before I got my first breath. It was half air and half water. I felt myself being pulled under again. With the next breath I stayed up, finally got my bearings and instinctively headed for shore, but only for a moment. I remembered that we were in a canyon and getting to shore wasn't much of a solution.

The canoe was between Wally and me. He was swinging toward the right shore, and I was near the left. I yelled to ask if he was going to swim the recovery rope to shore, then saw the throw bag floating about ten feet (3 m) upstream and on my side of the river. I swam to it, grabbed it and made for the left shore, which seemed closest. We were now riding the waves of the fourth rapids, the easiest in the canyon, but number five was yet to come. Looking downstream I saw the towering waves and knew the drop-off into the hole was on the right. I reluctantly let go of the throw-bag rope and kicked toward the left to miss the hole. As the waves engulfed me, I thought of Wally, whom I had now lost sight of. Either he was safe on shore or had been swept into the hole. I tried to relax as I was pulled through the waves, grabbing air when possible. The worst part was anticipating the waves of number five and, possibly, the hole. I surfaced, looked downstream and could hardly believe it. All I saw was dancing haystacks. I had missed the hole. I had made it!

The cold and fatigue hit me as the current swung me close to the right shore. I managed a few strokes and, at last, reached a ledge about a foot (30 cm) above water. I pulled myself up onto it and knelt there to catch my breath. The wet suit and paddling jacket enabled my body to warm the water next to my skin. The danger of hypothermia was passing. The air was cool but not cold.

I was worried about Wally. Why had he not appeared? I could only assume that he was able to reach the shore before the hole. The hole was big but not a keeper. I was sure that he would wash through, but where was he? Then I wondered about the two Gilles. Where were they? They must have stopped when

they saw us go over. That would mean they were trapped in the canyon above an unrunnable rapids or worse. Finally, I stood up to look over my own situation. The canyon was not nearly as deep here, but the walls were steep. The first part looked difficult, but then it appeared to get easier. I began the climb.

Much to my disappointment, all the rock was loose and rotten. The outcrops and hand holes were covered by debris. Each one had to be cleaned, and most were loose if I pulled on them. I continued upward but the going never got easier; it only looked easier. After 15 minutes of climbing, I came up under an overhang of loose rocks piled on edge like dominoes. I didn't dare to touch them. I moved to the right toward a pinnacle, which was also composed of rocks piled loosely on top of one another. I could go no higher. No one could climb that stuff.

I also knew I couldn't go down. Climbing up is much easier than going down, and I had pushed myself to the limit getting this high, climbing on adrenalin and desperation. I looked down on the ledge by the water and longed to be back where I had started. I had made a very stupid decision. I should have sat down and waited for a while. Only a rope from above could get me out of this mess. Where was everybody? Then I heard Alan. He was on the top of the rim across the canyon. I assured him that I was okay, but in big trouble. Alan said Wally was in the same predicament upstream of me, but still moving up the canyon wall. He had no idea where the two Gilles were; they had disappeared. Alan said not to move and he would get a rope. He turned to go, then said, "Do you want a picture?" Then, half jokingly he added, "It may be your last." I figured why not? What's another few seconds? As he proceeded to find a good location for the shot, the realization set in that it would be several hours before Alan could locate a rope, portage the third canoe to the end of the canyon, ferry across, walk back up my side of the river and lower a rope to me. And it would take more than himself and Bruce on the other end. Then I heard "Smile." Alan clicked the picture and raced off.

Standing on the narrow ledge was becoming increasingly difficult. In my position I couldn't rest; I had to go down. I lowered myself, groping for footholds and testing each one to see if it would hold. I remembered that rock climbers don't hug the cliff, they stand out and balance so they can see down and also so the force is straight down instead of out from the cliff. It was going much better than I had anticipated, but I occasionally had to take chances on loose footholds. Sometimes when I was testing them they broke loose and crashed down the cliff. Finally, with great relief, I stood once again on the ledge by the water.

Hood River expedition . . .

The prospect of jumping in and swimming across to an easier climb no longer seemed so formidable. I was thoroughly warmed up in my wet suit. As I was contemplating the swim I heard, "Mason, are you okay?" There above me was Wally peering down from the rim. From his vantage point, he agreed that I would have a much easier climb on the other side. I asked him if he had made shore before the hole in rapids number five. He described how he had but felt himself dropping into a hole in the fourth rapids. It pulled him down deep and the force of the water yanked his running shoes right off his feet. After he had surfaced, he was able to make shore just above rapids number five. He had made his climb in wet-suit socks. He doesn't use a wet suit, but prefers thick polypropylene underwear and a paddling jacket. He often wears rain pants over the underwear but, in this case, he was glad he hadn't. He was afraid the pants would have been pulled down, entangling his legs. Seeing him there brightened my day considerably.

I jumped in, swam across the river and pulled myself out onto a ledge downstream. The climb was much easier this time. I got into some shrubs and was finally able to make the top. I started out toward camp still wondering what had happened to the two Gilles. I could see the camp at the end of the canyon just over a mile (about 2 km) away. Then I counted three figures and a fourth coming toward me. Everyone was accounted for! Wally was walking along the other side of the canyon to a point opposite the camp. The person walking toward me turned out to be Alan.

How had the Gilles gotten to camp, when the last time I saw them they were sitting in an eddy upstream of rapids number two? They had not passed me in the canyon. With a big smile Alan told me how, after running rapids number two, they had seen Wally in the water and the capsized canoe. They couldn't see me, so they paddled to a ledge on the left shore to search for me. They leaped out of the canoe and clambered to a vantage point, but couldn't find any trace. Then, much to their

horror, they saw their canoe go drifting past them on the current. With no paddlers and no spray cover, it drifted into rapids number three (the one that had trashed Wally and me) and

proceeded to negotiate the rapids perfectly, all by itself, ending up bone dry. They had watched it dancing merrily on its way until it disappeared around a bend. The two had then looked up at the canyon walls. They are both skilled climbers, but it was an impossible climb even for them. They decided to swim down to just above rapids number three and attempt a climb farther along the canyon. It was difficult in the loose rock, but they managed it without incident.

Meanwhile, when Wally arrived at the shore opposite the camp, he could hardly believe his eyes. There, sitting in an eddy, was the Gilles' canoe, bone dry and with the paddles still in it. He jumped in and ferried across to the campsite. The ribbing that Wally and I endured was merciless. There we were with our complete spray skirt, and all our paddling skills — back ferry, high brace and low brace, pries and draws, pivots and backwatering — and we ended up swimming. And a canoe with no spray skirt and no paddlers ran the rapids without shipping a drop. It was agreed that we would have done better to just lie in the canoe. So much for fancy techniques! The canoe that Wally and I had lost was finally located on a rock, about two miles (3 km) downstream, by Gilles Couët. He managed to

get it off the rock by himself. The canoe was intact, but a little the worse for wear. The spray skirt was torn, paddles gone, and Wally's camera case was missing. Mine was still there.

Epilogue
Two weeks later, I wondered if the river was as dangerous as it had seemed at the time. When I remembered each rapids, I was sure we had run bigger stuff with floatation in the canoe and even played in it. So why was it such a harrowing experience? And why did I attempt to climb out of the canyon instead of jumping back in the water and swimming across to an easier climb? And the same goes for Wally. He was lucky not to have fallen.

What had made it harrowing was the sum effect of several factors. We were hundreds of miles from help. We had three irreplaceable canoes. The water was ice-cold and, once in the canyon, there was no way to avoid the rapids. The swim was bad enough even with a wet suit. Having made shore, I had no idea what had happened to the others. I was helpless as long as I was in the canyon. There was an irresistible urge to escape its confines. Interestingly, we all had the same blind urge.

There, again, was the old question, why did we take the risk? Was it worth it? The answer is very simple: Yes, it was worth it, because everything came out okay. Had one of us been hurt or killed, it would not have been worth it. It was an incredible experience to see that canyon from water level. It's a view I won't forget. And sooner or later someone will run it. In a kayak, or maybe even in a canoe, but probably in lower water.

There is one thing that Wally and I feel badly about. We'll never know if the two Gilles could have made the run. We think they would have. In any case, if you ever meet them on the streets of Chicoutimi, ask them, "How did you make out in your run down Wilberforce Canyon?" They can honestly say, "Oh, our canoe went through just fine. Hardly a drop of water in it."

Mountain River expedition

The Mountain River begins its journey about 150 miles (240 km) north of the Nahanni River and flows northeast into the Mackenzie River south of Fort Good Hope. After flying north from Fort Simpson for what seemed like a long time, our pilot put us down on a small lake nestled among the mountains. Two tributaries and two days' travel took us to the Mountain River.

We portaged out of the lake across a short plateau and into a stream that was only about as wide as a paddle blade and not deep enough to wet your feet. The canoes wouldn't fit. We dragged them along as best we could until the small feeder streams increased the flow. At last, we climbed into the canoes and started half paddling and half poling with our tough Mohawk paddles. We all had spare wooden paddles for the deeper water later. We were glad to have tough canoes, too. My partner, Chris Harris, and I were in a 16 ft. (4.8 m) ABS Mad River canoe. My other companions—Louise Gaulin and Wally Schaber, Judy Seaman and my son Paul—were all paddling 17 ft. (5.1 m) ABS Old Town Trippers. The bottoms flexed with the terrain, distributing the pressure evenly as we slid over the shallows. As much as I love my Prospector, these are the canoes for this type of travel.

We were heavily loaded with gear and food for three weeks—fresh food for the first three days. I would have preferred to start off with only dried food for such a strenuous beginning, but I didn't complain when it was time to eat. After about 6 miles (10 km) of poling and paddling, our little stream joined another and at last there was enough water to actually paddle.

About a quarter of a mile (0.5 km) downstream, the river turned sharply into the first of several canyons. It was the first time we had been down the little river, so every time it disappeared into a canyon we followed it with considerable apprehension. With the speed of the current and the sheer walls, there would be no turning back. Scouting along the top of the canyon, though, revealed easy Class 1 and 2 rapids.

Big but easy rollercoaster rapids, Mountain River

Mountain River expedition . . .

The two tributaries that led us into the Mountain River were a delight, as were the next few days on the Mountain River itself. The river, which was in flood because of heavy rains, carried us along faster than we wanted to go. Gradually the mountains began to close in on us, and from time to time, we stopped to climb. The view from the top of some of the peaks was worth the effort of reaching them. From an unnamed mountain of some 7,500 ft. (2300 m), we watched the river disappearing among the crags. A few more days would take us into the first of five canyons, all of which were runnable.

Many or most rivers that flow out of the western mountains are full of surprises. And these surprises come at 7 to 10 mph (12 to 16 km/hr). To steer clear of a sweeper or large waves in water moving at that speed, it's necessary to start the move far upstream. On such fast-flowing rivers back ferries and even front ferries can feel very ineffective. If you don't anticipate problems far upstream, you can end up going where no canoe should go, even if it is equipped with spray covers.

Chris and I rounded the corner of a hairpin bend in the fourth canyon. The next turn was to the right, so the obvious route was on the inside of the turn on the right. However, I figured I could get a great photograph of the other two canoes entering the canyon if we eddied out to the left. Chris, whose nickname is "Cool Hand Harris," as usual, nonchalantly agreed. We paddled furiously to reach the eddy, but were as ineffective as a matchstick drifting on the current. Giving up on the eddy, we swung around to face upstream so I could photograph the two canoes. Judy and Paul were hugging the inside of the turn. I got the shot but Louise and Wally were not yet in sight. I heard Chris suggest that maybe we had better start paddling. Looking behind us, I saw to my horror that we were being swept toward the cliff face on the outside of the corner and that the water was plowing straight into the cliff.

Memories of my Wilberforce Canyon swim flashed through my mind. I paddled furiously

and glanced quickly back at Cool Hand. He was paddling just as desperately. That's when I knew we were in big trouble. He yelled something that sounded like, "Look downstream." I looked, and wished I hadn't. The cliff was undercut. The water was racing under the cliff with about a foot (30 cm) of clearance, the last place any canoeist wants to go. Chris and I attempted to paddle upstream, at an angle away from the cliff, but despite our frantic efforts we made no headway. The canoe spun around on a divergent current and we ploughed into the cliff face, bow first.

Fortunately, we were still upstream of the undercut wall of rock. The canoe hung there for a moment, then swung sideways and was pinned against the cliff. We both overcame the instinct to lean away from the menace of the towering rock. Instead we leaned toward it,

keeping our upstream gunwale high. The last thing we wanted to do was to let the current grab the upstream gunwale. In that moment I thought of millions of places I would rather be.

I glanced back at Chris, who was sitting there leaning against the cliff surveying the situation. I remember thinking, "Well, if I have to be in this fix, there's nobody I would rather be with than Cool Hand." Since we were facing upstream, I reached out to draw my bow into the current. Nothing happened. Chris yelled, "Harder! Pull harder!" I did, but we weren't going anywhere. Chris, in a manner that befits his nickname, said, "Let's think of something else." The only "something else" was to back out downstream along the cliff, but that would have put us right into the undercut. As I turned to survey the possibility, the only thing that kept me from a state of panic was my view of Cool Hand sitting there thinking about it. His philosophy is that 98 percent of all worrying is unnecessary. That leaves only 2 percent to really get uptight about. I wanted to tell him, "Chris! This is it! This is the 2 percent. Do something!"

Suddenly I felt my end of the canoe sinking. I spun around just as my camera case, which was lashed to the bow, disappeared. The water then rushed up my chest, and still kneeling in the canoe, I found myself being

pulled under. The canoe rolled sideways and I kicked free. My first instinct in any upset is to get free of the canoe before it pins me. In this case, it could only have been under water and against the cliff. I waited for the crushing force of the canoe but it didn't come. I then decided it was time to make a try for the surface. I swam upwards but banged my head on the underside of the canoe. Trying to pull myself to

one side, I again crashed into the bottom of the canoe. I tried the other way and failed again. I had done a lot of swimming in rapids, but I had never been stuck under a canoe on a permanent basis. It was time for panic. Meanwhile, up on the surface, Chris was hanging out on a brace with the front half of the canoe down in the whirlpool. He cranked a

180° turn and the bow popped to the surface. But where was I?.

Suddenly I, too, popped to the surface. My first view as I gulped air was this sheer cliff face looming over me, then I heard Chris yell, "Hang on." I turned and there he was right beside me. I couldn't believe he was still upright; I had felt the canoe going over as I bailed out. I grabbed the stern, taking deep

breaths, because I expected at any moment to be pulled into the undercut with Chris and the canoe. But it didn't happen. We ran right through the haystacks beside the cliff. There the water was flat but swirling. Chris yelled, "Quick, can you get in?" I wasn't sure I could until he followed with, "It looks like there might be a falls ahead!" That did it. Downstream I

saw a cable stretched across the canyon, which in Ontario means a falls. I shot straight into the air and came down into the canoe frantically grabbing for the spare paddle.

We were three-quarters full of water, but the canoe was planing for shore. As we passed

under the cable, all we could see was flat, swirling water — no falls. And we had survived the cliff face.

As we pulled in to shore to empty, we anxiously looked upstream to see how the other two canoes were doing. Only Paul and Judy were in sight, and they seemed to be paddling along in absolutely placid water on the inside of the corner. Wally and Louise were

Mountain River expedition . . .

nowhere to be seen. I turned and asked Chris how he had managed to stay upright. He looked at me and said, "You think I'm crazy? No way was I going swimming in there. That was a whirlpool." He explained how he had seen the whirlpool spinning toward us along the cliff face. Before he could shout a warning, he saw me disappear along with my half of the canoe. Then the canoe went over on its side as it did a 180° turn. He held the canoe upright with a world-class brace. As the whirlpool disappeared downstream, the bow of the canoe resurfaced and there I was . . . gone. When I didn't appear he admitted that he had begun to get a little worried. However, when I finally broke the surface, I am sure it only confirmed his belief that 98 percent of all worrying is for nothing.

We wondered about the cable across the river and correctly surmised that it had to do with a river-level measuring device that sent a signal to a satellite. Anyway, it sure put a scare into us. The humorous side of all this is that Paul and Judy had been sneaking down the inside of the corner, so they couldn't see around the bend. When they looked across the river and saw us clinging to the rock face they figured that we knew something they didn't. Maybe there was a horrendous falls around the corner. So they gingerly edged around the cliff until all they could see was the continuation of flat water. They couldn't figure out what all the fuss was about. They saw me disappear, then finally reappear, alongside Chris. What really impressed them was how fast I catapulted myself back into the canoe.

They joined us on a boulder bar to wait for Wally and Louise. After a long and worrying wait, they finally came into sight, still upright. They, too, had tried to eddy out on the left to have a look before descending into the canyon. But like us, they couldn't reach the eddy, putting them on the outside of the corner and in great danger of being pinned against the cliff, but much farther upstream than we had been. They were able to ride a current through the big haystacks all the way

along the cliff. We can only surmise that the main current was not sweeping under the undercut cliff as we had been led to believe from our view upstream.

I relived the adventure many times over the next few days and then began to wonder if it had been that bad. When I asked Chris about it, he said he couldn't remember when he had been in a worse situation.

I don't want to give the impression that the Mountain is a difficult river. It was easy for experienced canoeists up to the first canyon. In low water, the canyons would probably be easy, too, but several days of rain had raised the river to flood levels. Some corners had interesting boils and divergent currents, as well as big waves on the outside of some of the bends. However, the big waves can almost all be avoided by staying on the inside of the corners. On other parts of the river, there were lots of beautiful big haystacks that couldn't be avoided. The haystacks were at about the limit of navigability for an open canoe, but were easily runnable with spray covers. In flood conditions, there were plenty of monster roller-coaster waves that could be run for fun with spray covers. The scenery on the Mountain River is second only to that of the Nahanni. And as an added bonus, the mountains, which rise right up from the river, can be easily climbed. The view from several of them is imprinted on my memory forever. I can hear the song just thinking about them.

Journey pastimes

An amazing number of people ask me, "What do you do out there for weeks or months at a time?" Most canoeists travel every day; for them the journey itself is important. But I sometimes stay in one place for many days. It's what I do along the way that's important. And for me there are never enough hours in a day.

Trip journal
Whether you prefer pictures or a trip log, some kind of record can be great fun both to make and return to over the years. Because I am visually oriented and rarely take notes, I record my trips with sketches, paintings and photographs. On several occasions, my son Paul has pointed out that perhaps that's why my stories seem to get better over the years! On some of our group trips, one person has organized the trip report along with pictures and cartoons from other members and then had copies sent to everyone. Many people who intend to take the trip have found these diaries very useful.

Still photography
There is a big difference between snapshots and photographs. Snapshots are banged off as things happen. Occasionally a snapshot can be a prize winner but not often. Serious photography requires time and effort. That's why much of my canoeing has been solo or with one other person.

Color slides are a very effective medium through which to share your trip with others. If you plan to put together a slide show, be sure to cover all the major events, including getting there. When you're on a trip with friends or family, think in terms of story line, just as you would a film. A closeup of each member of the expedition in a characteristic but natural pose, and a nice mix of long shots, medium-range shots and closeups are a good idea. For rapids-running shots, you need at least a 100 mm lens; a 200 or 300 mm is even better. A 300 mm lens is wonderful for taking close-ups around camp and photographs of any wildlife you might come across.

The forests of Canada and the northern United States are not over-populated with animals. That's what makes it so exciting when you do see one. I have got the world's greatest collection of animal photographs. You know the kind: "Over there, just to the left of the tree behind the rock, you can see one of his antlers." Animal shots taken on a canoe trip can be very disappointing. Many's the time I have clicked a prize-winning shot, with great light, sensational action and perfect background, and when it came back I couldn't find the animal. And if anybody needs a shot of the wrong end of a moose, bear, caribou, musk ox or wolf, just let me know.

Fishing

One of life's greatest taste treats is a fish taken from lake to pan to plate! Although I'm not an avid fisherman, I'm always first in line with my dish. I fish if I'm alone, but usually prefer to spend my time looking at the scenery, sketching and photographing. For a canoe trip, a rod that telescopes to prevent it breaking on the portage is essential. The only thing I know about fishing lures is, if you've got only one lure, make sure it's a daredevil. I use the heaviest possible line and just crank 'em in.

Other interests

Having a special interest can greatly enhance your enjoyment of the outdoors. The possibilities are endless. A woman I know always took her geology hammer with her. She was happiest chipping away at a pile of rocks. Recording sounds is another pleasant diversion. For some people, these special interests have led to full-time jobs. I know of photographers, sound recorders, writers, artists, carvers, geologists, zoologists, archaeologists and biologists whose lifetime work was a result of their early outdoor pursuits. My life and the life of my family has been shaped by the canoe and our journeys in it.

Fishing, Cascade River, Lake Superior ———

Running the Mars River canyon, Quebec

The very best equipment isn't much use if you can't keep it dry. It also isn't much use if you leave it at home, forget it at the last campsite or lose it in an upset. What you pack your gear in, and how you secure it to the canoe, are almost as important as the gear itself. You can get the expensive, high-tech waterproofing systems or get by with inexpensive but practical ones.

I might covet some of the superbly-designed, light, modern packs, but I will probably never own one. The way things are going, it looks like my old Woods canvas packs are going to outlast me. Some of them are 30 years old. I actually enjoy patching and replacing their worn leather straps and buckles.

Canvas packs

Canvas packs are commonly known as Duluth packs because they were first made by the Duluth Tent and Awning Company in Minnesota. Woods Bag and Canvas company has also been making a similar pack for many years. I prefer the 24 by 20 by 8 in. (61 by 51 by 20 cm) pack. Duluth Tent and Awning make a pack called the Northwoods Pack that is 20 by 22 by 8 in. (51 by 56 by 20 cm). These packs are equipped with a tumpline, which is a great help for carrying heavy loads over portages. Over the years, the quality of canvas packs has varied as companies change hands. Here's what to look for in a good quality canvas pack:

• The material should be stiff and heavy.
• The rivets should be well placed or centered and the ends should be well splayed.
• A piece of canvas should be stitched over each rivet head on the inside of the pack, so the jagged edges won't tear or wear through a waterproof liner. If the pack doesn't have the rivet heads covered, tape each one with duct tape.

Woods packs are readily available in Canada. For the original Duluth packsack, write to Duluth Tent and Awning, P.O. Box 16024, 1610 W. Superior Street, Duluth, Minnesota 55816.

Canvas Duluth or Woods pack

Portaging with tumpline

Day Packs

Because I carry a small day pack when canoeing, I never need to open my large pack during the day. My Woods Nessmuck has many exterior pockets for items such as sunglasses, sketching materials, map, compass, bug repellent, bits of rope, film, matches, toothbrush, raincoat, tracking lines, and so on. It has no frame, so it rolls up when not in use. I find it quite comfortable to carry when packed properly, but it can't compare with the new nylon day packs. On portages, it rides on top of the other packs.

Woods Nessmuck day pack

Canoe packs . . .

Nylon packs

Most nylon packs are very well designed and don't take on much weight when wet. The system of buckles and the method of tightening is usually excellent. It's a competitive business, so each manufacturer tries to outdo the others by adding pockets and gimmicks. They can get quite fancy and so can the prices.

Internal frame packs

Packs with frames, designed for hiking, are generally considered unsuitable for canoeing because the frames take up valuable space in the canoe. However, if a number of backpacking side trips are planned, it might be desirable to include an internal frame pack. Some of these packs are very sophisticated, with pockets and zippers for easy access to any part of the interior of the pack. This is a great asset for hiking. If you are trying to keep the costs down, a simple canoe pack will do the job.

Infant backpacks

Baby backpacks are a wonderful idea for portaging and for working around camp. The baby should never be left in a backpack in the canoe. In fact, a child should not be tethered in any way when in a canoe or left alone in a backpack at any time.

High-tech nylon pack with padded straps ——————

Internal frame hiking pack ——————

Infant backpack ——————

Waterproofing systems

For the wellbeing of everybody on a journey by canoe, it's important that each canoeist's waterproofing system works. If one person is in misery because of sopping clothes and equipment, everybody suffers. Keeping your stuff dry isn't easy, and I'm always looking for a better way. So are many of my friends and they have come up with some ingenious solutions.

Waterproof packs

Pack manufacturers have three problems to deal with when designing a waterproof pack. It is difficult to seal the seams and to make a waterproof closure. And, because packs inevitably suffer wear and tear, the material starts letting in water eventually. For these reasons, it is still essential to insert a waterproof liner with a dependable closure into your waterproof pack.

For canoeing you need a big pack. The one in the photograph has a high top with extra material to allow for a tight roll. The watertight closure is quick and practical. The big, snap buckles are quick to close and allow for tightening. The shoulder straps adjust easily and it has a tumpline strap. A stuff sack stitched to the back holds loose articles for the portage and a side pocket holds the axe. A partition on the inside for the sleeping mat provides padding for the portage. Unfortunately, the seams are not waterproof.

Plastic bag and stuff sack

The method for waterproofing that I still prefer is a waterproof liner inside a large, tough canvas or nylon pack. I've tried many different materials for liners. The 50 lb. (23 kg) plastic bags used for skim milk powder are excellent. Heavy-duty garbage bags are commonly used and some (Surtec, for example) are stretchier and more resistant to puncture than others. You can double or triple bag them. For an absolutely waterproof arrangement, place a nylon stuff sack inside your canvas or nylon pack. Then insert one or two plastic bags. Now place another stuff sack inside that and put in your gear. The plastic liner is protected from abrasion from both sides by the stuff sacks. Close the opening by twisting, folding and then securing each bag with a rubber band or a cord. They are not a long-term solution, but what is? Even the expensive high-tech bags have a limited life and must be handled with care. Don't use a liner that doesn't allow you to fill your pack completely; there is nothing more frustrating than a pack that can be only half-filled.

Indian pack basket

The traditional Indian pack basket is still one of the best methods for portaging fragile gear such as cameras or sound equipment. On our filming trips, we placed the basket inside a Woods pack. We then put a nylon liner inside the basket and a heavy plastic bag inside that, followed by another nylon liner. The camera gear was then placed in individual foam socks for protection. The liners were extra long for rolling up to make a reasonably watertight seal. It worked well but is not as bombproof as the plastic barrel system.

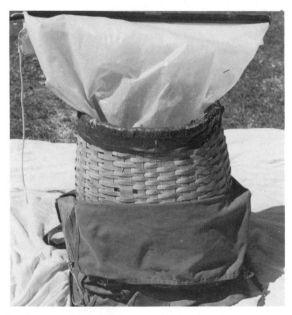

Indian pack basket ————————————

Waterproof pack ————————————

Plastic bag and stuff sack ————————

97

Waterproofing systems . . .

Commercial waterproof bags

Many manufacturers produce excellent waterproof pack liners or packsacks out of coated Dacron, heavy vinyl or coated nylon. Available in all shapes and sizes, they are commonly used individually as stowbags for sea kayaking or rafting. Here are points to check:

- Seams should be welded, not just stitched.
- The bottom must be smooth. (Cheap ones are folded inside.)
- The material should be heavyweight and coated.
- The top closure needs a triple system: 1. Velcro; 2. lots of extra length for rolling; 3. a trustworthy fastener system.

Some of the better-known bags come with straps and can be used as waterproof packs, but for rough use on portages, they will last much longer if you nest them inside a tough outer pack. To solve this problem, Ortlieb has made especially-large bags for the Trailhead stores to be used as pack liners. They can be ordered from Trailhead, 1341 Wellington Street, Ottawa, Ontario K1Y 3B8.

Ortlieb pack liner

Homemade liners

Joyce makes our liners out of waterproof nylon to fit our packs. She makes them extra big to avoid the strain of over-filling. Seam sealer is applied to all the seams. The liners are extra long to provide plenty of rolling for a tight seal. If the pack is filled to capacity, the liner tightly rolled and the straps pulled tight, it makes an almost waterproof pack. If the top is twisted, then folded and secured with elastics, it is absolutely watertight.

Homemade liner

Stuff sacks for each item

Regardless of what packs and liners you use, the sleeping bag, clothes, and so on should each be placed in a lined stuff sack for double protection. Use a heavy-duty plastic garbage bag between two nylon stuff sacks. Twist each bag and bend it over before securing with an elastic band. Label each stuff sack clearly. A better idea is to use a different colored sack for various articles.

I try to avoid having sharp objects come into contact with the liner. But sooner or later they do, so even these liners have a limited life. Periodic inspection on a bright day reveals pinholes that can be patched with duct tape.

Stuff sack

Commercial waterproof stuff sacks

There is a wide range of well-made stuff sacks on the market if you want to go to the expense. The aforementioned companies all make stuff sacks in many different sizes. They are too rich for my taste, but if you want a bombproof system, the commercial bags are excellent.

Waterproof closures

If a person could invent the perfect waterproof closure for pack liners and waterproof bags, the world would beat a path to his or her door. So far there are advantages and disadvantages in every system.

Sliding tubes   The sliding tube closure pinches the bag flat around a dowel, making a very waterproof seal. This type used to be difficult to manage, but is now quite easy to use. The bag must have a small mouth, otherwise the closing tube has to be much wider than the pack, making it unwieldy. Constant use does wear out the bag eventually.

Roll down with twist fasteners   This is a watertight closure, but a real pain to roll and secure.

Roll down tops with a buckle   This closes to form a handle. This seemed like the final solution, but much to my disappointment, they leak slightly if immersed. Nevertheless, they are my first choice in closures.

Elastic bands   For bags that are not too stiff, the twist, secure with an elastic, fold and secure again system still seems to work as well as anything.

Collar and buckle   The rubber collar that is secured around the top of the bag and buckled closed is a more sophisticated version of the elastic band. It is faster and better for bags made out of stiff, heavy material.

Sketching at Denison Falls, Dog River, Ontario ————

Jars and barrels

Plastic olive jars

Many of the trips that Black Fearther outfitters run are on the western mountain rivers where there is very little portaging. Several years ago, they began experimenting with plastic olive jars (photograph 1). The jars, which are 15 in. (37 cm) high and 10 in. (25 cm) in diameter, are about the right size for a sleeping bag, a tent or clothes, and are absolutely waterproof. Four jars fit in the large

1   Plastic olive jars

canvas or nylon pack (photograph 2). They found it made a good and reasonably comfortable load for portaging. The disadvantage is the wasted space in the pack created by the round shape of the barrels. A few items that don't need waterproofing can be stuffed in the space. The food for each day can also be packed in these barrels in the order that it would be eaten. As the jars become empty, they provide ideal floatation for the canoe in the big whitewater of the mountain rivers. These jars can be found at some delicatessens and restaurants, but the word is out and the demand is increasing. This book certainly isn't going to help the situation.

2   Four jars in a packsack

Plastic barrels

A larger alternative or companion to the olive jars is the plastic barrel (photograph 3). All your gear can be placed in one barrel and food in another or in as many as required. Straps can be fitted for portaging, or a more sophisticated pack frame can be designed. The lids are watertight and easy to open, and the barrels can survive almost any trip down a rapids. A 24 by 17 in. (60 by 37 cm) barrel is available from Trailhead in Ottawa equipped with a harness for portaging (photograph 4).

Northwest River Supplies of Moscow, Idaho, sells three sizes of barrel: the Papa Barrel is 36 by 21 in. (91 by 53 cm) with a 13 in. (33 cm) opening; the Mama Barrel is 24 by 17 in. (60 by 43 cm) with a 7½ in. (19 cm) opening; and the Baby Barrel is 17 by 10 in. (43 by 25 cm) with a 5¼ in. (13 cm) opening. The Papa Barrel is too big for portaging. There is a lot of merit to the larger barrels, but the best shoulder-strap system available still can't equal the comfort of a well-packed canvas or nylon pack. On our three-week Hood River trip, we used five food barrels, one as a wanigan for the basics, and the others for labelled poly bags containing each day's food. For his personal pack, Wally used the small plastic olive jars, four-to-a-pack system. The two Gilles used the large-barrel system and

Alan, Bruce and I used the pack-liner system. They all worked well, keeping everything dry.

I have been slow to switch to the jars or barrels, but have done so for trips involving little portaging. I am also enthusiastic about the barrels for the big whitewater trips where the extra floatation they provide is a great advantage. However, for my ramblings on rivers involving a lot of portaging, I'm sticking with packs.

3   Plastic barrels

4   Portaging barrels

Barrels provide floatation, Ecorces River, Quebec

Camera cases

Waterproofing for cameras has come a long way. Up until a few years ago the only waterproof bag you could depend on was the rubber-and-canvas ammunition bag, but it took forever to get into and a long time to reseal. For filmmaking, I used a Duluth pack lined with an Indian or wicker pack-basket and a double waterproof liner inside that (see page 97). The liner was very long, so it could be rolled to keep out the water. Each piece of camera equipment was placed in a foam sock to avoid abrasions and bumps. Still-camera equipment and sketching materials are not so voluminous, so I use a hard camera-case now.

Camera case lashed to bow deck

The Sport Safe (A)
Sport Safe, my personal choice for a camera box, is 14 by 11 by 5½ in. (35 by 28 by 14 cm), the right size for cameras, sketching equipment, wallet and other valuables. You can line it with foam so nothing rattles around. It has a small door that is the right size for a 35 mm camera with a lens up to 300 mm. Because of the size of the door, you are less vulnerable in rapids, waves or rain when you open it to grab the camera for a quick shot. The Sport Safe can be lashed to the bow deck

or the stern thwart for quick, easy access. I tuck the extra lenses, film and stuff away in the corner, and leave the camera near the lid. I can actually shoot between the waves. Another nice point about the Sport Safe is the size. It's perfect for slipping into a Duluth or even a day pack for portaging. And it's absolutely the best size for sitting on. Things have come a long way in the waterproofing department, but unhappily, the Sport Safe, the best container for canoe tripping, is no longer available. I list it here in the hope that someone will go into production again. If you do own one or are lucky enough to find one second-hand, look after it. I sure would hate to lose mine.

Pelican case (B)
I don't know of anything as waterproof or as strong as a Pelican camera case. It is the best solution at present for protecting your camera from water and hard knocks. Available in four sizes, it comes fitted with foam, and you can buy additional inserts. One disadvantage is its shape. It looks like a suitcase and needs a bit of room to open, making it vulnerable to spray or rain. When going canoeing mainly for fun, I take a small camera in the 8½ by 6½ by 3¼ in. (21 by 16 by 8 cm) case, and my sketching materials in another of the same size. If it's a serious creative trip, I use the 17⅜ by 11¾ by 6½ in. (44 by 30 by 16 cm) size.

Wally Schaber's Pelican case got away from him in Wilberforce Canyon on the Hood River and was retrieved the next day many miles downstream. The contents were bone dry. You can't do much better than that in the waterproof department. You might want to brighten it up a bit with paint or tape. We nearly went by it as it bobbed along the shore.

Small camera boxes (C) and ammunition box (D)
If you are carrying only one camera, there are several kinds of small waterproof boxes that work well. And there's always the old bomb-proof, metal ammunition box that seems to

show up everywhere. Some people think it's great for everything from cameras to toilet tissue and airline tickets! It's the poor man's Pelican case.

Various devices for carrying cameras (E)
Anything that is stiff and waterproof can be used for carrying cameras. Some makeshift arrangements are better than the so-called camera bags; for example, plastic food containers that come in all shapes and sizes.

Roll-top plastic bags (F)
I have tried waterproof plastic bags with roll tops for cameras, but don't like them because they don't afford any protection from knocks, and are difficult to open and close. Any camera container should be easy to get in and out of, or you're going to miss those once-in-a-lifetime shots!

Plastic olive jars (G)
Olive jars can be used as a very-cheap-but-waterproof container for cameras and film. Their screw top lids take a bit longer to open, but provide excellent protection.

Plastic pail with lid (H)
A plastic pail with a friction top can be used, although the best you can say about it is that it's cheap. It can be used as a splashproof day pack. Getting the top on and off is a bit difficult, but the pail isn't very watertight if the top isn't on tight.

Homemade camera case (I)
A paddler from Denmark, Michael Nielsen, recently sent me a homemade camera case that is as clever as anything I've ever seen. It's made out of the top third of a plastic barrel and has a plywood bottom and a lever-action lid closure. It opens and closes instantly and is completely waterproof. It has two strong handles and is the right size for a couple of cameras. The bottom is glued and screwed in place for a watertight fit. He has installed a piece of Ensolite on the lid for comfort when using it for a seat.

Waterproof camera cases

Preparing your canoe

An important part of canoeing is rigging your canoe properly for the conditions you might possibly encounter. A skilled canoeist should be able to deal with any situation, from capsizing far from shore to upsetting in wild rapids. Even if you don't intend to run rapids, you should be prepared to recover from unforeseen misfortunes, such as being carried into rapids inadvertently. By personalizing your canoe, you can be not only safer, but also more comfortable.

Knee pads and foot braces (A)

The most important modification for me is knee pads. A wet ABS canoe is one of the most slippery materials known. I glue either con-toured individual knee pads or a sheet of closed-cell foam into position with contact cement. The material must be closed-cell so it won't absorb water, or you'll be kneeling in a swamp all day. If you are canoeing sitting on a seat with your legs extended, then a foot brace is a great asset for power and stroke control.

Thigh straps and toe blocks (B)

Thigh straps really make you feel a part of your canoe. You can pull your canoe over into extreme leans more easily than by shifting your weight to one side. They are fun for fooling around, or hot dog canoeing, in whitewater. Toe blocks help to keep your thighs tight against the straps. Some canoeists never go anywhere without them, while others don't like them for fear of becoming tangled in them.

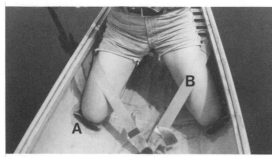

Knee pads and thigh straps

Throw bag (C)

The throw bag is often used as a recovery rope. The rope is attached to the canoe with a carabiner and the bag is secured by Velcro or a shock cord. In an upset, you grab the bag and head for shore hoping you get there before the line pays out to the end.

Secure spare paddle (D)

This is one of the most essential and simplest precautions. Always carry a couple of elastics around the shaft of your paddles. Secure the shaft to the thwart with the elastic band. In an emergency, just break the elastic. Be sure the blade end is under the thwart and the paddle will never float free in an upset.

Portage yoke (E)

This will take some of the agony out of portaging a heavy canoe. It can be as simple as a piece of Ensolite wrapped around the center thwart, or padded blocks or a beauti-fully carved and shaped wooden yoke. I use paddles for portaging. A cord is tied perma-nently on the center thwart so the paddles can be easily installed. For two people portaging, the cord is tied on the stern thwart. The secret to comfort is the extra Ensolite padding attached to all the right places in my life jacket (see page 122).

Tie-downs (F)

If your packs are secured to the bottom of the canoe, they will act as floatation unless they are heavier than water, which is unlikely. Wood-canvas canoes have the advantage of open gunwales. Ropes can be threaded through anywhere for a secure tie-down. If the gunwales are solid, eyebolts can be installed under the gunwales for tying in packs.

Stern thwart (G)

A stern thwart is a must for securing packs and for the strength of the hull. Don't buy a canoe without one.

Bailers (H)

For running rapids and paddling in waves, a good-sized bailer is indispensable. It can be made from a plastic detergent bottle, an antifreeze container or some such plastic vessel. Cut the bottom out of the container and fasten the screw top tightly. Tie a piece of very short cord to a carabiner and tie the other end to the handle. Fasten the carabiner to a pack strap or thwart. Also glue a piece of Styrofoam in the small end of the bailer for floatation in case it gets away.

Notice I said "very short cord" rather than rope for tying the bailer to the canoe. There is always the danger of becoming tangled in ropes in an upset or swamping. I recently swamped in a large rapids and managed to eddy out without sinking or upsetting. As I approached shore, I leaped out and fell on my face. My ankle was tangled in the bailer rope. Being dragged down a rapids by a canoe full of water isn't my idea of a good time. If preferred, you could use a piece of string securing the bailer to the thwart so it breaks if you get it tangled around your foot.

Bow and stern painter (I) not shown

This is a 12 ft. (3.5 m) rope for tying up to trees when scouting a rapids or checking out a possible campsite. Use an elastic band to keep it coiled and out of the way when running rapids.

Tracking ropes (J)

One or two 48 ft. (15 m) extension ropes or tracking ropes are handy to have, but they should be coiled and secured. No lengths of rope longer than 3 ft. (1 m) should be loose.

Center rope (K)

An overturned canoe with packs tied in is difficult to right. It's even tougher if it's an ABS canoe with no keel to grasp. One end of a 3 ft. (1 m) rope is tied to the center thwart at one of the gunwales and the other end left free in the canoe. If you can grasp the free end by reaching over the upturned hull, you can gain leverage and easily turn the canoe right-side up. Then you can climb back in and paddle to shore swamped, or even bail it out without going ashore.

Jam cleat
When my son Paul guides, he rigs his stern deck with a jam cleat. The last thing you want to do when making a rescue is to tie another canoe to yours in rapids. You might have to release it if you get swept into another rapids and the rope could stick. With the jam cleat you can release the other canoe instantly and then recover it at the end of the rapids. The rope must be fed through an eyebolt that is secured to the deck, so the pull on the rope will be from the right direction.

Seat pad
Your sitter-downer will be eternally grateful for a closed-cell pad attached to your canoe seat. If you tie the pad in place or install fasteners or Velcro the pad can be removed for sitting on around camp.

Map and compass case (L)
The map is carried in a clear waterproof bag with a closure, and is secured to a thwart along with the compass.

Camera case (M)
This is fastened on a short rope and carabiner for easy access and quick release in case you want to remove it from the canoe.

Waterproof accessory bag
Some canoeists prefer a small waterproof bag secured to the thwart for such items as sun-glasses, sun screen, bathing suit, notepad, and so on, rather than a day pack. The bag is left on the thwart while portaging. For fast rivers, where the rapids never end, some canoeists prefer a bum pack so the essentials stay with them rather than with the canoe.

Final preparations

Freeboard   A loaded canoe should have no less than 6 in. (15 cm) freeboard. Any less and you're pushing your luck in waves and rapids. If you look at a ruler, 6 in. (15 cm) isn't really very much. It is enough because a canoe is buoyed up by the waves so that the freeboard is relatively constant.

Trim your canoe   Use your packs to trim the canoe so it rides slightly stern heavy. If it's bow heavy, it will be difficult to steer.

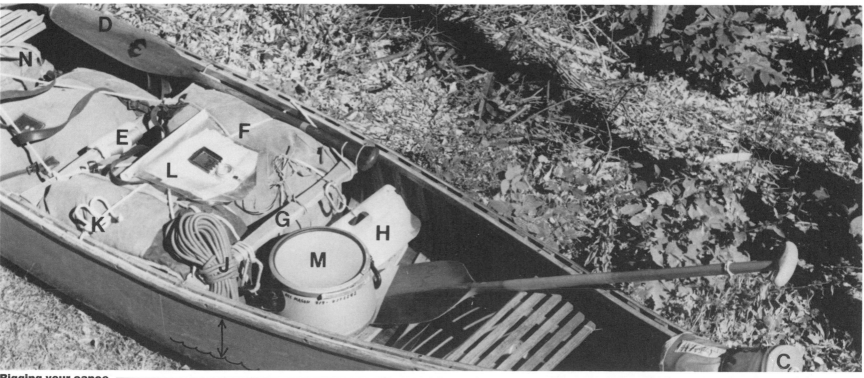

Rigging your canoe

Getting to the put-in point

Everything is packed and ready to go. Now all you have to do is get to the put-in point to begin your trip. There was a time when you could throw your gear and your canoe on a train and have it stop at your put-in point. Then the railways decided that they were taking up too much baggage room. Now your canoe has to be crated and shipped ahead of time. And today trains won't make stops at out-of-the-way places and sometimes they won't stop at many of the smaller stations. With a few exceptions, you now need a vehicle to get your canoe to the put-in point.

Five canoes on canoe rack

Bush vehicles
I have had a string of so-called bush vehicles and every one was a piece of junk. On the adversity scale, a broken-down vehicle way back in the bush rates about the same as a hopelessly pinned canoe—about a 9.9 on a scale of 10. The garage owner pleaded with me to take my all-terrain vehicle to some other place because it was so difficult to work on. Tests have shown that most of the high-wheel-base vehicles are far less stable on the road than a standard passenger car. And unlike passenger cars, they are not required by law to have reinforcing bars in the doors.

My last three bush vehicles have been run-of-the-mill passenger cars. When the doors fall off, we make a trip to the dump. All I want is a vehicle to get me, my gear and canoe or canoes to the river or lake.

A bush vehicle should have rain gutters for the roof racks and at least one dent. That first dent always hurts, but after that you won't feel a thing.

One modification that is required to turn your standard car into a bush vehicle is extra springs in the back to carry heavy loads. Preventive medicine is also essential. You need a local garage with a mechanic who has that sixth sense for what is going to go next. One final test for a bush vehicle is to stand back, look at it and ask yourself, "If this car was parked at the take-out point, is this the last car anybody would choose to swipe?" If the answer is yes, you've got yourself a bush vehicle.

The car shuttle
Trips that loop around to the beginning don't need a shuttle. On one-way trips you either have to leave a car at the end of the trip or hire someone to drive it from the put-in point to the take-out.

When you reach the end of the trip and walk over to the shuttle car, there is nothing worse than to watch your partner dig around in his or her pockets and packs for the keys, while your intuition says that they are in the car at the put-in point. When it comes to keys for cars, never trust anybody. Carrying the keys on your person or in your pack isn't the best idea, especially on a whitewater trip, but if you hide them, everyone on the trip should know where they are.

Canoe racks
The MXCC-003 (Mason Experimental Canoe Carrier Number 3) is a state-of-the-art all-purpose roof rack (photographs 1 and 2). The MXCC-003 is also one of the most functional devices ever invented, and I humbly take full credit for its present state of perfection. It can turn anything with four wheels into a truck. We

have carried canoes, packsacks, lumber, rocks, furniture, skis and even a fully-constructed dock down to the water's edge on it. The MXCC-002 on our old Chev used to carry six canoes and a kayak. It could have carried more, but I was afraid of causing an accident from people rubbernecking as we passed them on the highway. Our present Toyota can carry three on the highway and five on the back road shuttle. Packsacks can be carried under the canoes.

My canoe carrier used to have moving parts. I originally designed it so that handles made of broken hockey sticks could be inserted into the square metal tubing to provide extensions for carrying two canoes side-by-side on my small car. However, moisture got inside the tubing causing the hockey sticks to swell and seize up, so they can't be adjusted anymore. My next version, MXCC-004, will have adjustable bars.

As much as it pains me to admit it, there is one disadvantage to the MXCC-003: it cuts down on gas mileage.

For the canoeist who considers it a sacrilege to bolt, rivet, or nail down a roof rack permanently on his car, there are some well-designed carrying devices on the market (photograph 3). Special attachments make it possible to fit them onto cars without rain gutters. The high-tech roof racks have a lot of attachments that are functional, but easily lost or misplaced. That's one great advantage of the MXCC-003 over the high-tech models. There is nothing that can fall off.

Most of the better and more expensive makes have a locking system to protect the carriers or the stuff on them. The MXCC-003 so cleverly disguised as an eyesore that nobody would think of swiping it.

For the canoeist who is too lazy, or unskilled, to build an MXCC-003, and too cheap to go for the high-tech car racks, there are adequate el-cheapo racks. The car must have rain gutters for their installation. Avoid any form of roof rack that uses suction cups; they will slide around as the cups get older. Rain gutter clamps bolted to two-by-fours are a better alternative. Foam gunwale blocks aren't the greatest rig, but they will do (photograph 4). Be sure your canoe is positioned properly so that it doesn't shift and loosen the ropes. The straps and clips that come with the foam blocks will loosen and fall off if the canoe shifts.

No matter how secure the roof rack is, you must rope the bow and stern to the bumpers. Make sure your tie-down rings are very strong. As a safety measure, run a rope back to the seat in case the bow ring lets go. The trucker's hitch (see page 39) can be used, but with a wooden canoe you should be careful not to strain the decks by cinching the rope too tightly. Eyebolts on the bumpers are wonderful (photograph 5). They make tying and untying easier, and are gentler on your ropes than the sharp edge of the bumper. If you don't have eyebolts installed in the bumper, secure four very heavy, ¾ in. (2 cm) rope loops permanently under the bumper. This makes it possible to tie on your canoe without climbing under the car. The loops are convenient and prevent your tracking lines from being frayed or cut by the bumpers. Check the loops periodically for wear. Tape the knots. Tie-down ropes should be at least ⅜ in. (1 cm) braided nylon: it's dependable, strong and the easiest to work with. Sash cord swells and jams when it gets wet. The trucker's hitch is also the best method for tying a canoe to the roof rack. Never use shock cords.

1 The MXCC-003

2 Rear view of MXCC-003

3 High-tech roof racks

4 Foam gunwale blocks and straps

5 Eye bolts on bumpers

Equipment checklist

There is nothing quite so exciting as arriving at the put-in point on a lake or river. Everything I need to live comfortably and eat well outdoors is loaded in my packs or in my canoe and ready to go (photograph 1). Or I hope it is. For years I usually forgot something until I resorted to a checklist. Here it is.

Equipment pack

Pack A (photograph 2) contains:
   a. clothes
   b. sleeping bag
   c. sleeping mat
   d. tent poles
   e. tent
   f. candle lantern
   g. repair kit
   h. fly sheet or tarp
   i. groundsheet
   j. books
   k. flashlight
   l. first-aid kit
   m. saw
   n. axe
   o. ropes or extra guy lines
   p. extra plastic bags

Kitchen and food pack

Pack B (photograph 3) contains:
   a. food wanigan
   b. portable fireplace or grate or gas stove or reflector oven
   c. pot set
   d. food for seven days, each day separately packaged and labelled

Supplementary food pack

This pack (C, not shown) contains your partner's personal gear, sleeping bag, and so on. There is room for the supplementary bulk food for refilling the containers and also food for the second week since there is no camp gear. The Prospector canoe has room for yet another pack, that would contain food for the third and fourth weeks.

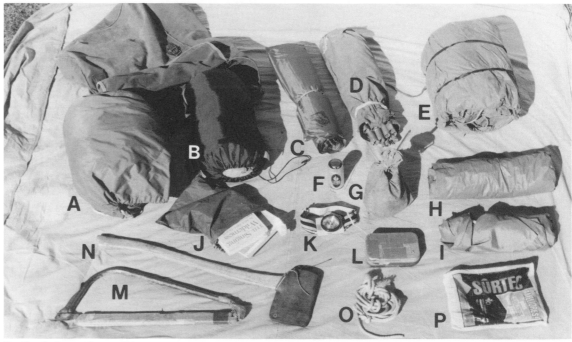

1   Canoe loaded

2   Pack A, equipment

Day Pack

Pack D (photograph 4) contains:

a. bug hat and bug jacket and repellent
b. raincoat, rain pants and hat
c. small camera case
d. duct tape
e. toilet paper
f. map and compass
g. binoculars
h. small case containing Swiss army knife, lighter or match case and a candle
i. short lengths of cord and various sizes of elastic bands
j. fishing lures
k. trowel for digging toilet
l. sheath knife
m. sunglasses, reading glasses
n. fishing rod and reel
o. harmonica or whatever
p. journal or diary, pencils
q. sketching materials
r. toilet articles and sun screen
s. knee pads if required (not shown)
t. travel permit, fire permit, fishing licence (not shown)
u. ouch kit (Band-Aids, not shown)
v. cup (not shown)

Other articles not contained in the packsacks

a. canoe
b. paddles (Don't laugh; once I put my canoe in Lake Manitoba and when I returned to my car for the paddles there weren't any there!)
c. PFD (Personal Floatation Device)
d. carabiner, whistle
e. tracking lines
f. throw bag
g. bailer

To continue the checklist refer to the following: wanigan contents, page 64; clothes bag contents, page 77; repair kit contents, page 133; first-aid contents, page 137. It's amazing to think that all this stuff will fit in a canoe. It's even more amazing when you realize that the native people would head off on a hunting trip of unlimited duration with a rifle, flour, tea, tobacco, axe, pot, blankets and the clothes on their backs.

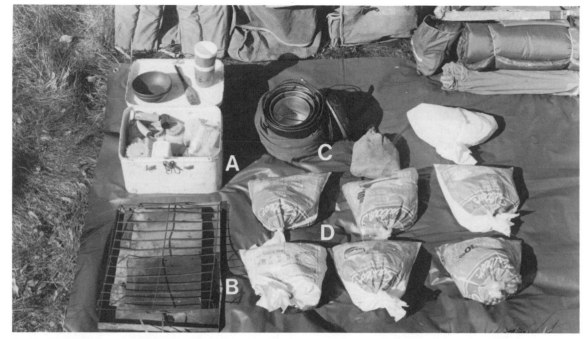

3 Pack B, kitchen and food pack

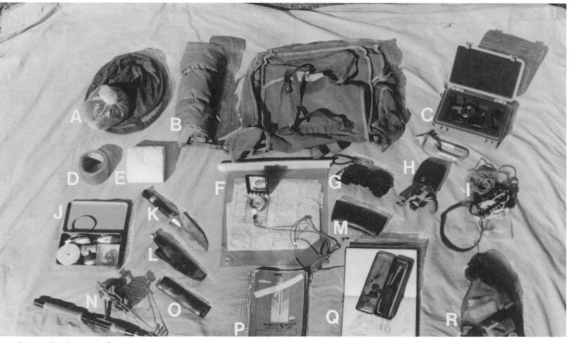

4 Pack D, day pack

Navigation

Navigation is the art of keeping track of where you are, and of figuring out where you're going. I agree with Calvin Rutstrum that there is no such thing as an inborn sense of direction. In his book, *The New Way of the Wilderness*, he described a scientific experiment in which people were blindfolded on a sunless, windless day and placed in a flat, soundless area. No one was able to walk in a straight line in one direction and everyone circled helplessly. The reason some people seldom get lost is because they have learned to think ahead or are naturally observant. Before you head into the bush for firewood or a hike, stop and think about how you are going to find your way back to the campsite.

Planning ahead
If you are camped on the north side of a river that runs from east to west, and you decide to head into the bush to hunt for firewood or a gold mine, to get back to the river, you head south. When you reach the river and the campsite isn't there, you can do one of two things—travel west or travel east following the river. If you travel east for a reasonable time and don't find the campsite, you then turn around and travel west for the same distance past the spot where you hit the river. One of the reasons people get lost is that they don't take note of the direction the river is running at the point where they camp. If they know the general direction is east to west, they are bound to hit it if they travel south.

In summer the sun rises in the east, is in the south at noon, and sets in the west. That's all you need to know to find a river. To be more accurate, you can point the hour hand on your watch toward the sun. Half-way between the hour hand and twelve o'clock will be south. To locate the sun when the sky is overcast, try closing your eyes for a while, then open them quickly and stare at the sky. You might be able to perceive a bright spot in the gloom.

On a clear night, you can navigate by the North Star; use the two pointing stars of the Big Dipper to find it. It's fascinating to think that of the billions of stars in the sky, it is the one that stays constant. To travel south, go away from the North Star.

What I have described is the simplest possible situation, but the same strategy applies to many others. The river could be the shore of a large lake, a road, a railway line, power line, survey line or a ridge of hills. If you travel with the sun, stars or moon as a reference, you will travel in a straight line and, sooner or later, you will cross something. And when you do find a landmark, follow it.

It is more serious to be lost in an area where there are no rivers, roads or large lakes to use as landmarks. If you know that someone will come looking for you, it's better to stay in one place rather than to move aimlessly in circles. You might want to move to a location such as a hilltop to improve your chances of being seen. If you are on a long trip, and you know no one will be looking for you for a while, pick one direction and don't deviate from it. Your chances of finding a way out depend on travelling in that one direction, and luck. Staying alive depends on conserving energy and making commonsense decisions. The most deadly mistake when lost is to travel in circles until you succumb to fatigue.

Recently, I read that there are only three places in the United States that are farther than 10 miles (16 km) from some type of road. This information isn't much help if you are in northern Canada. On our Mountain River trip, if we had journeyed east, we probably wouldn't have crossed a road until we came to Norway.

Maps and Wilderness Canoeing is a Canadian brochure written by Eric Morse to meet the specific needs of canoeists. It contains a wealth of information, such as map scales for wilderness canoeing, lists of topographical maps, hydrographic charts and aerial photographs in various scales, plus diagrams and photographs illustrating the proper use of compass and maps. The reverse side of the brochure provides an index of the 1:250,000 map series of Canada. The brochure (MCR 107) and indices for the east, west and north areas of Canada are free from the Canada Map Office, 615 Booth Street, Ottawa, Ontario K1A 0E9. Maps of the United States for states west of the Mississippi River and Alaska are available from the US Geological Survey. Denver Distribution Branch, Federal Center, Denver, Colorado 80225. Maps for states east of the Mississippi River are available from the US Geological Survey, 1200 South Eads Street, Arlington, Virginia 22202. In the United States, index maps can be obtained from the National Cartographic Information Center, Reston, Virginia 22092.

The indices describe the maps (which are not free) and the scales they are available in. I'm a sucker for maps. If I had unlimited wallspace I would paper the walls with maps! Some of them are beautiful works of art. One masterpiece is the Canada Relief Map. It is a multicolored topographical map. To order it, request the geographical map series No. 1-1976-MCR 88. An atlas you might enjoy poring over before a wilderness trip is the *National Atlas of Canada*. It is loaded with every conceivable type of information. It has many maps, each containing one specific type of information, such as average rainfall or snowfall in any month, anywhere in Canada; or every power dam and potential power site; or profiles of all the major rivers showing their descent to the sea; or geological maps. You can view the book in any library and order individual pages. Another book that should excite canoeists with an interest in the history of Canada's waterways is the *Historical Atlas of Canada*.

The topographical maps show lake outlines, stream courses and land contours. Large-scale topographical maps might show rapids and falls, but you can't always trust the markings. The large-scale maps can also be useful for locating access roads to the rivers and lakes that might not be shown on the usual road maps. Map scales that concern the canoeist are:

1:50,000 or about 1¼ in. to 1 mile (1 cm to .52 km)

1:125,000 or about 1 in. to 2 miles (1 cm to 1.3 km)

1: 250,000 or about 1 in. to 4 miles (1 cm to 2.6 km)

For most trips, the 1:125,000 scale is adequate, but I like the 1:50,000 scale for problem areas such as canyons, falls or a section of heavy rapids. Carrying the 1:50,000 scale for the entire trip would require a stack of maps. Contour lines, the lines that define altitude, can tell you a lot about a river. They give a three-dimensional aspect to the map.

Some people make a game out of map reading: it's called orienteering. My orienteering skills aren't much better than my knot-tying skills. My knowledge is easy to share with you and it's enough to allow you to find your way on lake and river trips. And I haven't been lost, at least not for very long! To set out on a trip without a compass, detailed maps and a basic knowledge of how to read them could lead to considerable adversity.

Entering the mouth of First Canyon, Mountain River ————————————————————

Contour lines—river

About ten years ago, two friends, and my son Paul and I were running the Dog River (formerly known as the University River) which flows south into Lake Superior east of the cliffs. I had attached my map to the thwart in front of me. I was able to find my place on the map at a glance, as I had marked our route on it prior to the trip. With a transparent marker, I had run a line down each side of the river about an inch (2.5 cm) away from it. Starting from the put-in point, I had marked off each mile (1.6 km) with a number and circled it. These numbers went on one side of the river. Then I had numbered the contour lines crossing the river and had marked them on the other side, with an arrow drawn to the exact location.

As I studied the contour lines, I began to get some sense of what the river would be like. The river was 40 miles (64 km) long. The contour lines, each representing 50 ft. (15.2 m), crossed it 14 times. The total drop therefore was 14 times 50, or 700 ft. (213 m). I divided 700 ft. (213 m) by 40 miles (64 km) and got an average drop of 17½ ft. per mile (3.3 m/km). However, the first contour line crossed at 15 miles (24 km), which meant that the river was flat to that point. Dividing the total drop of 700 ft. (213 m) by the remaining 25 miles (40 km) gave an average drop of 28 ft. per mile (5.3 m/km). The map indicated that more than half of the total drop occurred in two short sections of the river. At mile 30 (kilometer 48), I saw that the river went crazy. Further study of the map revealed that contour lines 6, 7, 8, and 9 crossed within a distance of less than 2 miles (3.2 km), giving an average drop in this section of 100 ft. per mile (19 m/km) (photograph 1). The map indicated a falls above the place where contour line 6 crossed the river and a second falls above contour line 7. The height of the falls wasn't given, but I knew there were a couple of portages and probably very difficult rapids.

As I reached mile 37 (kilometer 59) on the map, I saw that the river dropped steeply again (photograph 2). Contour lines 11, 12, 13, and 14 crossed within a distance of less than one quarter of a mile (400 m) which

meant a drop of over 200 ft. (60 m). And herein lies the reason why I chose this river. It meant hard work lining, portaging and running difficult rapids, but it also meant spectacular scenery with canyons, falls and rapids. The map did tell me that the height of the falls was 100 ft. (30 m), so that left another 100 ft. (30 m) in this section unaccounted for. Several other falls and maybe some rapids would probably make up the difference. From contour line 14 to the river mouth, we could anticipate runnable rapids all the way.

Some maps indicate a falls with a single line and a rapids with two lines. More recent maps indicate a falls with a line like this] and rapids with a single line. Big falls have names. Rapids are marked, but sometimes rapids turn out to be falls and falls turn out to be runnable rapids. The land is too vast for the mapping department to mark all of them accurately. Actually, many canoeists prefer it that way. We take our maps and compasses, but we don't mind a few surprises.

Wilberforce Falls

An area that intrigued me for several years was Wilberforce Falls and Wilberforce Canyon on the Hood River, in the Northwest Territories. Before our trip, we talked to people who had been there to confirm the existence of the canyon. One of the group suggested it might be possible to run it. The Hood River map was available only in the 1:250,000 scale. The contour lines were at intervals of 100 ft. (30.4 m). As we studied the lines we found that three of them crossed the river in less than 1 mile (1.6 km) (photograph 3). That's a drop of 300 ft. (91.4 m)! The name Wilberforce Falls confirmed that most of the drop was a falls. The contour lines indicated a canyon below the falls. Rivers like the Hood lose a lot of their total drop in falls. There were many unrunnable rapids and one with a dangerous approach that was likely to be unrunnable. We marked it carefully but, despite our caution, one canoe was swept into it.

On a river, it is difficult to get lost, but it's easy to lose track of where you are. Knowing

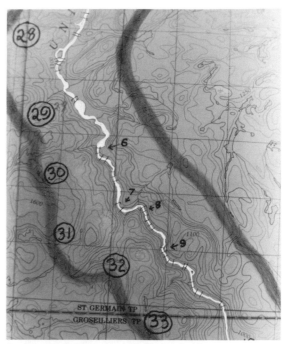

1   Contour line crossings marked

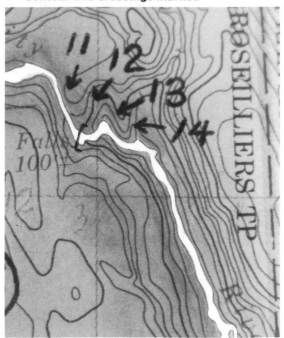

2   Contour crossings close together

your location is important if there are dangerous rapids and falls. When you round that tight bend, it's nice to know what's around the corner. As you gain experience, you know what to expect as you study the maps, but there are always surprises. You will notice that all contour intervals that cross a river point upstream. At least I've never seen one that points downstream. Falls and rapids wear their way upstream over eons of time. That's why a river rarely falls directly into a lake. Usually, you have to travel upstream between high banks to reach the falls. A wonderful exception to this rule is Cascade Falls on the Cascade River, which plunges directly into Lake Superior. It's another of my favorite places. By contrast, the mighty Denison Falls is almost 5 miles (8 km) up the Dog (University) River at the head of a canyon. The canyon was left behind when the falls cut its way upstream.

Sometimes it's fun to look at aerial photos with a stereoscopic viewfinder. It's like looking at the area from an airplane. It takes time to get the glasses positioned properly, but when they are, you will be knocked off your chair! The glasses exaggerate, so canyons appear to be seven times their actual depths. But you don't have to tell your friends that when you show them the mountains you've climbed and the canyons you've run. The purchase of the glasses might be a group or club project as the cost is over $60. They can be purchased at survey equipment stores or at the larger art stores. Most university libraries have stereo map-reading glasses. The stereo aerial photos cost about $10 a pair. Request high-quality prints for stereo viewing when you order your aerial photos from the Canada Map Office or the US Map Office.

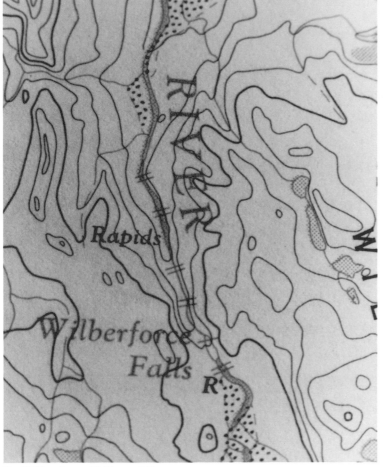

3 Wilberforce Falls and Canyon

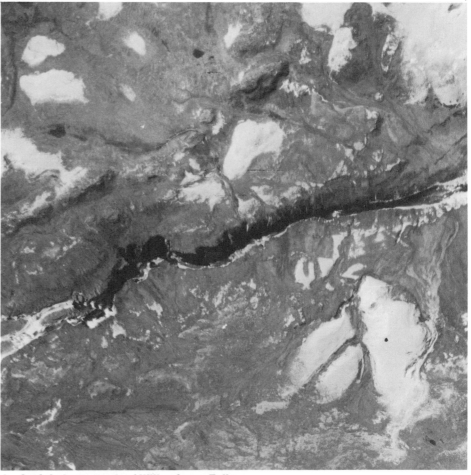

4 Aerial photograph of Wilberforce Falls

Setting the compass and plotting a course

In 1962 I was planning a trip along the north shore of Lake Superior and I hadn't found anyone who had made the trip. I had heard, however, that there are some places that are so steep you can't come ashore for several miles. Studying the 1:50,000 topographical maps gave me a clear picture of what to expect. First, I found the contour interval in the lower margin of the map. It indicated that the vertical height between each contour line was 50 ft. (about 15 m). At point A near Tamarack Bay, the rise from water level seemed to be no more than that. There would be no problem pulling my canoe up if the wind began to blow. Also, there were a large number of bays into which to escape. As I travelled west, however, the closeness of the contour lines indicated a sheer cliff face for at least 3 miles (4.8 km). At B, I counted 13 contour lines, which indicated a cliff face soaring 650 ft. (198 m) straight out of the lake! It would be great for photography, but a tense hour-long paddle; longer if a head wind came up. A bit of a promontory was indicated at C. It suggested the possibility of a landing, but I didn't want to count on it. I would probably have to round Point Isacor before attempting to land.

And that's the way it worked out. I camped east of Tamarack Bay and set out early in the morning to make the run to Point Isacor. A head wind developed about halfway, but I was able to paddle against it. It's a lot of fun and quite a challenge to read the land by means of contour lines.

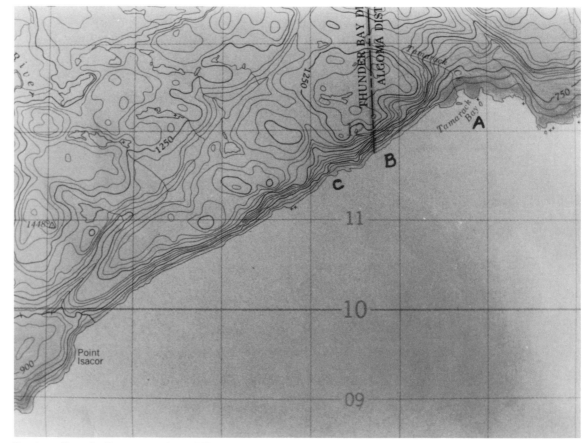

Contour lines indicate soaring cliffs ───────

Compass

The compass I use for canoeing and hiking is the Silva Type 15 Ranger. It has everything you'll ever need to get you there and back: a screw for setting magnetic declination (A); a dial with 360 degrees marked on it, that rotates for setting your course (B); a straight edge with a scale (C); a cover with a mirror (D); and a sight (E) for pinpointing your destination by line of sight. When you have set your compass, the line scratched on the mirror (F) points in your direction of travel. A black orienteering arrow (G) is inscribed on the base of the dial. Also there are some red lines (H) for lining up with the meridians on the map. Finally, and most importantly, there is the compass needle (I). The red end points north.

Rotating dial ——————————————

Declination

The first thing you must check on a map is declination. The compass needle doesn't point toward the North Pole or true north. It doesn't even point to a magnetic pole, but aligns itself with the magnetic lines of force that exist in any given place. In the eastern part of North America, the needle can point west of the North Pole, by as much as 40°. In the west, the needle can point east of the North Pole by as much as 40°. This is what is known as declination. The amount of declination from true north varies across the continent. For an accurate compass reading, you can't ignore declination, which is printed in a box on the margin of each map. The figure will indicate the number of degrees the compass needle is pointing to the west or east of true north. For example, if your figure is 7° 15' east, then the needle is pointing 7° 15' east of true north.

The easiest method to allow for declination is to use the adjustment screw on the dial of your compass. Use a screwdriver or the tip of a knife to turn the screw (A) until the black inscribed arrow (G) is pointing 7° 15' east. The distance between adjacent declination adjustment lines represents two degrees, so 15 minutes can only be estimated by a very small adjustment. Similarly, if the declination is 20° west, you move the arrow to point to 20° west of north. And now that you've adjusted for declination, you can forget about it, as long as you are in the area described by that map. Don't forget to adjust your compass when you plan a trip in a location far from your usual tripping area.

Silva Type 15 Ranger Compass ——————————————

Setting the compass and plotting a course

Marking up the maps

The compass is essential on large bodies of water, especially if they are studded with islands. And it is useful for finding the inlet of a river across many miles of open water.

In 1965, I was travelling south through the Lake of the Woods country in western Ontario. I was in a 25 ft. (7.6 m) simulated birchbark voyageur canoe guiding a group of seven paddlers. We were doing a survey of the Lake of the Woods portion for the 1967 cross-Canada canoe pageant. I'd known the area well so far, but we were heading into unfamiliar country, in the open water of Big Traverse Bay (see map, opposite page). Now I was depending on my compass because I didn't want to suffer the embarrassment of having to search 20 miles (32 km) of flat shoreline for our destination, the outlet of Rainy River. As we passed Sugar Point (A), I looked out across Big Traverse Bay and saw a watery horizon. The far shoreline was low, so the curvature of the earth put it out of sight.

1. The declination for this area is 7° 15′ E, so the black arrow engraved on the base of my compass was set at 7° 15′ E by turning the adjustment screw.

2. To set my compass for my direction of travel, I spread out my map and drew a solid line from where I was (A), Sugar Point, to where I wanted to go (B), Rainy River. This is exactly along the border of Canada and the United States.

3. Then I placed my compass on the map. The inscribed line on the mirror was going to be my pointer. I pointed it toward my intended direction on the map. But to get an accurate reading, I laid the edge of my compass along my intended route (A to B).

4. It seemed unlikely that we would hit the river opening dead on, regardless of how careful I was. When we got near shore, I would have to decide whether to travel left or right to find the opening (B) and what distance in either direction. I decided to aim to the east (C) by about a mile (1.6 km). In this way, when I reached the long island, I would only need to travel west to find the opening (B) between the islands on each side of (B) and thence into the outlet of Rainy River.

5. I lined up the edge of my compass with A and C, drew a dotted line on the map, and pointed the inscribed line on the mirror in the proper direction. Then I turned the dial until the black arrow on the base of the dial was pointing north on the map. For accuracy, I positioned the red lines on the base of the dial with a meridian line on the map (H). But it wasn't in the right place to be of much help, so I drew a line between corresponding longitudinal numbers from the margins on the top and bottom (E). (Don't confuse the longitudinal lines with map grid lines which can vary from true north by several degrees.)

After this was done, I could put away my map. I rotated the whole compass until the north end of the needle (red) was lined up with the black arrow inscribed on the base of the compass dial (black). The inscribed line on the mirror pointed in the direction I wanted to go. I placed the compass in the center of a thwart pointing directly at the bow and made sure there was no metal near the compass to throw off the reading. Then I steered the canoe so the compass needle lined up with the black arrow on the base of the dial.

By keeping the arrow lined up, I should have arrived at (C), but in reality it is impossible to keep it aligned perfectly. We actually reached shore east of (C), so we had to paddle about a mile and a half (2.5 km) to find the inlet (B). If I had not set a course with the compass, we could have arrived at Windy Point (D), Zippel (F) or Long Point (G). And at Zippel we could have travelled a long way up a river before realizing our mistake.

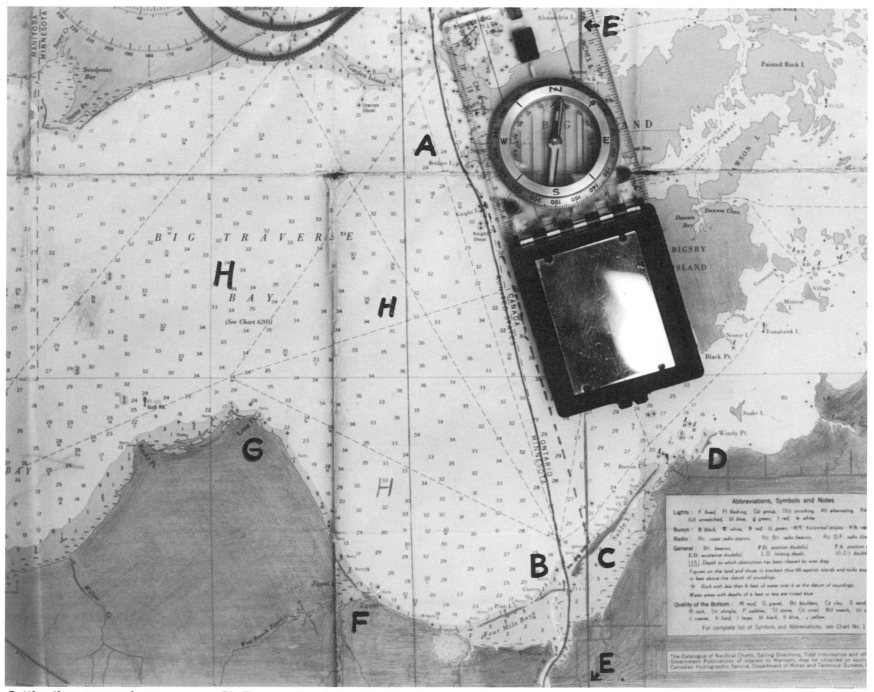

Setting the compass for a run across Big Traverse Bay, Lake of the Woods

Setting the compass and plotting a course . . .

Hiking inland along the shores of Pukaskwa National Park, Ontario

Taking a visual sighting with the compass

A few days later, we found ourselves on a lake where the distant shore was hilly, with the occasional white pine towering above the surrounding trees. The outlet we were looking for could have been one of several pronounced dips in the tree line. We set our compass in relation to the map, but this time we took a visual sighting on the distant shore. The mirror and notch on the compass lid make a very accurate sighting possible. Holding the compass at eye level, I folded the lid down halfway, until I could see the dial reflected in the mirror. Swinging the compass until the north end of the compass needle lined up with the black arrow in the mirror, I then looked through the sight on the cover toward my destination; it happened to be a distinctive dip in the hill, so I could put away the map and compass.

Locating the portage with a compass sighting

Orienting the map with the compass

Several years ago, I was standing on the top of one of the highest rocky points on the Pukaskwa River. I was making a film about Pukaskwa National Park and wanted a shot looking down on the river, panning up and following it as it snaked across the land. It disappeared behind a series of hills before it reached Lake Superior, many miles away. There were gaps in the rugged shoreline, but I didn't know which one was the mouth of the Pukaskwa.

To find the mouth of the river, I laid my compass on the map and adjusted the screw to make the declination correct for the area. The declination was 4° 20′ W, so I turned the screw until the black arrow pointed to 4° 20′ W on the red declination adjustment scale on the base of the dial. Next I lined up the edge of the compass with the hill I was standing on (A) and with the mouth of the river (B). The line etched on the mirror pointed in the direction I wanted to go. Then I rotated the dial until the red lines on the base of the dial lined up with the meridian lines on the map (D). (When there are no meridian lines, I draw a longitudinal line by joining the corresponding meridian numbers at the top and bottom of the map, in this case 50° (D).) To orient the map to the surrounding country, I rotated it carefully until the black arrow lined up perfectly with the red, north end of the compass needle (E). Now everything on the map related perfectly with the surrounding landscape. I could see the place where the East Pukaskwa River joined the Pukaskwa River, even though the river was hidden from view, and I knew exactly where it emptied into Lake Superior.

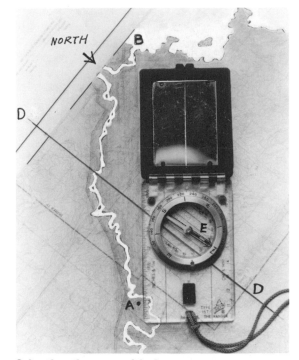

Orienting the map with the compass

The best way to stay alive and well and away from adversity in the wilderness is to be aware of what can go wrong and make sure it doesn't. If you anticipate correctly the type of terrain, weather conditions and potential dangers you might experience, you will have the equipment you need. Even if you don't need it, someone else may. There are articles in my repair and first-aid kits that I have been carrying for many years, and have never had to use, but it is reassuring to know that I have them.

Paddling a canoe is as safe as reading the newspaper or as dangerous as playing Russian roulette. It all depends on your paddling skills, where you choose to go and the weather conditions. If you can sit or kneel in a canoe wearing a PFD (Personal Floatation Device, or a life jacket) without falling out while paddling a pond, small lake or quiet stream, then canoeing is as safe a pastime as there is. On the other hand, rounding an unscouted blind corner in a deep-water rapids without shore eddies, or crossing a long flat water stretch between headlands or islands in unpredictable weather, are high on the danger scale. Just hearing about a friend who did a 10 mile (16 km) crossing from an island to the mainland on the icy waters of Lake Superior sends shivers up my spine. Yet, I've paddled in huge waves on Lake Superior, very close to shore, and wouldn't consider that especially dangerous.

As with many other things about canoeing, there is no one answer. Canoeing is a safe sport if you can accurately assess your skill level, and that of your partner and companions, and predict the difficulties you might face on the water. If you don't have an escape plan in the event of a capsize, then you are entering the danger area. You are on the brink.

In recent years we've seen more and more kayakers firing themselves over 30 to 50 ft. (10 to 15 m) falls. Although it looks insane, most of those people know exactly what they are doing. It's not as dangerous as two inexperienced canoeists making a lake crossing in cross waves, in icy water conditions, and without floatation secured in the bottom of the canoe. If they tip and no one is around to rescue them, they are dead.

What you should know to keep yourself on the safe side of the brink
- When paddling solo, the most dangerous place to be sitting, in a non-loaded canoe, is on the stern seat.
- When paddling double, the stern paddler should get out first. If the bow paddler jumps out first, the stern paddler is left sitting in the canoe at a point where it is only 18 in. (45 cm) wide instead of almost 3 ft. (1 m) wide at the bow paddler's position.
- A non-loaded canoe is more likely to tip, but less likely to take in water over the gunwales in waves and rapids, than a loaded one. It is also more responsive to paddle strokes, and suffers less damage when run into rocks or obstructions.
- If packs are secured so they don't float free, it is possible to paddle a canoe that is completely swamped (see page 126). The packs are lighter than water, so they float. An overturned canoe with packs tied in can actually be righted, reboarded and paddled to shore. A swamped canoe without floatation secured in place is tippy, sluggish, and will sink if you try to stay in it.
- A throw bag (see page 128), secured to the stern deck with a carabiner and held in place with Velcro, should be standard equipment on all canoe trips. This also applies to bailers.
- Know the water conditions that you will be paddling on, or be sure you can trust the knowledge of the person who is leading. Don't be lured into running a rapids because someone else made it look easy.
- Cold water is very dangerous. You either have to get out of it quickly, or be suitably dressed, to avoid hypothermia. In cold, rough water, keep in mind that if you upset, the often repeated advice, "Hang on to your canoe," won't save your life. The survival time in water of 30 to 40°F (0 to 5°C) can be as short as 15 minutes. The distance anyone can swim in these temperatures is very limited.
- Trying to rescue a swamped canoe in big waves in cold water also puts the rescuer in great danger. In adverse weather and water conditions, it's wise to select your companions carefully.
- Paddling in cold water *and* cold air temperatures is very dangerous. Add to this wind and waves, or wind and rapids, and you have the most dangerous situation of all. This is the place for the wet suit, dry suit or some other kind of cold-water protection.
- Rivers and the approaches to portages are usually most dangerous in high water. Although difficult rapids sometimes disappear in high water, they can also become a maelstrom of waves. In low water, there are other problems: it's tough to drown in 6 in. (15 cm) of water, but it might be a long walk if there isn't enough water to float your canoe. You have to know your river or go with someone you can trust.
- If you are not an experienced paddler, there is usually safety in numbers, especially under knowledgeable leadership. The best possible way to learn is with an instructor, and the safest way to travel on a potentially dangerous river is with a professional guide or an experienced friend. Consider joining a canoe organization. Paddlers are usually a gregarious bunch and will welcome you into their midst.
- If you are a skilled paddler, the old adage of safety in numbers doesn't always apply. In large waves or rapids, and in cold water conditions, an inexperienced canoeist could get both partners killed.
- Be sure that you and your companions learn first aid, artificial respiration and rescue techniques (see page 128).
- It's also possible to learn almost everything you'll need to know about safe paddling from a book or by trial and error. It just takes much longer, and there is more risk involved.

Personal floatation devices

In earlier days they were called life jackets, because they looked like jackets and were meant to save your life if you fell in the water. At camp, if a kid got into a canoe without his life jacket, you just yelled, "Hey, put your life jacket on." Not anymore. Now you yell, "Hey kid, put on your Personal Floatation Device." The kid looks at you and says, "Put on what?" So it's been shortened to PFD.

The one thing I remember from camp more than anything else is, "Don't sit on your life jacket!" Sitting on your life jacket was an unpardonable sin. There was a good reason for this rule. The life jacket consisted of a cloth covering over a plastic bag filled with kapok. If you punctured the bag, the water got in and soaked the kapok. It could take three kids to lift a water-soaked life jacket. If you fell in the water with one of those on, you went straight to the bottom. Then there was the life jacket that was made up of narrow plastic tubes filled with air. You'd see kids walking around in them at camp with 12 of the 14 tubes as flat as a pancake.

Years ago the jackets approved by the US Coast Guard and the Canadian Department of Transport were designed to hold you up with your face out of the water. Paddling in them was very difficult. Finally PFDs designed for paddling were approved.

Synthetic foams have revolutionized the life-jacket industry. One of them, Ensolite, is a durable closed-cell material that doesn't absorb water and is very comfortable for paddling in and for sitting on around a camp fire. Everyone still hollers, "Don't sit on your PFD. It could save your life." Mine has saved more than my life. It's been saving my bottom from wear and tear for years. There are very few people who would openly admit that they abuse their PFD by kneeling or sitting on it. Well, I'll tell you right now, the world is full of liars, because I've never met anyone who doesn't. The only way to avoid sitting on your PFD is to carry a square of Ensolite to sit on. I sometimes do that, but can never seem to find it. Someone else is always sitting on it!

Although there are five different types of PFDs, only two are of interest to paddlers. A well-designed Type 3 PFD is comfortable to wear and doesn't restrict the canoeist while paddling. When in the water, the jacket does not automatically keep the swimmer's face out of the water, as the Type 1 and Type 2 PFDs would. To be government approved, the adult Type 3 PFD must provide at least 15½ lb. (7 kg) of buoyancy. Not all Type 3 PFDs are designed for paddling canoes or kayaks. Ask around to find out what satisfied paddlers are wearing.

For children who weigh less than 30 lb. (14 kg) and are not actively paddling, the Type 2 PFD is required. The most common Type 2 PFD is the horse collar. It doesn't look very comfortable, but it is one of the few designs that really does keep the face out of the water. When you buy a PFD for your child, test it as soon as possible to make sure it really works.

If you do upset with a child on board, it isn't likely to be in ideal conditions, so you don't want to be dealing with a jacket that isn't doing the job. This is particularly true if you have more than one child on board.

With so many PFDs on the market, it is difficult to say which one is best for canoeing or kayaking. I can, however, tell you what I like about mine:

- It allows complete freedom of movement when paddling.
- It doesn't chafe at the neck or arms. It doesn't have plastic trim around the arm-holes and at the neck that will crack in time.
- It has good ventilation because it's not too snug.
- The zipper is still working after many years. Plastic zippers are much more durable than metal, and don't jam as readily if they get sand in them.

Swimtime on the Ottawa River

Personal floatation devices . . .

- The material on the outside is tough and dries quickly.
- I float in a comfortable position for swimming when I end up in the water. Unfortunately, it rides up, but this hasn't prevented me from swimming after my wayward canoe on many occasions.
- It is a panel-type PFD, one panel at the back and four at the front, which explains why it is so comfortable to sit on.
- It keeps my upper torso warm in cold, wet weather when I wear thick pile under it.
- The absence of straps and buckles makes it very easy to climb into my canoe after an upset. My PFD happens to be a Mustang Floater, but I'm sure there are other good ones. You might prefer a snug-fitting jacket to avoid having it ride up when swimming and chafing the arms and neck when paddling. Adjustable straps help to eliminate this problem. In some models, the adjustable straps can be tightened for increased insulation or loosened for better circulation of air. Beware of elastic. It eventually loses its elasticity, making for a very floppy fit. Netting on the inside is a good idea for quick drying and good ventilation.

By law, there must be a PFD for everyone in a boat or canoe. There was a time when a stigma was attached to actually wearing one, but not anymore. Now that they are so comfortable, there is no excuse for not wearing a PFD. In fact, life jackets must be worn at all times when canoeing under the auspices of some organizations. There are good reasons for this. The following scenario shows one of the major causes of drowning. When people fall out of their canoe, it often rights itself without shipping any or much water. The wind then blows it out of reach much faster than the paddlers can swim, leaving them stranded. The difficulty of swimming with clothes and shoes on can come as quite a surprise if you are not used to it. Finally, paddling with young children without wearing life jackets is negligent in the extreme.

There is one slight modification that you can make in almost any PFD to take the pain out of portaging. Without removing any of the floatation, simply add some Ensolite padding to the top of the shoulders and behind the neck. Some PFDs have padding over the shoulders, but not enough. Unfortunately, a modified life jacket is no longer a certified PFD, so to play by the rules, you must carry another one.

A wet suit can be a great asset in whitewater. It not only keeps you warm but, while running rapids in early spring, it also provides a considerable amount of extra floatation. In addition, it helps protect you from bumps and scrapes on the rocks.

The perfect PFD hasn't been made yet, but they've come a long way since the old "keyhole." It's important to remember that you don't have to be in a boat to need a PFD. A couple of years ago, a man drowned while dipping water beside a rapids. Others have died while tracking or wading.

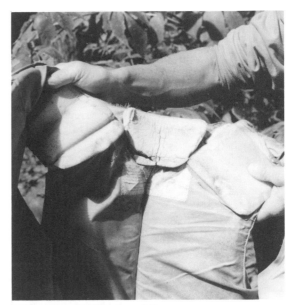

PFD with additional padding ⸻

A bewildering array of PFDs ⸻

Spray covers

The subject of spray covers is a controversial one. There are times when they are a definite asset, and there are times when they are more trouble than they're worth. Spray covers have made many rivers accessible to canoeists of moderate skill. At the same time, those same rivers have been canoed by paddlers who used skill rather than spray covers to keep themselves afloat.

Wally Schaber and Louise Gaulin ran the Mountain River without spray covers by skillfully maneuvering through very wild and turbulent stretches. On the entire river, they had to line only one short stretch that had no clear route through. My son Paul, Judy Seaman, Chris Harris and I put our spray covers on for the canyons and were able to plow through the largest of waves for a thrilling roller-coaster ride.

In the fourth canyon of the Nahanni (the canyon below the falls), almost everyone uses spray covers. Because of the wilderness nature of the Nahanni, the canoes are always heavily loaded, and it's difficult to avoid all the big waves. Without a spray cover, it only takes one of those waves to put you under. On the Little Nahanni (a misnomer if ever I heard one) I doubt if anybody could make it through the canyons with a heavily loaded canoe without spray covers in medium to high water. When we canoed the Little Nahanni, one of our party, Gilles Couët, made it without a spray cover, but he was running solo and with great skill. I can only guess that before the advent of spray covers, many of these wild mountain rivers, as well as countless rivers in the Shield country, were not navigable without long portages around the canyons.

Spray covers are not without their problems, however. Although they will keep the water out of your canoe, they won't keep you from upsetting. A spray-covered canoe full of water weighs close to a ton. That's a lot of weight to manhandle out of a strong current. When you do get it into an eddy, it is much more difficult to empty than a canoe without a spray cover. Unfastening one side of the cover makes it possible to tip out the water or bail it out of the cockpit.

Another disadvantage of spray covers is the difficulty they present for portaging. They add weight, and it is impossible to see where you are going, so you have to remove them or go to the trouble of adjusting them. On a river with many portages and only a few rapids that require a spray cover, I would choose to leave the cover at home, and portage the questionable rapids. For lake travel, spray covers add immeasurably to safety and comfort. In waves they will keep you dry, and in rain you won't have to do much bailing. They also cut down on wind drag by streamlining the load. On the big, cold, portage-free rivers of the mountains, I also prefer spray covers, but in the rock-studded rivers of the east with their many portages, I use packs for floatation and bail in the eddies. Sometimes I use spray covers in the east when the rivers are in spring flood.

Spray skirts

One decision that has to be made concerning spray covers is whether or not to also equip them with spray skirts. The spray skirt fits tightly around the body and keeps the water out of the cockpit. Many people are afraid they will be trapped during an upset and refuse to wear them. Their fears are valid. People have drowned as a result of becoming tangled in a spray skirt. Homemade rigs can be particularly dangerous. It's much more difficult to design a foolproof cowling on a homemade spray cover for a canoe than it is for a kayak.

There are two kinds of spray skirts. One is the kayak type that is worn around the waist like a skirt. The bottom of the skirt is secured to the cockpit cowling. In an upset, you eject from the canoe by pulling the spray skirt free of the cowling. Some canoeists are afraid that it might not come free, so adjust it loosely. However, if it's too loose, it will cave in when hit by a large wave.

The second type of spray skirt is secured permanently to the spray cover, comes up around the paddler's chest and is held there with an elasticized closure. The paddler falls free of the skirt in an upset, but if he twists while tipping, the sleeve can bind and tangle him. At the very least this can be a frightening experience; at worst it could be fatal. Even if you have someone to help you, it is difficult to right a capsized spray-covered canoe, and even more difficult with someone caught in the spray skirt.

Spray-decked canoe on Mountain River ————

Spray covers . . .

Wave-deflector cockpit
For their whitewater trips, Black Feather outfitters has devised a spray cover with open cockpits that have a deflector that sheds all but the largest waves (photograph 1). At the front of the cockpit, a sleeve is sewn around the edge of an extension of the spray cover (illustration 2). When a flexible plastic rod is pushed through the sleeve, the nylon fabric of the extension is stretched and pops up to form a wave deflector in front of the cockpit. The deflector must either be tight against your chest, or be far enough forward so it doesn't interfere with your paddle stroke. In an upset, there is no danger of becoming tangled and it is easy to step in and out of your canoe—no fiddling with attaching or detaching a skirt.

Attaching spray covers to canoe
The cover should be attached securely to the canoe, because if it comes loose during an upset, you can become tangled in it. Snap fasteners are the most common method used. In *Path of the Paddle*, I suggested Velcro for fastening the cover to the canoe, but it comes loose far too easily. You can use that page for starting your next fire!

Equipping canoes with spray covers is a real problem for outfitters. They have canoes of different sizes and shapes, and the spray covers get mixed up. After many failed attempts to figure out a system, Wally Schaber arrived in the north one spring to discover that his partner, Chris Harris, had drilled all their canoes, old and new, full of holes. The holes were about 1 ft. (30 cm) apart and ran the length of the canoe just under the gunwale. Ropes had been fed through them to form loops. The spray covers had been made in two sections. There was an extra length of material at the center thwart that could be rolled to adjust to the length of either a 16 or 17 ft. (4.8 or 5.2 m) canoe (photograph 3). The center join of the two sections allowed easy access to the packs. The rope loops alternated from the inside to the outside along the length of the canoe, and were large enough to receive the clips on the spray cover wherever they happened to come. The spray covers would never come off the canoe inadvertently.

Most people would be reluctant to drill holes in their canoe, but it does work. Little or no water enters through the holes if they are the same diameter as the rope. The loops on the inside of the canoe have the added advantage of providing tie-downs for the packs, which provide a certain amount of floatation for a swamped canoe. A canoe equipped in this manner can be righted and bailed in the middle of the river without going ashore, a great asset on a fast-flowing river where recovering a swamped canoe is very difficult.

The cover should be equipped with a pocket to hold the spare paddle blade, and a strip of Velcro for securing the handle. Also, there should be a means of attaching the throw bag to the stern.

State-of-the-art homemade spray covers
In my travels, I have met some paddlers who have made a hobby of designing and making their own spray covers. We met one such party on the Mountain River (photograph 4). Their spray covers were works of art. They were adjustable for their oversized packs and had pockets for the spare paddles, maps and recovery ropes. They were neat and taut as a drum. Their spray skirts were of the sleeve type with a Velcro fastener to keep the spray skirt tight around their chests. The covers were attached to the canoe with snap fasteners.

We were very impressed, but still didn't like the idea of having to undo the Velcro in an upset. It can get confusing, hanging upside down in churning whitewater. Because they were familiar with the escape procedures, it is perhaps unlikely the skirts would present a problem for them.

Upsets with a spray-covered canoe
Upsets on a wilderness trip with a heavily loaded canoe are much less frequent than when you are practicing or learning with an empty canoe. However, a loaded canoe dives much more deeply into the waves, hence the need for spray covers. If you decide to use spray covers, it is important to load up your waterproof packs, secure your spray cover, upset your canoe, and go through the procedures in shallow water close to shore. It will take some practice to right the canoe and climb back in. How quickly can you bail it out? Is your bailer easy to get to? Did your recovery rope stay in place? Try towing your upside-down loaded canoe with your recovery rope. Testing spray skirts should also be done in shallow water with someone standing by to help if you get into trouble.

A heavily-loaded covered canoe is very hard to turn right-side up, especially an ABS canoe. There is no keel to grab onto. You have to reach across to grab the far gunwale, so you are lying across the canoe and have no leverage. Practice righting the canoe with the 3 ft. (1 m) rope tied at the gunwale amidship. You can literally stand on your canoe and pull it upright with this rope.

In an upset, where you want to use a canoe-over-canoe rescue (see *Path of the Paddle*), you must remove the spray cover and the packs. This could be difficult, especially in large waves. The spray cover makes bailing a good option for recovery. If your packs are tied in securely, they will add freeboard to the canoe even though it's swamped, making it easier to bail. If you are too far from shore to drag the canoe, bailing is your only option, other than abandoning the entire outfit and swimming to shore. Contrary to what all safety organizations preach, swimming is sometimes advisable. I once upset in very cold water with no hope of rescue and headed immediately for shore. My outfit came ashore many hours later as I warmed myself beside my fire. If I had tied my packs in the canoe, I could have righted it and paddled to shore swamped (see page 126).

For hot dog canoeing in rapids without packs, I fill the canoe with floatation. Floatation has a couple of advantages over spray covers. A canoe equipped with floatation floats high in an upset and is easy to recover. You roll it over, climb in and bail it out without ever coming ashore.

1   High open cockpit spray cover

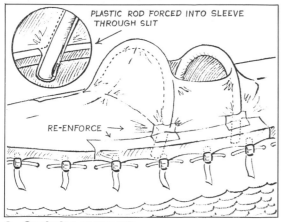

2   Cockpit construction

PLASTIC ROD FORCED INTO SLEEVE THROUGH SLIT

RE-ENFORCE →

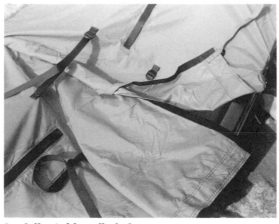

3   Adjustable rolled closure

4   State of the art sleeve-type cockpits

PFD for your canoe

In *Path of the Paddle* I suggested securing all packs on a tether so they could be easily removed for a canoe-over-canoe rescue (see page 146). Because the contents are in waterproof bags, the packs are buoyant and will float at the end of the tether while the canoe is being emptied and then recovered. I have since changed my mind because of what I have learned in hot dog canoeing (photograph 1). To play in rapids, we tie inner tubes under the center and stern thwarts of the canoe. (It is also possible to buy air bags to fill the entire canoe except for the cockpit.) When we swamp or upset, we either perform a roll or we just climb back in and bail the water out without going ashore. The floatation buoys the canoe up, so that even when it's full of water, you have about 3 in. (8 cm) of freeboard, making it possible to bail the remaining water. Even without a bailer, you can stay upright in the canoe and paddle to shore. The canoe is slow and sluggish, but you can still make it without sinking or rolling over.

When you are playing in the waves and begin to take on water, a canoe buoyed by inner tubes becomes amazingly stable. The water in the canoe buoys up the inner tube equally on both sides, and the canoe begins to feel like a raft. With floatation, you can actually run a rapids, albeit with limited mobility, while completely swamped.

Keeping this in mind, let us replace the inner tubes with packsacks as would be the case on a wilderness journey. Packs are always lighter than water (photograph 2). So if they are tied in securely (photograph 3), the packs will buoy up a swamped canoe (photograph 5) and you can maintain some degree of floatation and mobility. If the packs are released by cutting the ropes, the canoe sinks from the paddlers' weight (photograph 6).

I am not suggesting that you should run rapids in a loaded canoe for the sake of buoyancy in an upset. In difficult rapids, a loaded canoe is much more sluggish and easier to swamp. In reasonable rapids, up to Class 2 or easy 3, we regularly run loaded.

But for the more difficult stuff we portage the packs.

Very recently, I have begun to keep the lightest pack secured amidships, and already there have been several occasions when it buoyed me up enough to stay in the swamped canoe and work it into an eddy. The pack must be secured right to the floor to be effective. I wedge it under the center thwart. This also means one less pack over the portage.

If you swamp or upset a loaded canoe with the secured packs in waves on a lake, you can right the canoe, climb back in, and paddle it. This can save your life in cold water conditions because you are able to get out of the water immediately. However, if you aren't carrying secured packs, the canoe doesn't have sufficient buoyancy to hold you up.

When rescuing a pinned canoe in rapids, it is important to remember that a swamped canoe loaded with packs is actually lighter than one without. If there are rocks in rapids, stay well away from the canoe until you reach deep water, then right your canoe and bail it or get in and paddle it swamped to shore or into an eddy. Three packs weighing 180 lb. (81 kg) would probably displace about 500 lb. (230 kg) of water. Your net gain in lightness is about 320 lb. (150 kg). You are better off attempting to free a swamped, loaded canoe rather than an empty one, so leave the packs in the canoe as long as it is completely submerged. The canoe will float even higher if it is upside-down because the canoe is riding up on top of the packs. I always laugh when I see a film where the hero goes through the ice and is carried to the bottom of the lake by his pack. He then struggles out of his pack and swims to the surface. I've never seen a pack that was heavier than water.

1   Running dangerous rapids with floatation-equipped canoe

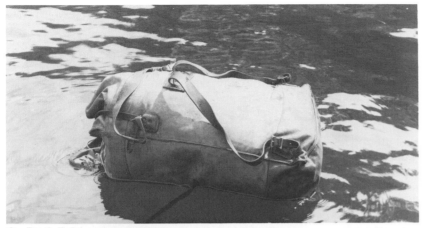
2 Pack lighter than water

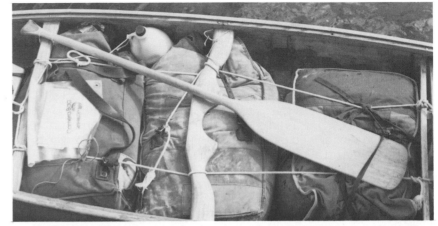
3 Packs lashed securely in canoe

4 Allowing canoe to fill with water

5 Swamped canoe buoyed by packs

6 Cutting packs free — canoe sinks from weight of paddlers

Rescue techniques

Throw bags

The techniques for rescuing a pinned canoe or a paddler stranded on a rock in the middle of a rapids above a falls could fill volumes. As skills, techniques and equipment improve, people are running rapids that would have been considered suicidal a few years ago. The result is people make mistakes and get themselves into difficult predicaments. This is especially true of guided trips where people are often canoeing at the limit of their skill level. Everybody in the group should be prepared to perform a rescue from shore.

The throw bag is an ingenious but simple device that can be used in many ways. It consists of a nylon bag stuffed with 50 to 100 ft. (15 to 30 m) of special, tangle-free braided nylon rope that floats. A drawstring closes the top just sufficiently to keep the rope from falling out. A throw bag should be secured to the stern of each canoe by means of a carabiner for instant release in an emergency, and one should also be worn by the guide or leader. The throw bag has several advantages over a coiled rope: it is very compact, less likely to tangle, instantly available and easier to throw accurately. The throw bag rope is also less likely to be used for securing packs or tying a canoe to shore because of the length of time it takes to stuff it back in the bag.

There are some inherent dangers in using a throw bag. When you take a throw bag in your hands, you should be aware of these dangers and be thoroughly familiar with the following procedure for making a rescue:

1. When choosing the place on shore from which to attempt the rescue, look for a spot free of overhanging branches and with good footing.

2. Loosen the drawstring on the bag, grasp the loop in the end of the rope in the non-throwing hand, pull out a couple of feet (0.5 m) of rope and get ready to throw the bag.

3. Don't throw until you make eye contact with the victim. It is essential that he sees where the rope lands.

4. When you have eye contact, throw the bag and yell, "Rope!" This is not only for the victim, but also to inform other people that the rope has been thrown. The victim should back-scull against the current to slow his descent, and to keep his feet downstream and up near the surface, to avoid entrapment between rocks. It's better to throw it too far rather than too close.

5. The victim grabs the rope, but should be reminded not to wrap the rope around his hand. Ropes should never be secured to any part of a swimmer's body in a current. The rope could jam between rocks holding the swimmer underwater.

6. If the victim is knowledgeable about throw-rope rescues, he will stay on his back, holding the rope to his chest and over the shoulder farthest from shore. This decreases the tendency to roll over onto the stomach, pulling the head underwater.

7. The rescuer can lessen the drag, and make it easier for the victim to hang on, by walking downstream along the shore.

8. The rescuer attempts to work the victim into a shore eddy. Only when the victim is in the still water of the eddy should he attempt to stand up.

9. If the rescuer misses, or the rope falls short and out of reach of the victim, he pulls the rope in quickly, with the coils falling neatly on the rock by his feet. The bag is filled with water for weight, the drawstring is closed and another throw is made. It would take much too long to restuff the rope into the bag. The loop on the bag should be small to discourage the victim from putting his hand through it; he must be able to let go easily.

Paul is the expert with the throw bag, having put it to good use on many occasions. One time, a canoe belonging to a party of canoeists just ahead of him on the river dumped. The water and air temperatures were cold, and he hoped the victim would swing into a large eddy not far above a 6 ft. (2 m) falls. He unsnapped his carabiner and took off through the bush with the throw bag. When he emerged from the trees, he saw the victim in the eddy. He yelled "Rope!" to attract the victim's attention as he threw the bag. The bag landed about 10 ft. (3 m) beyond the victim with the rope dropping right on his head. He grabbed the rope and Paul began reeling him in. Just then, the other members of the party, who hadn't seen Paul, arrived around the corner. All they saw was the strange sight of their companion streaking to shore leaving a wake!

Throw bag rescue

Throw bag secured to stern with carabiner

Self-rescue of canoe

The throw bag has many other uses. It can be used for self-rescue when a canoe upsets or swamps. As someone who seems to do a lot of swimming, I have used it on many occasions to save my canoe. It goes like this. The canoe gradually takes on water until it disappears beneath the waves and rolls over (no canoeist ever admits he or she tipped). I push myself well clear of the downstream side to avoid being pinned on a rock, then approach the stern from the upstream position. I reach under and yank the throw bag free of the shock cord that has secured it on the stern deck. The loop on the free end of the rope is secured to the deck with the carabiner. I head for shore, but slightly against the current in a sort of back ferry. I swim on my back with the frog kick. The rope pays out without snagging.

The canoe continues on down the river, but usually I reach the shallows before the full length of the rope is out. I work the canoe out of the current and stop its downstream descent. If necessary, I cinch the rope around a tree to stop the canoe and pull it out of the current. I would never wrap the rope around my hand or body. Sometimes, in a strong current, you have to let the rope go and recover the canoe at the end of the rapids.

Canoe-to-canoe rescue

Paul has rigged up a useful arrangement on his stern deck for rescuing his clients' canoes. In an upset or swamping, he paddles over and secures the free end of the rope to the swamped canoe with the carabiner (photograph 1). He then heads for shore with his throw bag secured to his stern deck by means of a sailing cleat (photograph 2). For the cleat system to work, the rope that's secured directly to the bag itself, not the free end, must be fed through the eyebolt so the pull is from the proper direction to hold it in the cleat. Note that the loop on the throw bag has been untied. The rope pays out of the throw bag. When he reaches the end of the rope, he continues to work to get the swamped canoe out of the current. If he fails in the attempt, and the canoe threatens to pull him into the next set of rapids, all he has to do is yank on the rope to free it from the cleat (photograph 3).

This is a good system because, once a rope is pulled taut, it is impossible to untie. Even a carabiner is difficult to unhitch when the rope is taut. The last thing you want to have happen is to be dragged down a rapids or over a falls backward by a wayward canoe!

1 Secure carabiner to swamped canoe —————

2 Throw bag secured to rescue canoe by cleat —————

3 Cleat enables quick release —————

Rescue techniques . . .

Z Drag

A skilled guide has the knowledge and equipment to deal with almost any crisis on the river. For a personal trip, there is a limit to how much equipment you can carry. We have gotten along with several lengths of strong rope, and an axe and saw for cutting stout poles as levers for freeing a pinned canoe. However, we are always looking for easier and better ways to do things, and the Z Drag is definitely that!

Because the throw bag rope is very strong, it can also be used for winching pinned canoes off rocks by using carabiners as pulleys. I've seen swamped canoes that four strong people couldn't budge that came off easily with the pulley system known as the Z Drag. It's safer than using levers, because once the rope is secured to the canoe, the recovery is made from shore. The Z Drag pulley system increases the pulling power by almost three times. You need the throw-bag rope, maybe more than one if the canoe is far from shore, at least three carabiners and a 3 ft. (1 m) prusik loop (a thin but strong rope).

The rescue canoe is ferried out to the pinned canoe and pulled into the eddy behind the rock the canoe is pinned on. The bow paddler steps out onto the rock if the rock is above or at water level. The rope must be secured to a thwart and brought up, around and over the bottom of the hull and then to shore (illustration 1). If the rope is tied directly to a thwart, seat or deck without passing it around the hull, it will probably pull them off. Ferry your canoe to shore feeding out the rescue rope. Tie a short length of rope to a solid tree or rock and attach a carabiner. Put the rescue rope through the carabiner, then attach a prusik rope to the rescue rope at least 10 ft. (3 m) from the tree (illustration 2). Attach another carabiner to the prusik rope and run the rescue rope through the carabiner. (If you run out of rope, you tie it off with another prusik and position another carabiner and repeat the procedure.) You are ready to pull. The more people pulling the better.

If both the canoe and rock are submerged,

you've got a real problem. Try standing in the eddy below the rock. You could try securing the line on the swamped canoe from your canoe, but this is a tough one. Downstream of the canoe is a dangerous place to be. If the canoe shifts, it could pin you.

There are many other refinements that you learn by practice, such as the angle of pull. Hopefully, you won't have much cause to use the real thing, so practice on canoes that aren't pinned.

Some people enjoy the challenge. I've actually seen Paul's eyes light up when he comes sweeping around a corner and sees a canoe pinned on a rock in the middle of a river. We have three hopelessly mangled canoes in our backyard that Paul found pinned and deserted. They are totally useless, but they are like trophies. Some people collect moose heads; my kid collects mangled canoes!

3   Securing rope to pinned canoe

4   Pulling canoe free of current

1   Rescue rope secured to canoe

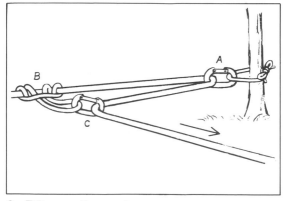

2   Z Drag pulley system

5   One more trophy for Paul

Canoe emergency repairs

Into my sixth year of owning my first canoe, I found myself swimming down a rapids being chased by my swamped canoe. It was broadside to the current and every time it hit a rock there was a sickening crunch as it rolled up and over. I tried to swim away from it, but it seemed to pursue me. Each time it rolled up and over a rock there was another piece missing.

Finally the current slackened and the canoe became docile once again. I rolled it over, climbed into what was left and with my spare paddle, paddled it to shore. My beautiful Plycraft canoe, made from molded plywood, was ripped three-quarters of the way around in two places, and the thwarts and seats were torn loose and broken. The gunwales were pulverized in several places. The canoe appeared to be a write-off. I had just been given a lesson in the tremendous power of moving water in rock-studded rapids.

This happened a long time ago and yet the memory of the adventure is extremely vivid. It was a feeling of exhilaration, because I had survived without injury. I retrieved my gear from the head of the portage, since my canoe had been empty, built a fire and studied my map while eating lunch. It would be a day's walk out to the nearest road. I pulled up the canoe (or what was left of it) and hid it in the trees. The sad part of the story is that, knowing what I know now, the canoe could have been salvaged. The following summer a friend convinced me that it could be repaired with fiberglass, but when we returned for it, we discovered that someone had torn the bow off and thrown it into the rapids. I regret losing that canoe because it was my first one.

The subject of canoe repairs could—and does—fill volumes, because of the different materials used in their construction today. For wilderness repairs, you need only one thing to make it possible to refloat your canoe, regardless of how badly it's damaged, assuming that you still have all the pieces. If you're missing parts, that presents another problem.

We had reason to use our emergency repair technique one fall on the Petawawa River. It

Nothing a little duct tape can't fix ─────────

Duct tape repairs ─────────

Canoe emergency repairs . . .

was late in the season and the river had very little water in it; its average depth was about 4 in. (10 cm). As we approached a set of rapids, we could see some canoeists standing on the shore. We stood up in the canoe to line up with the V, knelt down and entered the rapids. The river was so low that we were often touching and scraping the rocks. After an enjoyable run, we pulled in and landed on a gravel bar halfway down the rapids for lunch. Soon the canoeists who had been looking at the rapids earlier paddled by, like us, banging into just about everything. Lunch finished, we pushed off and ran the rest of the rapids. When we reached the end, we spotted the canoeists with one of their canoes on shore. Their very light Kevlar canoe looked like a truck had run over it. It was hard to believe that a river with so little water could do so much damage, but once swamped, the canoe had drifted down the rapids out of control. With a ton of water in it, each rock had just pulverized it. After having a look at the damage, we assured them that we could make it float well enough for them to get home.

Paul went looking for the one thing that could put this jigsaw puzzle back together — duct tape. Silver duct tape will stick to anything if it's warm and dry. If you use it properly, it is very strong. The bad news was that we couldn't find any. For the first time in years, we had forgotten our roll of duct tape. We proceeded to remove duct tape from our paddles, camera case, packsacks, anything that had been repaired. Most of it came from my camera case. I always place about ten overlapping strips along the side of my case for easy access. We actually stuck that canoe back together so it would float.

Duct tape will do in an emergency, but canoe repair tape is preferable — it sticks better and lasts longer. It should be available at any good canoe store. On a place where there is excess stress, fold one piece with the sticky side out and then place another piece over it to hold it in place. Canoe tape or duct tape that is folded over once is extremely resistant to tearing. On a long trip where the damaged canoe would be coming under a lot of stress, the tear should be repaired by drilling holes along the tear and lacing it back together with cord or wire. To strengthen and make it waterproof, epoxy a cloth or fiberglass patch over the tear. Splintered or broken gunwales should be taped, so you don't cut your hands. Seat bolts can break or the nuts fall off, so carry spares. Very sophisticated or even permanent repairs can be accomplished with the repair kit on page 133, but unless you are on a long trip, you only need a temporary repair until you reach your destination.

Fiberglass or epoxy repairs ——————

Taping it all back together ——————

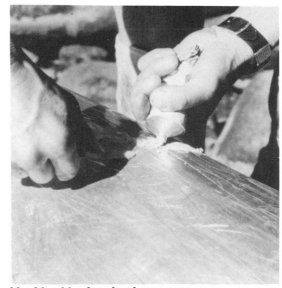

Liquid solder for aluminum canoes ——————

Emergency gear

Repair kit

A packsack strap pulls away from the rivets; a paddle splits; someone puts a nick in the axe. There's great satisfaction in getting out the repair kit in the evening and putting everything back together again. My repair kit is almost the same for long, extended trips as it is for a short weekend trip. It contains many items, and yet is very small.

Accessories (A)   I carry a small tin or plastic vial containing the following items in various sizes. It takes up very little space and the weight is negligible.
SCREWS (G)   For repairing splintered gunwales, seats, thwarts or paddles.
NAILS (G)   If you carry a few, you'll find a use for them.
BOLTS (G)   For fast repair of a broken packsack strap. Also good for broken gunwales, thwarts, and so on.
RIVETS (G)   For repairing shoes, packsacks, and so on.
SPARE FLASHLIGHT BULB

Five-minute epoxy (B)   For repairing paddle tips, splicing a broken shaft and for canoe repairs. It can be used to repair anything that doesn't flex.

Tube of seam sealer (C)   For sealing seams in pack liners, tents, tarps and clothes.

Copper wire (D)   Very handy for holding together a rip or break in the side of a canoe. Also for splicing a broken paddle shaft or a thwart.

Seat bolts (E)   Special bolts are required to attach seats to gunwales.

Cord or string (F)   There never seems to be enough.

Contact cement (H)   Will stick a patch on almost anything.

Small needle-nosed pliers (I)   For tightening nuts on canoe seats; also nuts on bolts used to repair packsack straps or gunwales.

Piece of beeswax (J)   Strengthens thread and waterproofs seams in cotton material.

Matches (K)

Piece of Egyptian cotton or nylon (L)   For tent repairs and repairing a hole or rip in a canoe.

Piece of soft leather (M)   For repairing shoes, gloves, packs.

Stitching awl (N)   A great tool for repairing shoes, packs and gloves. Will stitch almost anything.

Whetstone (O)   For sharpening knives and fish hooks.

Axe file (P)   For sharpening the axe, but can also shape wood.

Needle and thread, safety pins (Q)

Duct tape   Carried in the day pack for easy access, duct tape is used for patching canoes, tents, packs, clothes or almost anything. The broken item must be absolutely dry. If the tape is heated, it adheres more permanently. Rub well.

Swiss army knife   Carried in day pack. I used to think it was a gimmick, but now I wouldn't go anywhere without it. It will make holes in anything, sharpen pencils, cut and file fingernails, carve paddles, saw through a three-inch (7 to 8 cm) piece of hardwood, remove a hook from a fish gill, measure the length of the fish, skin it and prepare it for frying (I prefer my belt knife for that though), file through a piece of wire, repair a camera, remove slivers, tighten screws (slot or Phillips), open cans and bottles (shouldn't be necessary on wilderness trips). It's even got a toothpick.

Awl punch   For making holes in leather or softwood.

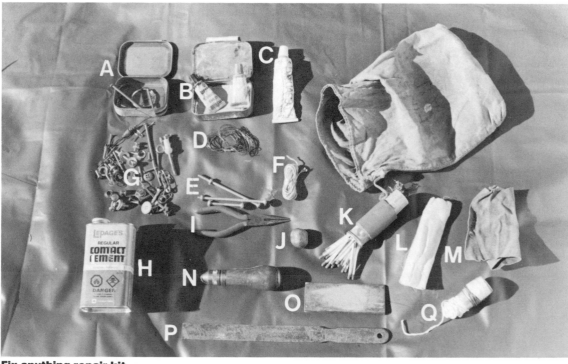

Fix anything repair kit

133

Emergency gear . . .

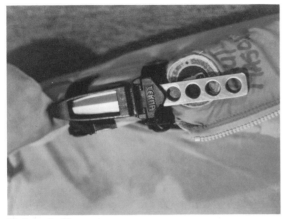

Tekna knife

The well-equipped guide or leader

Rescue knives

Although I rarely have loose ropes to get tangled in hanging from my canoe, from time to time it's necessary to handle ropes in fast water, for example when lining, tracking or making a rescue. I have always worn a sheath knife on my belt for easy access, and have suffered a considerable amount of good-natured abuse about my "bear huntin' knife!" Countless outdoor magazine articles talked about how the sheath knife went out with hand-to-hand combat. Well, if you've been reading those same magazines, you'll discover the sheath knife is coming back. It's in the form of a lethal-looking "rescue knife," with a double cutting edge, that is secured in a plastic sheath attached to the PFD. The Tekna knife, which costs as much as I paid for my first canoe, is becoming very popular among whitewater guides. Designed for emergency rescues, its serrated top edge could saw a pinned canoe in half to free a trapped paddler. For my personal use, I still prefer my belt knife because of its versatility. I can cut bread, split wood, sharpen tent pegs or do any number of jobs with it.

Emergency gear for trip leaders

I do think the rescue knife and all the other paraphernalia are a good idea for anyone burdened with the responsibility of leading people through whitewater. A well-equipped guide carries a whistle, throw bag, prusik ropes, and several carabiners attached to his PFD. Matches in a waterproof container, or a disposable lighter, and a candle for lighting a fire quickly should always be carried in a jacket pocket. With all the essentials secured to the PFD, they are instantly accessible. Increased safety-consciousness and good equipment are largely responsible for the low accident rate in relation to the tremendous increase in whitewater canoeing and kayaking.

Radios and location-finding devices

I find it hard to be enthusiastic about having radio communication of any kind when I am enjoying a wilderness experience. Even with the latest in technology, portable radios are still heavy for canoeing and hiking. Worse, they are completely undependable. Of the ten times I have used radios in my film work, they only worked on two occasions.

I have found that having a set pick-up date or reporting in at the end of the trip is an adequate precaution. For anyone who doesn't want to be out of reach of emergency services, there are many trips that parallel roads, railways or are frequently paddled by other canoeists. For example, the wild and lonely shores of Pukaskwa National Park on the north shore of Lake Superior are not all that lonely any more. You can flag a boat almost any day of the week.

Commercial guiding outfits are finding it necessary to be equipped with an emergency location device. Once triggered, it sends out a signal that can pinpoint the location to within a few meters. These devices can prevent a costly search, but once triggered, you can't change your mind.

Coping with bugs and bears

There's nothing much between the tiny bug and the large bear that presents a problem for the camper. Poisonous snakes live in several areas across North America, but in all our years of camping, we've never seen one.

Biting insects

When we think of adversity, we immediately think of bugs. We can deal with extreme heat and cold if we are well equipped and have the knowledge and skill to deal with their effects. However, bugs are almost unavoidable when we are outdoors at certain times of the year. Usually they are at their worst in spring and in early summer when it's hot, humid and windless, but they are unpredictable. I have occasionally enjoyed almost bug-free trips in spring, only to find them much worse in summer, when their life cycle is supposed to be over.

There are several ways to combat biting insects. One is to dress so they can't get to you, and the other is to practice psychological warfare. During the day, I try to ignore them. Sometimes, the more you let them get to you, the harder they seem to bite. I don't like using chemical warfare, particularly spray repellents. I have always believed that anything that is bad news for bugs is bad news for me. My suspicions have been confirmed by recent medical reports that indicate that insect repellents, including the most effective ones — diethyltoluamide (deet) and ethyl hexanediol — may cause allergic or toxic reactions, especially when used in high concentrations. It is probably wise to avoid prolonged or excessive use of any insect repellent unless you are allergic to insect bites.

The best defense against all forms of biting insect is proper clothing. Prospectors, trappers and loggers knew this a couple of hundred years ago. Even in summer, they wore heavy clothing that bugs couldn't bite through. I prefer to cover up with light, but tightly-woven, materials that insects have a tough time penetrating. Clothes should be loose fitting, but have tight cuffs. I like a hood to keep them off the back of my neck and ears — that's where the blackflies go every time. When I do resort to repellent while sketching, painting or filming, I put it only on my clothes, bandana, pant and sleeve cuffs and around my hood. Another reason for putting it on your clothes is that perspiration washes it off your skin.

Sometimes I wear a bug jacket, which is made of a mesh material soaked with repellent. You can put it on and take it off as required. I always wear light clothes and a hat under the jacket, so the chemicals don't come in contact with my skin. It does keep the bugs from behind the ears. If you use a bug jacket, store it in an airtight bag so the repellent doesn't evaporate. It can be rejuvenated by soaking it in replenisher solution. When the bugs are unbearable, I resort to the head net.

Insects are not much of a problem to canoeists when on the water, but are bothersome around camp or on a portage. It's unfortunate that insects work in shifts. In early summer, blackflies come on duty about 8 AM, work a 12-hour shift and leave about 8 PM. They aren't a problem inside a tent, because, like a dog or cat, as soon as they get in they turn around and want to go right back out. At 8 PM the mosquitoes check in. There's a double shift when the no-see-ums or sand flies show up after dark. Considering their size, it's unbelievable the size of lump sand flies can raise. At night, they get in your hair and burn like fire. After 35 years of having normal netting on my tents, I've finally smartened up and installed fine-mesh netting, even though it inhibits both the view and air movement. I take great delight in lying there looking through the netting watching the ravenous hordes going crazy for my blood.

In recent years, allergies to bee and wasp stings seem to be increasingly common. For some, an Anakit and medication are sufficient treatment, but for others, an insect sting can be life-threatening. If you suffer a violent reaction to a wasp or bee sting, you should consider taking shots to build up your immunity.

Without portages and hordes of biting insects, there would be no wilderness. Think about that the next time you're on some swampy, bug-ridden portage. You probably won't hear the song on the portage, but it will come in all the more loud and clear later. Some people can't or won't tolerate bugs, and would never go on a trip where bugs would be a possibility. Which is okay, too. Someone has to keep the motels, hotels, resorts and tours in business.

Bug hat and jacket

The infamous Barren Lands mosquitoes

Coping with bugs and bears . . .

Bears

One of the most dangerous animals you are likely to encounter anywhere is the human who feeds bears. Anyone who feeds a bear, or is responsible for leaving food or garbage around, is taking an active part in creating a potential killer. Bears are not always afraid of people. If food is easy to get from humans or from garbage dumps, bears will quickly overcome any fear they might have had in order to get it, and they will eat almost anything. Bears are fast and unbelievably strong. When a bear wants something, it just walks over and takes it. There are two ways to avoid bears. Never camp within miles of any village or town that has an open garbage pit. Never camp with or near anyone who is stupid enough to feed bears.

Algonquin Provincial Park in Ontario is advertised as a wilderness park, yet scattered throughout it are logging camps, which used to have open garbage pits. On a film trip, I ran across a logging camp where the cook fed a bear every day at the cookhouse door. A few years later, someone was killed by a bear not too far from the area. This was one of the very few deaths from a bear attack in eastern Canada. All dumps in Algonquin have now been closed and buried and garbage is trucked out.

I have read so many articles about how to protect your food from bears that now, after 35 years, they've even got me worried. I have always left the food packs in the door of my tent, with one wing of the Campfire tent draped over it, but now I'm not so sure. Maybe I've been lucky, apart from that one experience, and I blame that on the dump. For years I've been reading that the only way to keep your food from bears is to sling it high off the ground between two trees. Recent articles indicate that the old tree trick doesn't work. If the bear really wants it, he just climbs up and gets it. The best possible defense is to keep the site spotlessly clean. Burn all tins before flattening them and putting them in the garbage bag to carry out. Divide the food into several packs, and secure the food packs in

plastic. Place them about 50 ft. (15 m) from camp, in opposite directions. Although it's claimed that the bears won't be able to smell the food through the plastic, I wouldn't bet on it.

A bear that has not become spoiled by garbage is likely to move off at the sight of people. If he doesn't, then it's wise to shove off yourself. Noise will sometimes scare a bear away, but then he'll think about it for a while, decide that it wasn't all that bad, and wander back into camp to have another listen. A louder noise might work again, but the procedure repeats itself until the bear actually begins to enjoy the performance.

The only other animal that causes me much worry is the polar bear. Biologists walk among them to study them, but even they admit the odd one might decide to have them for lunch. I have done a lot of filming in polar bear country and have never had a problem, but it is becoming necessary to carry a gun in certain areas, such as northern Manitoba, where there is a heavy concentration of polar bears. The recommended weapon is a twelve-gauge shotgun. (Anything smaller is considered inadequate for bears and more dangerous than no gun at all. In Canada, handguns are illegal and of no use against bears.) The first few slugs can be rubber to deter the bear. In most cases, the rubber slugs have been sufficient to scare off the animal. In other instances, the bear has returned and had to be killed.

Some books suggest that if a gun is carried on the trip, everyone should be given instructions on how to use it. I disagree. People have been known to blast away at noises and even shadows.

On one of my film trips we were camped on the sea ice. It was a large expedition, and one of the crew was given the responsibility of protecting us from polar bears. He was a weapons expert and delighted in showing off his artillery. In his friendly way, he was describing the kind of slug he would use on a full-sized bear. First he fired a normal bullet at a huge slab of ice that was standing on edge.

It looked like he had missed, but he showed us a clean little hole. He explained that a bear could kill you before the bullet would stop him. Then he fired a bear-stopping, soft lead, hollow point bullet and the huge slab disappeared. Then he began to give instructions about reloading. I thought, "Wait a minute! A gun like that you shouldn't have to reload!" I told him that I would rather take my chances with a bear anytime, rather than stand within range of someone waving a bear-stopping gun who wasn't familiar with firearms.

In polar bear country the safest place to be is with native people who make a living by hunting. This is especially true if they are travelling with dogs. Dogs are the best protection against polar bears. Firecrackers or flares might work at first, but when the bear realizes they haven't hurt him he might just go over, prepare a snack from your food box, pull up a packsack for a backrest and sit back to enjoy the show. I heard of one instance in which the big bang of a firecracker was really effective. The problem was the man threw it over the bear's head and it went off behind the animal, which then ran right over the man and his camp while trying to get away!

The inevitable question is, what do you do if a bear charges? Every book and article I've read about bears says not to run. The next thing they tell you is to roll up in a ball, cover your stomach, head and neck, play dead and pray a lot. And what do you do if these suggestions don't work? Nobody ever talks about that! I'd like to think that the person who wrote this advice did so after the attack, not before. It's advice like this that makes me break camp and move on when a bear shows up and looks like he's going to join (or have) me for lunch.

First aid

For years I have carried a fairly complete first-aid kit. Fortunately, I have never needed anything more than an antiseptic for cuts and tweezers for slivers. However, I dare not leave any of it behind, because the time I did would be the time some mishap would require everything I've got.

First-aid courses

A detailed course on first aid is beyond the scope of this book, and if the truth must be known, beyond my abilities. I've taken several courses in wilderness first aid. They were excellent courses, and I recommend them to anyone who goes far afield, but because I don't get to practice much, I have difficulty retaining the information. And unless you do things in the proper order—for example, when applying CPR—you can do more harm than good. Even though you may forget much of what you have learned in a wilderness medicine course, there are books to help you recall how to deal with a specific problem. One of the best is *Wilderness Medicine* by William W. Forgey, M.D., Indiana Camp Supply Books, Pittsboro, Indiana.

One of the things that did stay with me from my courses was the importance of being able to make the right decision on a wilderness trip after the victim of an accident has been patched up. On the one hand, you have to err on the safe side, but on the other hand, no one would be very happy about needlessly spoiling a trip, especially a trip that everybody, including the patient, had looked forward to for a long time. The patient is the only one who can tell you how he or she feels; however, the patient is not always the best one to make the decision. Often the decision has to be made by the trip leader in consultation with the group if the patient is reluctant to abort the trip. Permanent damage is the thing you have to worry about. If the patient is obviously seriously injured, the decision is not whether to abort the trip, but whether to take him or her out, send for an aircraft or helicopter, or bring the doctor in.

One of my friends was leading a trip. While they were loading the aircraft at the beginning of the trip, a client tore a ligament loose in his arm. Strangely, it wasn't too painful. The departure point was remote, so medical advice was not available. A decision had to be made immediately because they were about to board the flight. If the client were to leave, his paddling partner would have to leave as well, because a replacement was not possible. The patient insisted he wanted to go, so they took off. When the trip was over the ligament had deteriorated and couldn't be reattached properly. In retrospect, the client wishes that somebody had insisted he not go on the trip.

First-aid kit

You won't be much help if you haven't got the tools to work with. Fortunately a well-stocked first-aid kit isn't too cumbersome. Even if you never need any of the supplies—and it's amazing how seldom you do—it gives a sense of security knowing it's there, along with the necessary information to deal with the problem. Paul tells me that he has never needed his first-aid kit for himself, other than the odd Band-Aid, but over the years he has had the occasion to use the following for his friends or clients: tetracycline (for infection), Tylenol 3 (for pain), 3 by 4 in. (8 by 10 cm) Telfa pads, tweezers, Band-Aids, tape, Elastoplast, alcohol prep pads, Caladryl (for stings and bites), first-aid antibiotic ointment, Molefoam (for blisters), Second Skin (for burns and scrapes) and butterfly bandages. To this list you might want to add many other things, depending on how accident-prone you or your friends are, and how remote the location.

A basic first aid kit

The Prospector, Cascade Falls, Lake Superior

The first thing you have to understand about a canoe is that it is not a lifeless, inanimate object. A canoe is a bit like a horse: it has a mind of its own. If you don't believe me, try paddling a canoe into a stiff head wind, when you are sitting on the stern seat, solo. It can't be done. The canoe will swing around and head downwind every time, like a horse heading for the barn. In a lively rapids, a canoe will dump you overboard and continue on down the river by itself. Get between the canoe and a rock in a fast river and the canoe will kill you. All of which makes you wonder why people become totally and incurably addicted to canoes, but they do.

If you are going to become a canoe addict, you have to decide what kind. There are go-fast canoes for racing; big, heavy-duty canoes for wilderness cruising; sensitive canoes for hot dog canoeing in big rapids; and light canoes for the long, portage-type of tripping. There are old classics in natural wood, which would look good hanging in the National Gallery, and which are used today for solo free-style paddling.

To understand the differences in canoe design, and why there are so many different kinds, we should go back to the Indian birchbark canoe, where it all began. The Indian craftsmen would visualize the shape of the finished canoe, because they didn't build their canoes on a mold. They built the planks and ribs within the bark skin and held it together with root lashings. Just after the turn of the century, cedar canoes began to be built on a mold. To keep out the water the craftsmanship had to be flawless. Then someone conceived the idea of covering the canoe with canvas. This resulted in a tougher and cheaper canoe. Around 1920, hundreds of different kinds of canoes were made in an explosion of canoe manufacturing.

It didn't take long for manufacturers to realize that if you made a canoe with a straight keel, it would be fast, although difficult to turn. If you made it narrow and long as well, it would be faster, but even more difficult to turn. I have an old, straight-keel, cedar-strip canoe

that takes half the width of a lake to make a 180° turn. Conversely, canoe builders also discovered that if you made the canoe with a rockered keel, it would turn very quickly, almost within its own length. Everyone agreed that if the canoe had nicely upswept gunwales, at the bow and stern, it would be aesthetically pleasing and keep the water from splashing in over the bow. A high bow and stern were more susceptible to wind, but aesthetics were a high priority, so most canoes had a high bow and stern. The Old Town canoes had a particularly beautiful upturned bow and stern. In fact, many of the canoes from that era are works of art.

Back in the good old days when somebody asked me for advice on what canoe to buy, I would drag out my latest Chestnut catalogue and point out the pros and cons of each model. There were six different models to choose from, and most of them were available in several lengths. In the last Annual Buyer's Guide in *Canoe* magazine, there were 1,500 canoes listed. With the new space-age materials, there has been an explosion of new canoes in every conceivable shape and size.

Traditional canoes
If I could have only one canoe, it would be the original Chestnut wood-canvas 16 ft. (4.8 m) Prospector. There are faster, slower, tougher, less stable, more stable, more beautiful and less beautiful canoes than the Prospector, but none that do everything as well. The high bow and stern, or the curving up of the gunwales at the bow and stern, are what makes the canoe so aesthetically pleasing to me. Also it enables the bow to cut through a wave without taking on water over the gunwales. Another thing about the bow of the Prospector is the beautiful curve of the stem. The rocker along the keel line adds to the beauty of the upswept bow. From a practical standpoint, the rocker makes the canoe very agile and enables it to turn, pivot and sideslip across the current quickly. However, with the high bow and stern and the rockered keel line, it takes skill to track a straight course, especially in wind.

The Prospector is deep overall, which provides a greater carrying capacity for its length. To maintain the ease of paddling that is characteristic of the Prospector, the bow has a sharp entry at the waterline, then flares out a few feet back to provide volume at the waterline. This enables the canoe to be buoyed up by the wave after the bow has cut through it. The tumblehome or "sloping in" of the sides near the gunwale amidship adds to the beauty of the canoe. Unfortunately, tumblehome also allows the waves to climb the side of the canoe and splash in. When sitting in the center of the canoe it can be heeled over on its side, making it easy to reach water. With the shortened waterline, the canoe turns, pivots and sideslips beautifully. If you know how, you can more or less sail the canoe and use the wind to your advantage. The Prospector is difficult to paddle against a head wind. I might be windbound more often than the new straight-keel canoes, but being windbound isn't such a bad thing.

One of the advantages of the high position of the Prospector's seats is the diversity of possible paddling positions. The many paddling positions keep you from getting stiff. The basic kneeling position, whether it be one knee down or both, is much easier on the back than sitting. In waves or rapids, kneeling is a must because of the high seat position. In solo paddling, the cane seat enables you to sit close to the gunwale making it easy to reach the water.

You trim traditional canoes with the packs. If you are paddling empty, you trim by shifting your paddling position.

Recently, I attended a canoe symposium in the United States. There were canoes from most of the major US canoe manufacturers and a few from Canada. Every conceivable type of canoe was there: long, short, wide, skinny, very skinny, bi-symmetric, asymmetric, round bottom, V bottom, flat bottom, straight keel, rockered keel and even a banana boat. I tried all of them and had a lot of fun. For the first time, the reason for the popularity of low-profile, straight-keel canoes in the US became obvious to me. Everyone paddled these canoes by sitting on the seat, or kneeling braced against the seat position, as though they had a destination. No one sat on their heels with the canoe heeled over on its side. I had a wonderful time cranking turns and sideslipping, but I found it interesting that no one else did anything like this with the canoes.

It was the same at a gathering of wooden canoe enthusiasts that I attended several years ago. The enjoyment seemed to be in owning these marvellous, old traditional canoes, admiring their beauty and sharing them with fellow admirers. Performance was not much of a consideration. I have always believed that the two should go together. In Canada, we use canoes for going somewhere, too, but as Mole said in *The Wind in the Willows*, "there is nothing — absolutely nothing — half so much worth doing as simply messing about in boats."

I love to get the canoe going as fast as I can and then crank a 180° turn with a one-handed pry. It's done with the canoe heeled over on its side while sitting on your heels. When you achieve that, you can go up into a high kneel to add to the fun. Then there is the power sideslip, toward or away from the paddle side, and pirouettes. Doing these maneuvers while moving backward makes endless possibilities. It's called free-style paddling, or solo ballet or classic solo. It's what makes canoeing the beautiful art it is. Paddling any kind of canoe flat when using the switch-side method or the J stroke is okay for going somewhere, but for messing around, it is a bore.

The traditional canoes, such as the Chestnut Prospector, don't track as well as the straight-keel canoes, but they are ideal for classic solo paddling or for "messing about in boats." The tumblehome makes them very sensitive and tippy in the leaned position, which is what you want in classic solo paddling. It's your skill that keeps you from falling overboard.

Straight-keel canoes

There is a great array of superbly designed canoes to choose from in the straight-keel department. Many of them are designed by racing enthusiasts who use test tanks and computers to get the edge over their competitors.

Most straight-keel canoes have a low bow and stern profile to cut wind resistance. The bow and stern are slightly flared out near the gunwale in order to prevent waves coming in over the bow. Adjustable seats for perfect trimming at the waterline are a common and important feature for ease of steering and to cut drag. Some of the solo canoes are meant strictly for the switch-sides paddling style (see page 150). The bucket seats are centered and won't adjust far enough back for an effective J or Canadian stroke.

The workmanship in many of these canoes is superb, and the lay-up and materials are of the highest quality. Beauty is in the eye of the beholder and, for the manufacturers of these canoes, the beauty is in the clean, no-nonsense lines, practical design and placement of seats. Many of these canoes don't have bow and stern decks. Some have only a carrying bar or a plastic cap, which is too practical for my taste.

I am a bit concerned by the growing interest in straight-keel, low-profile canoes. However, my paddling orgy in these narrow, high-tech canoes at the symposiums has forced me to reconsider the possibilities. When I removed or ignored the seats and sat on my heels, leaned to the gunwale, or went into the high kneel, the canoes were very tippy, a little more maneuverable and great fun to paddle. Extreme maneuvers are not possible because, even when leaned, the entire length of the keel remains in the water.

It was a real challenge making these canoes do things they were not meant to do. I fell out of a skinny Sawyer attempting a bow pry from the high-kneel position, and climbing back in was a challenge. I also sank a Lotus, but as the saying goes, "If you're not flyin', you're not tryin'." I found myself heading again and again for the Mad River Pearl, the We-no-nah Whisper, the Sawyer Starlight and the Lotus Bucktail. They were all fun to paddle in the extreme leaned position. When sitting on the seats, or kneeling braced against the seats the way they were meant to be paddled, these canoes were stable and fast, but not much fun.

I can't help wondering what would happen if you took one of these narrow, sensitive canoes and gave it some rocker, put some poetic-looking lines in the gunwales by curving them up, added some oil-rubbed mahogany decks and installed a Mike Galt seat from his Egret canoe and some traditional thwarts. That would be one hot canoe for "messing around in," and it would be beautiful.

Other types of canoes
In sharp contrast to the fine-lined, low-profile, fast canoes, American manufacturers also produce most of the heavy-duty, large volume, wilderness tripping canoes. The Old Town, Blue Hole and Mad River ABS canoes are almost indestructible. Nearly all outfitters have switched over to these canoes for whitewater canoeing because they slide over rocks without sticking. Old Town, Blue Hole and Mad River also make high-performance rockered canoes for hot dog canoeing. They are ideal for surfing and playing in the big whitewater and going where open canoes were never meant to go. The most popular hot dogging or solo whitewater play boat is called the Whitesell. It was designed and is manufactured by Nolan Whitesell in the United States. In Canada this canoe is made by Western Canoeing Inc., under the name of Clipper Canoes.

Canoe design characteristics

Straight keel line (1A) The entire length of the canoe is in the water.
ADVANTAGES Fast and tracks well, which means it doesn't veer off course easily. Less steering action required on each power stroke.
DISADVANTAGES Not very maneuverable; difficult to turn quickly; doesn't sideslip easily.

Rockered keel line (2A) Keel rises so bow and stern are out of the water. Rocker can be slight or extreme.
ADVANTAGES The more rocker, the more maneuverable the canoe. This is an advantage in whitewater and solo freestyle. It's easier to turn and, with less of the canoe's length in the water, easier to sideslip.
DISADVANTAGES With the bow rising out of the water, it doesn't cut through the water as efficiently, so is slower. With less of the canoe's length in the water, it veers off course more easily on each power stroke, requiring more steering action. Steering action causes drag, so some energy is wasted.

Low bow and stern at gunwale (1B)
ADVANTAGES Not adversely affected by wind. Less drag on the canoe and not easily blown off course.
DISADVANTAGES Not as aesthetically pleasing to traditionalists. Waves splash over a low bow and stern. Many manufacturers attempt to overcome this problem by flaring the bow out near the gunwale to deflect the waves. The effectiveness depends on the extremity of the flare.

Rising bow and stern at gunwale (2B)
ADVANTAGES For traditionalists the rising bow and stern are what makes the canoe aesthetically pleasing. In waves and rapids, less water splashes into the canoe if the rise is a gradual one from amidship to the bow and stern. If the rise is sudden near the end it is mainly for aesthetic reasons.
DISADVANTAGES Wind drag increases with height of canoe out of the water. More easily blown off course by side winds. This tendency can be compensated for with skill and knowledge.

Depth amidship of shallow canoe (1C) Twelve inches (30 cm) or less, measured from bottom to top of gunwale.
ADVANTAGES Less wind drag. More fun to paddle.
DISADVANTAGES Can only carry a small load. Not suitable for doubles on a long wilderness trip with large waves or difficult rapids. A minimum of 6 in. (15 cm) of freeboard is necessary when loaded. (This is measured from waterline to top of gunwale.) Paddling solo, I have used the smaller, shallow canoe for extended wilderness trips and installed a bow deck to shed water in rapids.

Depth amidship of deep canoe (2C) Thirteen inches (32 cm) or deeper.
ADVANTAGES Can carry a heavier load while maintaining the minimum 6 in. (15 cm) of freeboard. This is one of the most important considerations in wilderness cruising.
DISADVANTAGES More wind drag. Paddling empty, it is very susceptible to wind. Takes a great amount of skill and knowledge to handle in wind.

Narrow canoes (3A) Thirty-three inches (84 cm) or less.
ADVANTAGES Fast and easy to propel through water; sensitive and fun to paddle; requires some skill.
DISADVANTAGES Low carrying capacity; more likely to be unstable, but many manufacturers overcome this with a low seat position.

Wide canoes (3B) Thirty-three inches (84 cm) or more.
ADVANTAGES Greater carrying capacity; more stable when paddled flat; fun to paddle in the extreme leaned position.
DISADVANTAGES More wind drag, especially when paddling without a load. In the leaned solo paddling position, more canoe out of the water to be affected by wind.

Sharp, narrow bow and stern (4A)
ADVANTAGES Cuts water well, so is very fast, especially if canoe has a straight keel line. Cuts through waves.
DISADVANTAGES Because bow cuts through wave it dives deep rather than being buoyed

up. Waves will come in over gunwales. Flaring of the bow near gunwale can help to solve this problem, but effectiveness is a matter of opinion.

Wide, full blunt bow and stern (4B)
ADVANTAGES   Bow is buoyed up when it plunges into a wave because of greater volume near the bow. Waves are less likely to splash into canoe.
DISADVANTAGES   More voluminous bow thuds into wave so canoe is slowed down.

Flat bottom (5A)
ADVANTAGES   Very stable. Many articles show diagrams depicting how a flat bottom canoe rolls in waves more than a round bottom canoe. In reality there is nothing more stable than a flat bottom canoe. They also draw less water than a round or V bottom canoe.
DISADVANTAGES   Flat bottom canoes are slower than round and V bottom canoes.

Round bottom (5B)
ADVANTAGES   They are much faster than flat bottom; tracking is good.
DISADVANTAGES   The rounder the bottom, the less stable it is. They also draw more water.

V Bottom (5C)
ADVANTAGES   Faster than round or flat bottom; tracking is very good.
DISADVANTAGES   Not as stable; draws more water and is more difficult to turn than a flat bottom.

Tumblehome (6A)   Tumblehome describes the amount of slope of the sides of the canoe near the top of the gunwale.
ADVANTAGES   It is easy to paddle a wide, large-volume canoe with tumblehome because you don't have to reach out far over the gunwale. Canoes with tumblehome are more pleasing aesthetically to the traditionalists. They are also more voluminous and therefore can carry heavier loads. With more width at the waterline, the canoe has good initial stability. This means it is stable until leaned way over.
   When leaned over, so the waterline is right to the gunwale, the canoe has poor latent stability, which means it is very tippy. This is what makes it so much fun to paddle as a solo freestyle canoe. When paddled flat it becomes a stable, heavy-duty, tripping canoe. In other words, you get the best of both worlds in one canoe.
DISADVANTAGES   Waves climb the side of the canoe and splash over the gunwales. When the canoe is leaned way over and riding on the rounded bilge, it then becomes unstable.

Sides that flare out (6B)
ADVANTAGES   Excellent latent stability, which means that the canoe actually gains stability as it is leaned or tipped to the gunwale. Deflects waves away from canoe so water is less likely to come in over gunwales unless waves are extreme. It's very easy to empty by means of the shake-out. These canoes can be nested one inside the other if the decks, seats and thwarts are removed; a great advantage for reducing shipping costs.
DISADVANTAGES   More difficult to reach over the side of the canoe for paddling. This is a serious drawback.

Extended bow and stern (7A)
ADVANTAGES   Possibly adds slightly to buoyancy of bow. The main advantage is that along with flaring out or straight-sided canoes, canoes can be nested for shipping.
DISADVANTAGES   Not as pleasing as the traditional recurving bow and stern, but only a matter of opinion.

Recurved bow and stern (7B)
ADVANTAGES   In the eyes of a traditionalist, it is more aesthetically pleasing.
DISADVANTAGES   Canoes can't be nested for shipping.

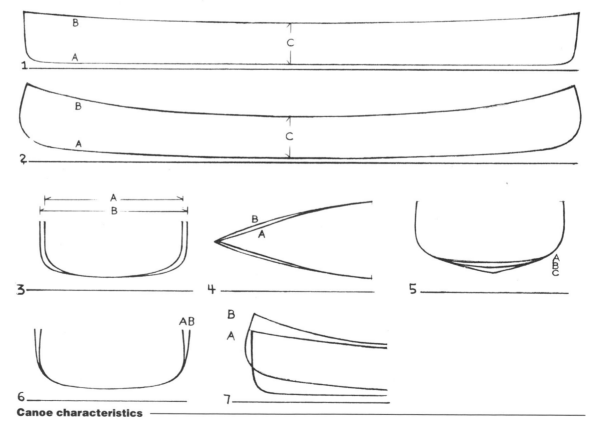

Canoe characteristics

141

Materials for tripping canoes

The materials that are used in canoes also have their advantages and disadvantages. There is no universal material.

Wood, canvas
ADVANTAGES   The most traditional and aesthetically pleasing materials (photograph 1). Tougher than most people think. Available in the most beautiful shapes. Reasonable to very expensive because of the high labor costs.
DISADVANTAGES   Usually heavier than canoes made with some of the modern materials. Wood soaks up water, so becomes heavier on a trip. Minor scrapes and cuts are easy to repair, but canvas must be removed to repair broken planks and ribs. They require painting and varnishing. They should always be stored under cover and off the ground.

Stripper   These are made with cedar planking sandwiched between fiberglass layers (photograph 2). The types of resins that can be used are too numerous to be listed here. I always refer to *Canoecraft* by Ted Moores and Merilyn Mohr.
ADVANTAGES   Beautiful to look at. Very light if well made and much stronger than they look. Can be made in any shape. Easy to repair and require minimum maintenance. By far the easiest kind of canoe to make at home.
DISADVANTAGES   They aren't as strong as aluminum, ABS or Kevlar. Breaks must be repaired right away or water will get in to saturate the wood, causing it to rot.

Fiberglass
ADVANTAGES   A strong, modern material that is easy to repair (photograph 3). These canoes range from heavy to moderately heavy. Can be aesthetically pleasing, but many are not. Easy to manufacture in any shape. Little maintenance and usually moderately priced.
DISADVANTAGES   Most of the worst-looking canoes come in fiberglass, so be careful — know what you're buying. Fiberglass will crack and break. Avoid all cheap canoes that are made with chopped fiberglass.

Kevlar   Kevlar and epoxy canoes are a subject in themselves (photograph 4). Some manufacturers combine layers of nylon, foam core and other materials with the Kevlar for strength and rigidity, and there is an endless list of epoxies. It's wise to buy from an established manufacturer and have them explain what you are getting.
ADVANTAGES   Very light, extremely tough and tear resistant. Can be manufactured in any shape. Easy to repair and require little maintenance. More scratch resistant than fiberglass. When made with the vacuum-bag technique, they have less resin and are lighter and stronger.
DISADVANTAGES   Ultra-violet rays are harmful to them. Kevlar and epoxy materials are very expensive.

Royalex ABS
ADVANTAGES   The toughest of all materials (photograph 5). Consists of a foam core sandwiched between tough, flexible, slippery plastic. Bends without breaking or creasing. Has a memory, so can be bent completely out of shape and will spring back with only slight creasing. It is almost indestructible if equipped with vinyl gunwales with aluminum cores. Very scratch resistant, but even this material will cut. Easy to repair. Little or no maintenance.
DISADVANTAGES   Difficult to mold in pleasing, functional shapes. So far, it hasn't been possible to make a sharp bow and stern. Material is flexible so bottom of canoe is not rigid. This is a disadvantage in maneuvering the canoe, but an advantage in avoiding damage sliding over rocks. When heavily loaded, the bottom becomes more rigid. ABS canoes are heavy and expensive.

Aluminum   Aluminum canoes come in varying thicknesses, so toughness varies (photograph 6).
ADVANTAGES   Standard thickness canoes are very tough and rigid. Absolutely no maintenance required. Most have flat bottoms and are very stable. Prices range from moderate to expensive.
DISADVANTAGES   Least aesthetic canoe. Noisy. Will dent but can be pounded out. They stick on rocks and this can get you into trouble when running rapids. Aluminum will tear if bent severely out of shape, but can be repaired on the trip. Weight ranges from moderately light to moderately heavy.

Polyethylene   Many canoeists and canoe manufacturers believe polyethylene is the material of the future. As Kevlar, fiberglass, resins, ABS material and labor escalate in price, polyethylene canoes may become the most practical and affordable canoes. They are just as heavy as ABS, almost as tough, but easier to mold into graceful lines and cheaper to make in volume. Previously, polyethylene has been used mostly in kayaks because it's been difficult to make a broad-beamed canoe with a rigid bottom without a lot of clumsy bracing. Old Town's Crosslink 3 TM has overcome this problem with a rotational molding process which consists of a cross-linked outer layer, a foam core central layer and a cross-linked inner layer. This material will probably be the popular heavy-duty canoe for some time to come.

1 **Wood canvas Prospector**

2 **Stripper Prospector**

3 **Fiberglass or Kevlar Prospector**

4 **Straight-keeled Kevlar**

5 **Royalex ABS heavy duty canoe**

6 **Grumman aluminum canoe**

Canoe dimensions

Length

16 ft. (4.8 m)   This is the average length of canoes. They can be paddled solo or double. Suitable for wilderness travel if they are wide and deep.

14 or 15 ft. (4.2 or 4.5 m)   Anything under 16 ft. (4.8 m) is too small for wilderness travel for two paddlers. Short canoes don't track well, but can be a lot of fun for solo freestyle paddling and hot dogging.

12 or 13 ft. (3.6 or 3.9 m)   Short, small canoes are wonderful for teaching children to paddle. Our children learned just about every maneuver in a 12 ft. (3.6 m) birchbark canoe before they were ten years old.

17 or 18 ft. (5.1 or 5.4 m)   This size of canoe is ideal for the long wilderness trip and big water. Even with a load, they have enough freeboard to stay afloat in the big stuff. Weight becomes a problem on the portages. Long, narrow canoes are fast, and therefore popular for racing.

Over 18 ft. (5.4 m)   Anything this big is usually paddled and portaged by several paddlers. They are known as voyageur canoes and often have high bows and sterns to simulate the historical voyageur canoes (see page 12).

Width

33 in. (83.7 cm) or less   Anything under 33 in. (83.7 cm) is considered narrow. Narrow canoes are unstable but fast. They are popular for racing.

34 to 36 in. (86.2 cm to 91 cm)   This is the width of most canoes. This width is desirable for a wilderness tripping canoe where rapids will be encountered. For lake travel, some paddlers prefer length over width to gain volume. This makes for a faster, but less maneuverable canoe. An 18 ft., 33 in. (5.5 m, 83.8 cm) canoe with a straight keel line would be very fast for lake travel, but not suitable for difficult rapids.

Over 36 in. (91 cm)   Anything this wide is considered big and stable. However, stability has as much to do with a flat bottom as width.

Depth

12 to 13 in. (30 to 32 cm)   This is the depth of most canoes. It is measured from the floor of the canoe amidship to the top of the gunwale.

Under 12 in. (30 cm)   Shallow canoes are fun to paddle solo or freestyle. Heavily loaded, they don't have enough freeboard for wilderness travel in waves and rapids unless decked over with a spray cover.

Over 14 in. (35 cm)   This depth is good for remote wilderness travel. It allows for a heavy load with ample freeboard. This deep canoe can be heavy for the portages and is susceptible to winds if not heavily loaded.

Dimensions of the 16 ft. (4.8 m) Chestnut Prospector

There are many canoes that are similar to the Chestnut Prospector. The amount they can vary and still be called a Prospector is a matter of opinion. I prefer them to be as close to the original as possible for reasons of aesthetics, performance and tradition. But, remember, everything is a trade-off.

The measurements in the illustration are taken from my original Prospector and the Prospectors of several friends. There are many canoe manufacturers making canoes that they call Prospectors. If you want the true Prospector shape, take along this page and a tape measure. If it varies a little, it doesn't mean it's not a good canoe; it's just not identical to the original Prospector. If it varies a lot, then it is definitely something else!

Some measurements, such as seat position, can vary to suit the weight and preference of the individual paddler.

Some manufacturers don't install a stern thwart unless it is requested. It adds strength to the canoe and is essential when you tie in your gear and secure floatation when you fool around in rapids. It's also handy when you tie in your paddles for the portage. A stern thwart helps to create the gunwale line shape that is unique to the Prospector. The seats should be hung by bolts off the gunwales. This strengthens the canoe and holds the shape of the gunwales.

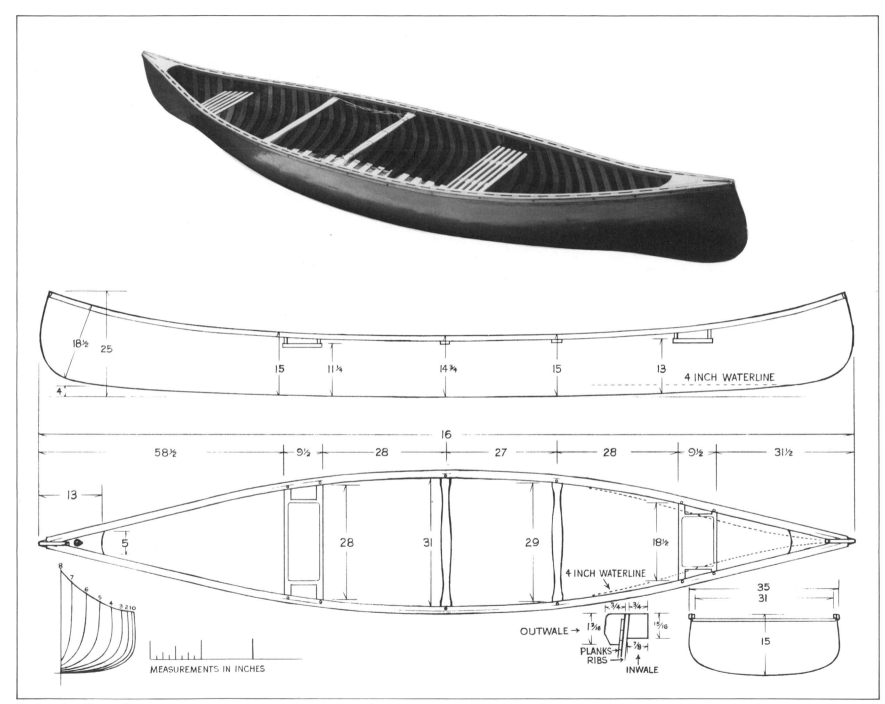

18½ 25

4

15   11¼   14¾   15   13   4 INCH WATERLINE

16

58½   9½   28   27   28   9½   31½

13

5   28   31   29   18½

4 INCH WATERLINE

OUTWALE → 1³⁄₁₆   ¾   ¾   ¹⁵⁄₁₆   35
                                                    31
8
7
6   15
5
4 3 2 1 0   PLANKS→   ⅞
                        RIBS →   INWALE

MEASUREMENTS IN INCHES

Prospector dimensions

145

Beauty is in the eye of the beholder

A careful study of the above characteristics should confirm the fact that everything is a compromise. It is the reason I am so adamant about not altering the dimensions or shape of the most versatile canoe, the Prospector. The Prospector is now even more versatile, because it is available in a wide range of materials.

Many small companies are making wood-canvas canoes from the Chestnut molds. The Muskoka Fine Watercraft and Supply in Ontario has bought the name "Chestnut" and is making a canoe that is very similar to the original Prospector. The workmanship has to be seen to be believed! It is probably better now than it was in the heyday of Chestnut. Another manufacturer, Cedarwood Canoes in Ontario, also makes wood-canvas canoes off the original Prospector molds. And Fletcher Canoes in the Yukon makes an excellent wood-canvas canoe that closely resembles the Prospector. For lake travel, and even reasonable rapids and portaging, there is something wonderful about wood and canvas. The cost of a wood-canvas canoe is very competitive with the cost of one in modern materials.

If you intend to do a lot of rapids running and lugging over portages, the fiberglass or Kevlar Prospector is a great all-round canoe. There are several canoe companies making Prospectors in these materials. Trailhead in Ottawa, Montreal and Toronto makes a canoe in Kevlar or fiberglass that is identical to my original wood-canvas Prospector. The Voyageur Canoe Company in Millbrook, Ontario, also makes a superb canoe similar to the Prospector.

The "stripper canoe" method of construction is the choice of most do-it-yourself canoe enthusiasts. Canoecraft, a book by Ted Moores and Merilyn Mohr, tells it best and includes a Prospector among the canoe plans. There are many commercial canoe makers producing Prospector canoes with the stripper process. Buy from someone who guarantees their product. Theresa and Ric Driediger of Horizons Unlimited, in La Ronge, Saskatchewan, make a beautiful Prospector stripper canoe. They also offer a whitewater version, with a Kevlar and epoxy bottom that is resistant to abrasion. I thought strippers were fragile, but their canoes have proven me wrong. The strippers made by The Muskoka Fine Watercraft and Supply are works of art. They make four kinds, but the Sundance is the closest to the Prospector in shape.

For canoeing rock-studded rapids, or for shallow rivers, the ABS canoes such as Mad River or Old Town are ideal. On big northern rivers, where the only way home is in your canoe, the ABS canoes are the only ones that can remain relatively unscathed after being pinned or wrapped around a rock. Grumman and other aluminum canoes are tough, but stick on rocks, and tear when they've been bent. They can be easily patched, though. The 17 or 18 ft. (5.1 or 5.4 m) Grumman is very safe and stable for lake travel or deep, high-volume rapids. It's not suitable for shallow, rock-studded rapids. We used one for lake trips and deep rapids when our two children were very young. It could easily carry all of us with our gear. We called it the Queen Mary.

If you like the idea of getting to where you want to go with as little effort as possible, the high-tech, go-fast canoes such as Sawyer, Wenonah, Lotus and many others might suit your needs best.

A nice canoe for pleasure canoeing around the cottage or lake is the Chestnut Pal, which used to be one of the most popular canoes. The Pal is being made by Cedarwood Canoes. I used the Pal canoe in my films Path of the Paddle, Solo Flatwater, Solo Whitewater and in my feature film, Waterwalker. If you've seen the films, you will appreciate just how seaworthy that canoe can be. I used it in whitewater for years before I bought my Prospector. There isn't a rib or plank that isn't cracked. In fact, it is so beaten up that I had to finally remove the canvas and put a fiberglass skin on it. From the outside it looks as good as new. Inside it looks like a tank ran over it, but I love that old canoe. Every cracked rib, plank and hole reminds me of a time and a place, and brings the memories flooding back. If it were not for the fiberglass skin now holding it together, that old Pal would have gone where all good old canoes should go, the Kanawa Canoe Museum, RR#2, Minden, Ontario K0M 2K0. Kirk Wipper, the museum's founder, despairs that the canoe is going to outlast him, and that he won't be around to welcome it to the museum. If you've got a canoe with a story to tell, and it's ready for a resting place, give Kirk a call. He can be contacted through the Canadian Recreational Canoeing Association (see page 181 for the address).

Choosing the right canoe for the occasion is fundamental to having a good time. You can get by with a poorly designed tent or inadequate sleeping bags and even lousy food, but you can get into serious trouble by choosing the wrong canoe.

Paddles

The growth in recreational whitewater canoeing has allowed many manufacturers to produce high-quality paddles from wood or synthetic materials or a combination of both.

There was a time when I wouldn't touch anything but a long Clement laminated spruce paddle. I had a 7 in. (18 cm) wide blade for flat water and an 8 in. (20 cm) blade for whitewater and for the occasional regatta race (B). Then I rediscovered the joy of a shorter, razor edge, hardwood paddle (C and D). I remembered using them at camp as a teenager, and wondered how I had ever gotten away from them. I adopted the hardwood paddle for cruising on flat water, and the wide Clement for whitewater. I've snapped the end off many Clements by catching the tip on rocks doing pries and power strokes.

Not too long ago, I began experimenting with plastic Mohawk paddles (E). They are tough, but not very aesthetic. I don't like the feel of them. They are ideal for shallow, rock-studded rapids, and for commercial outfitters, because they are so tough.

To compete with the synthetics, manufacturers such as Grey Owl have developed many types of reinforced wood paddles. Grey Owl makes a paddle called the Black Feather Guide Series (F) exclusively for this outfitter. It's about as tough as they come, and yet has the warmth and beauty usually found only in wooden paddles. Two of its best points are the abrasion-proof shaft and comfortable grip. In rapids, I like its big blade for grabbing lots of water, and for a stable brace. Muskoka Fine Watercraft also make a hardwood paddle with a blade that is wide enough for whitewater (A).

For a pleasurable pace in long-distance canoeing on flat water, I usually opt for the razor-edge hardwood paddle. In recent years, these paddles have made a comeback. Craftsmen have rediscovered the art and joy of making fine paddles. The selection of wood for these paddles takes great skill. Before you buy a paddle, check it carefully by sighting down the shaft to make sure it isn't warped. A fine, hardwood paddle is a beautiful object, and deserves the extra care that must be taken in using and storing it. Leaving it lying on damp grass in the sun might warp it.

The bent-shaft paddles (G) have become very popular in recent years. I don't use them because I prefer versatility in a paddle, just as I do in a canoe. I love pry strokes, and like to roll the paddle blade over a lot, especially while doing tight maneuvers. However, the bent shaft has a great advantage in efficiency, because it enables the paddler to apply maximum power in the strongest part of the stroke, without lifting up on the water at the end of the stroke which wastes energy and causes the canoe to porpoise.

Laminated wooden paddles should be reinforced at the tip with fiberglass if they are used on remote wilderness rivers, or in shallow rock-studded rapids.

Paddles with a somewhat rounded tip seem to enter the water easily and with less splash, and handle best in steering. I might get some argument on that. Paddle shapes like paddle materials are a matter of personal choice.

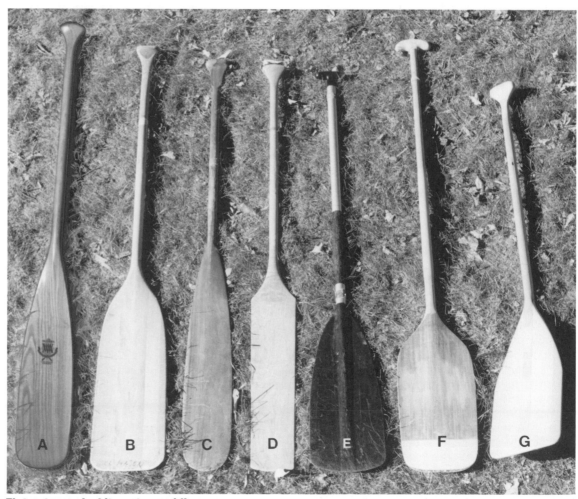

Flatwater and whitewater paddles

Catamarans and trimarans

There are very few things in life that are free, but drifting on a current, and being blown along on the wind are two sets of circumstances in which you really do get something for nothing. On some of the mountain rivers, you can travel with the current for hundreds of miles and hardly paddle a stroke, and on journeys that are predominantly flat water, you can sometimes use the prevailing winds to cover scores of miles for free.

I enjoy paddling for the physical exercise, but I'm not one to look a gift horse in the mouth. Lashing canoes together to form a catamaran or trimaran for drifting or sailing is a wonderful way to add fun and diversity to a journey by canoe. The possibilities for rigging catamarans and trimarans, or any number of canoes, are limited only by the imagination. The canoes should be lashed 3 ft. (about 90 cm) apart, and toed in at the bow to minimize the water build-up between the canoes when underway. Two poles are used; one is lashed to the back of the bow seats, and the other one to the stern thwarts. If you rig a mast using a tent pole or sapling, lash it to the pole behind the bow seat in the center canoe. Mainstays are required from the two stern thwarts and bow of the center canoe. A groundsheet can be used for a sail, and the simplest method is the square sail rig. Lash one side of the groundsheet to a pole that is used as a yardarm, and tie a rope to each side of it. For raising and lowering the sail, run a rope from the center of the rope on the yardarm through a pulley or carabiner at the top of the mast. The angle of the sail is controlled by the two lower corners.

On our Mountain River trip, we rigged a truly elegant trimaran when we hit the Mackenzie River. It improved as we went. Over two days we added a crowsnest, ratlines, and a bowsprit on which we placed gravel, for our firepit. We sipped tea and hot soup all the way down the Mackenzie, and took turns enjoying the scenery from the crowsnest.

Two canoes lashed securely together are very stable. You can swamp in a storm or rapids, but you can't tip. Often I have lashed two canoes together for safety when travelling in waves with children. But don't be lured into a state of complacency about the waves and weather. On a fast-flowing river, sweepers can be very dangerous. When paddling a catamaran or trimaran against the wind, the waves often splash off the bow of one canoe and straight into the other. Constant bailing is necessary or spray covers have to be rigged. When sailing with the wind, spray isn't much of a problem.

Sailing a solo canoe with a jerry-rigged sail, and a paddle as a lee board, requires some skill and caution to avoid capsizing. With this arrangement, you can sail with, or even across the wind, but not into it. To tack into the wind you need a properly-cut sail. On a wilderness trip, bailers are secured to the canoe and the packs are lashed in tightly, so they will act as floatation to enable me to bail in case of an upset. I'm not very keen on solo wilderness sailing when the water is ice-cold. I've never upset a wilderness sailing rig, but I've come close to it. I go swimming regularly when sailing an empty canoe with a real sailing rig in big winds. "Hey look! There goes crazy Mason with his oversize sail on his old wooden canoe," they laugh as they zoom by in their Lasers or sailboards. But then, they'll never know the fun, excitement and challenge of sailing a canoe.

Trimaran with square-rigged sail, Mackenzie River, NWT

Sailing through the Ramparts of the Mackenzie River ————

Becalmed in the Ramparts ————

A septmaran on the Nahanni ————

11 PADDLING AND PORTAGING SKILLS

Various styles of paddling evolved along with canoe design but, like the canoe, it all began with the native people. A long time ago, the Indians discovered that a canoe could be steered on a straight course, without changing sides, by means of a ruddering action at the end of the power stroke. This evolved into the J stroke, where the steering action begins halfway through the stroke. Then someone discovered that the steering could take place during the recovery part of the stroke, by knifing the paddle forward underwater. It became known as the Knifing J, or Canadian stroke. It was discovered that when paddling solo, what you do at the beginning of the stroke is almost as important as what you do at the end. For example, a bit of a draw in toward the bow at the beginning of the stroke meant less effort in the steering part of the stroke at the end. This became known as the C stroke. The possibilities are endless.

Paddling a canoe solo or double with the traditional steering strokes is fun. In fact, it can be an art. But if my main interest were getting to my destination as fast as possible without resorting to a motor, I would use the double-bladed paddle. Around the 1930s the double-bladed paddle was quite popular, but then interest in it died. In recent years something akin to the double-bladed paddle has become very popular, although it does make for a wet ride. Racing paddlers have discovered that by changing sides every few strokes, all the power could be used for propulsion rather than steering. One set of muscles gets a rest between changes. The bent-shaft paddle was developed for maximum efficiency. This style of paddling also favors the tractor seat slung low, with the feet extended against a foot brace. The canoeist sits dead center to facilitate changing the paddle over. The canoes tend to be narrow and have a straight keel line from bow to stern.

There are many reasons why people are adopting the switch-sides, power-paddling technique and the fast, straight-keel-line canoes. Because of the straight keel, the canoe tracks well and you can get six to ten power strokes in without a steering stroke, before the canoe veers off course. To bring it back on course, you switch sides. To turn away from the stern paddler's side, you keep paddling. To turn the other way, you change sides. It couldn't be simpler. For violent turns, you need the more sophisticated strokes, such as cross-bow-draws and bow and stern draws and pries, but for the average lake trip, you can get by with a few maneuvers.

The growing interest in this new way to paddle a canoe doesn't surprise me. It's in keeping with the pace of our society. Recently I read an article in a canoe magazine extolling the virtues of the high-tech canoes, the bent-shaft paddles and fast-change paddling technique. The writer told how he arrived at the put-in point late. He loaded up his go-fast canoe and pushed off with his partner. They used the fast, quick strokes of the changeover method. Easily outdistancing all other canoes, they arrived at the designated campsite and chose the best one. Eventually the other canoeists began to straggle in. The story illustrates a philosophy about being outdoors that is different from mine.

Embarking and landing

The aluminum and ABS canoes can take a lot of abuse, while the more beautifully designed and lighter Kevlar and canvas-cedar canoes require considerable care. Canvas-cedar canoes should be loaded while floating, and emptied before pulling up onto shore, unless the shore is smooth and slants into the water. One end can be lifted onto shore for easy unloading, but avoid sliding the canoe.

To land, use a strong backwater stroke to stop the canoe just as it touches shore. If paddling doubles, the bow paddler steps out and holds the canoe while the stern paddler walks forward and steps ashore. The bow paddler should not drag the canoe up while the stern paddler is still in, as the canoe might roll over. When landing in big surf, you must keep the canoe at a right angle to the shore. Jump out before you hit, keep the canoe aligned, and get it up onto shore as quickly as you can. A little dragging is better than having a big wave dump on you. If the shore is rocky and the surf is high, you've really got a problem. Slow the canoe down as you approach shore and jump out just before it hits. You can either dump the packs overboard and carry the canoe to shore, or lift and slide the canoe to shore as quickly as you can before the next wave hits.

To embark from a shallow, sandy shore, hold the canoe at a right angle to the shore, climb into the stern and, with your hands on the gunwales, walk to the bow. Your weight will float the end on shore free. If you're paddling solo, wait until the end on shore floats free, then move back to your paddling position. If paddling double, the other paddler steps in and joins you in the bow until the end floats free.

These are the little niceties that are being lost with the new indestructible battleships. With the Grumman and ABS canoes you just clomp on board and shove off. If this sounds rather disparaging toward the tough modern canoes of today, I don't intend it to be. These canoes have made possible many trips that would have been impossible or would have destroyed my canvas-cedar canoe or my extra-light Kevlar.

Embarking or landing in big surf is not easy whatever you are paddling. The price of error is just greater in a fine canoe. To embark, the canoe is loaded on the beach just above where the waves are breaking. Wait for a lull, then go for it, half dragging and half lifting. You must get out beyond the breakers before more big ones roll in. If the canoe swamps, avoid getting between the canoe and the shore. A large wave can pick the canoe up and dump it on you. With the water-filled canoe weighing almost a ton, you can be hurt badly.

Drifting

A canoe is a marvellous place to write, paint, read or just drift. This is being written while I am drifting downwind. It might be hard to believe, but even drifting in a canoe takes skill.

For example, if you want to drift slowly, you sit on the bottom of the canoe with your back propped with towels or extra life jackets against the center thwart. The canoe drifts broadside to the wind. To drift faster you sit on the bottom, but with your back against the stern seat. This raises the bow out of the water. The wind catches the bow and under the bow deck, swings the canoe downwind, and propels you along at a pretty good clip. If the sun is in your face and you want it at your back, turn around, face the stern and sit with your back against the stern thwart.

It might seem ludicrous to be going into all these details about drifting in a canoe, but a complete understanding of how wind affects even a slowly drifting canoe is an important element in canoeing. The two ends of a canoe are identical except for the placement of the seats. The force of wind on an empty drifting canoe is equal on both ends, so it drifts sideways. If you sit or kneel in the middle of the canoe, it will still drift sideways, because the force of the wind will still be equal on both ends. If you sit in one end of the canoe, that end will be deeper in the water, where the wind can't affect it as much. Conversely the other end will be raised out of the water, where the wind can get at it. Now the force of the wind will blow the raised end faster than the end deeper in the water. Thus, the high end always wants to swing around and drift downwind. This principle can be put to good use by the paddler. Time after time, even after instruction, people forget, and get blown around and down the lake. That's why very few people can paddle a rockered canoe solo into the wind without switching sides every couple of strokes. They sit too far back, and the wind grabs the bow and swings it downwind. Instead, they should move forward, so the canoe is riding level.

There are a few tricks to flat water cruising that you can't use in the bent-paddle switch method. For good cruising, junk the old idea of sitting in the center of the seat an equal distance from the gunwales. In rapids, kneeling in that position provides stability; however,

the objective in easy, comfortable paddling is to sit as close as possible to the gunwale. The closer you are to the water, the easier it is to paddle and the more efficient the stroke.

This applies to both double and solo. In paddling solo, you might want to put your pack on the opposite side of the canoe, so the canoe doesn't tilt too far. In paddling double, the canoeists balance each other. You shift around a bit, depending on the weight of the respective paddlers, until it feels balanced. Packs can also be shifted to provide an even keel. I often have a loose one that I kick back and forth to trim the canoe. Because the bow seat is wider than the stern, the bow paddler is sometimes unable to be right beside the gunwale. I much prefer kneeling on one or both knees in any case. Once you get used to it, it's very comfortable. If you extend one leg, be sure to toe in and extend the leg furthest from the gunwale. When you change paddling sides, alternate the legs for a rest. In cruising, you change sides when you feel like it. It can vary from not at all, to once every ten minutes; seldom more often than that. When you change sides, you slide across your seat so you will be close to the water. Although some teamwork is required, with time, much of what I have described here comes naturally.

It's a nice idea to change ends in the canoe for diversity, unless of course you end up with a partner who prefers the opposite end to you. Partners like that are hard to come by.

Coping with wind

Very few forms of transportation are more affected by wind than the canoe. Wind causes waves. The size and shape of them depend on the size and depth of the body of water. The waves of Lake Superior sometimes resemble an ocean swell, while shallow lakes such as Lake Winnipeg in Manitoba and Big Traverse Bay, Lake of the Woods, Minnesota have waves that are steeper, closer together and break more easily. They are also difficult to paddle in. Even the most skillful open canoe paddler cannot paddle a canoe through a breaking wave without upsetting or swamping.

It is very dangerous to set out across a lake from a lee shore in a wind. No matter how strong the wind is blowing, there are no waves along the lee shore. However, the farther from shore you paddle, the larger the waves will be. Out in the middle of the lake, the waves could be breaking, but you won't know until you get there, and then it will be too late to turn back. Be careful not to be led out into this sort of situation by a member of your party who isn't aware of the danger.

Air currents Sometimes wave conditions can be avoided by paddling at night or in the early morning. Local onshore winds are created when the sun is high in the sky and heats the air over the land. The warm air rises and brings in the cooler air from over the water, which is then heated and in turn rises. Strong local winds are thus created which can result in wave action.

Controlling canoe in strong wind

151

Flat water steering strokes

How to paddle and control a canoe in all conditions of wind, waves and rapids could fill volumes. This section is chiefly designed to teach you how to have full control of your canoe to avoid being carried into rapids inadvertently. For white water canoeing, refer to *Path of the Paddle*.

The switch — steering a straight course
The canoe always veers away from the stern paddler's side. If you are paddling a canoe with rocker, it will veer off course in three or four strokes. If you are paddling a straight keel canoe, it will take six to ten strokes before it veers off course. One method that has become popular in recent years is for both paddlers to change sides every six to ten strokes. The side to paddle on for the desired turn will become obvious immediately. The marathon racers prefer this method because all the power of the stroke goes into propulsion rather than steering; the canoe is allowed to zigzag.

The J stroke — stern paddler
The traditional method of staying on course is to use a steering stroke. There are several you can use but, for simplicity, we will use the basic J stroke. It's called the J stroke because the J describes what the paddle does as you take a stroke. Very few people do it instinctively; most people turn the paddle the wrong way at the end of the stroke. To simplify things, place a piece of tape on one side of the paddle and call it the power face. The power face is the side that pulls against the water, so as you take a stroke, the power face is what makes the canoe go. It will face the stern as you execute the stroke. As you near the end of your stroke, you will notice that the bow is veering away from your paddle side. To bring the canoe back on course you need to pry away from the canoe at the end of the stroke. To accomplish this, roll your upper hand over so your thumb points down. This will turn your power face away from the canoe. Now pry the paddle off the gunwale holding the blade underwater until the bow swings back on

course. As you get better at it, the stroke will smooth out into one continuous motion. The bow paddler supplies the power.

There is a school of paddling that believes the shaft should never touch the gunwale, but I could never figure out the logic of that. Everyone knows that the lever makes a task easier. As for wearing out the gunwales, I guess I've lost maybe an eighth of an inch (30 mm) off mine in the past 20 years.

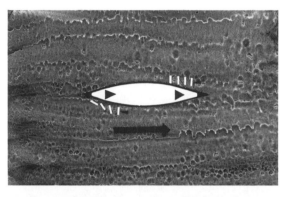

Turning strokes

The heavy J — the turn to stern paddler's side
To turn the canoe toward the stern paddler's side, increase the force and duration of the pry off the gunwale. Once again, check to see if the thumb on your upper hand is pointing down. This will make the power face turn away from the canoe. The harder you pry, and the longer you keep the paddle in the water, the more extreme the turn. As you become proficient, you will be able to make a tight turn to your paddle side without breaking the rhythm of your stroke. If you get some help from your bow paddler, the turn will be more effective. The bow paddler shortens his stroke and does a heavy J off the gunwale in the same manner as the stern paddler.

Sideslip strokes

Stern sweep—the turn away from the stern paddler's side

This is the easy one. If you paddle without the J stroke, the canoe will gradually veer away from the stern paddler's side. The canoe always veers unless you've got a gorilla in your bow. To increase the turn, sweep your paddle out to the side and around to the stern of your canoe. If the bow person reaches out away from the bow at about a 45° angle, and pulls the paddle directly toward his body, the turn will be more abrupt. This is called a diagonal bow draw. It's more effective and much more fun to work together in steering the canoe.

Stern draw, bow pry

The stern paddler reaches out and does a draw with the power face. The bow paddler does a pry off the gunwale with the non-power face, pushing against the water. If you work as a team, the canoe will sideslip laterally toward the stern paddler's side without turning.

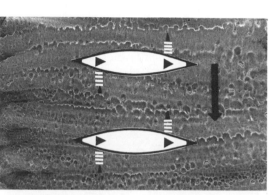

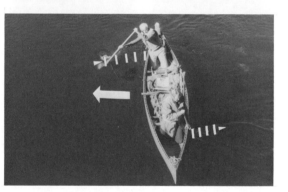

Stern pry, bow draw

The stern paddler does a pry off the gunwale, with the non-power face pushing against the water, and the bow paddler does a draw with the power face. The canoe sideslips without turning if you don't overpower each other.

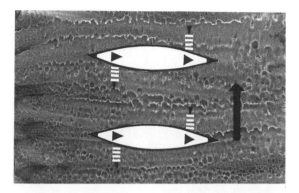

Pivot strokes

Bow and stern draw
To pivot the bow of the canoe away from your paddle side (the stern), both paddlers reach out at 90° from the canoe as far as they comfortably can. Now place the paddle in the water with the power face toward you, draw the paddle toward your body and right to the side of the canoe. The bow will pivot away from your paddle side. Practice by continuing with as many draws as you need to make a 360° pivot.

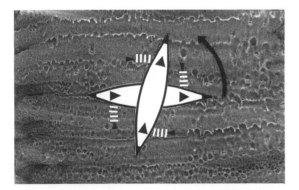

Bow and stern pry
To pivot the bow around to your paddle side, both paddlers place their paddle in the water, with the blade parallel to the canoe and the power face toward the canoe. Make sure the paddle is right up against the canoe, or even a little under the canoe. Now pull the upper hand toward your body to pry the paddle off the gunwale, with the non-power face pushing against the water. The bow will pivot toward the stern paddler's side. To continue the pivot, lift the paddle from the water and slip it back into the water beside the canoe. Repeat as often as necessary. Practice by doing 360° pivots.

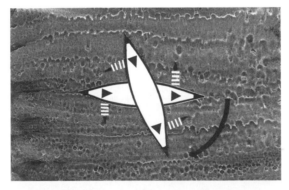

Pivot with cross bow draw
For the stationary pivot toward the stern paddler's side, the bow paddler has the option of doing a cross bow draw. The bow paddler reaches across the bow without changing hand positions, and places the paddle in the water as far out as possible. The paddle is then drawn toward the bow with the power face pulling against the water.

Now to make things interesting, start doing these maneuvers when you are moving forward, slowly at first, then gradually increasing the speed. You will find that the forward momentum of the canoe greatly enhances the turns or sideslips. If you don't brace yourself when you do a pry, you'll find yourself catapulted over the bow into the water! Cranking turns and sideslips are not only fun, but also necessary, if you find yourself in a current or difficult winds and waves.

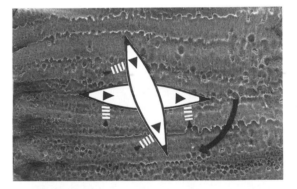

Backpaddling

Backpaddling straight

Backpaddling is an essential stroke for whitewater. When running rapids, the trick is to slow down the canoe to give yourself time to maneuver around the rocks. The bow paddler controls the direction with a reverse J stroke.

Reverse J

When backpaddling, the non-power face of the paddle is pushed against the water. To do a reverse J, the bow paddler rolls the NON-power face away from the canoe and pries off the gunwale, just enough to keep the canoe moving backward without turning. The stern paddler can assist by doing a draw toward the canoe or a pry away.

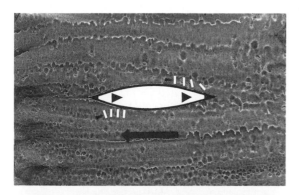

Backpaddling turn toward bow paddler's side

To turn the stern toward the bow paddler's side, the bow paddler does a heavy reverse J. To accomplish this, the bow paddler pries hard and keeps the paddle in the water longer. The stern paddler can assist with a pry at the beginning of the backpaddle stroke.

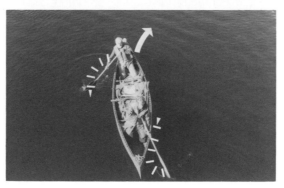

Backpaddling turn away from bow paddler's side

To turn the stern away from the bow paddler's side, the bow paddler backpaddles by sweeping the paddle wide, and ends the stroke by sweeping the paddle right to the bow. The stern paddler can assist in the turn by doing a diagonal draw toward the stern, followed by a backpaddle.

There are many refinements to these strokes to make them more efficient. As you accomplish these maneuvers, you will feel more comfortable in your canoe, and will be better prepared for unforeseen circumstances.

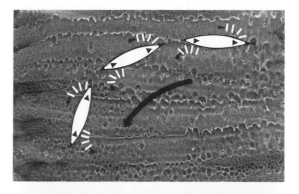

Canoeing rivers

The foregoing paddle strokes and maneuvers should keep you out of trouble if they are executed with reasonable skill. For those who are interested in learning to run rapids, I would recommend my book *Path of the Paddle*, and my four films of the same title. The films are now available on cassette at video stores. There are many other good books on the subject of whitewater technique, and excellent whitewater clinics across Canada and the United States.

Many people enjoy wilderness canoeing without running rapids. They are quite content to take to the portage trail. However, an alarming number of accidents, and even deaths, occur when canoes are swept into rapids inadvertently. It takes considerable skill to maneuver a canoe out of a strong current, and into an eddy beside the shore, for landing. (An eddy is the calm water downstream of any protrusion from shore, or downstream of any rock showing above the surface.) In low water conditions, there is little danger of being swept into rapids or over a falls, but the possibility increases proportionately with an increase in flow. When my partner, Ken Buck, and I were making the canoe film series, we did much of the filming in early spring, when the rivers were at their highest level. Often we camped beside the most interesting rapids, because it could take several days to complete a sequence. We witnessed many missed landings at Little Thomson Rapids on the Petawawa River in Algonquin Park, and spent a lot of time fishing people out of an eddy, and collecting their gear below the rapids.

Making a safe river landing

Eddy turn landing   Imagine that you are canoeing a river (illustration 1A) and there are rapids ahead. You are in the stern paddling on the right. The portage is on the left. To get to shore and into an eddy (D), the bow-first eddy turn landing, or the stern first landing, can be used. To do the former, pivot the canoe around toward shore by drawing on the right as the bow paddler draws on the left (B). As

you approach the shore, look for the head of the portage or a shore eddy (D). As your bow enters the eddy, the stern, which is still in the current, will swing around downstream (C). Be prepared for a sudden lurch as the canoe crosses the current line between the eddy and the current. As the canoe enters the eddy, it will be facing upstream.

If there is no eddy beside the shore, the bow paddler must make sure the bow touches shore first, and stays there! Don't let the bow swing back out into the current. The bow paddler must step ashore first (upstream end) while holding onto the bow. He or she steadies the canoe while the stern paddler gets out. If the stern paddler gets out first, the bow will ride deep in the water and can be yanked by the current out into the river and down the rapids.

The canoe is narrow under the stern seat. This makes it very tippy when you are sitting in the stern of the empty canoe, so before the bow paddler gets out, move forward onto your knees. This is a good habit even if you are carrying a heavy load.

The stern first or back ferry landing   You are now paddling down the river (illustration 2A) in the stern, on the right side of the canoe. The map indicates the portage is on the left. The river is turning to the left with a strong current. To anticipate the back ferry to shore, pry your stern over to the left, as the bow paddler pries the bow to the right (B). This allows you to drift on the current with the stern angled toward shore (C). If you want to move closer to shore, backpaddle (D). If you want to move away from shore to avoid some rocks or shoals, paddle forward (E). You will be amazed at how quickly you can move the canoe to or away from shore. If there are rocks where the passage is narrow, straighten the canoe with the pivot (F), run between the rocks and then pivot the canoe back into the back ferry position (G).

As you round the corner, you see the rapids ahead and the portage. All you have to do is backpaddle the canoe (H) enough to put the

stern over to shore right at the portage (I). The head of the portage might or might not have a shore eddy, but either way, you are in control. As the stern touches shore, step out and hang on (the upstream paddler gets out first).

Practice these moves at your leisure in flat water, and then in gently moving water. For these maneuvers, canoes with rockered keels are superior to ones with straight keels.

Sideslip the canoe into shore   If the distance to shore is short, you can sideslip the canoe to the landing in flat or moving water. It's slow, hard work to move a canoe sideways through water. You are running close to shore because you know that there's a rapids just ahead (illustration 3A). You are paddling stern on the right side. When you see the portage, do a series of pry strokes while the bow paddler does a series of draw strokes. If you work as a team, without overpowering each other, the canoe will sideslip over to the shore (B) and into the eddy (C). You can't move as quickly or as far as you can by pivoting the canoe around into a back ferry.

The maneuvers that I have described have been with the stern paddler on the right and the bow paddler on the left, with the canoe moving to the left shore. For the opposite direction transpose all the directions.

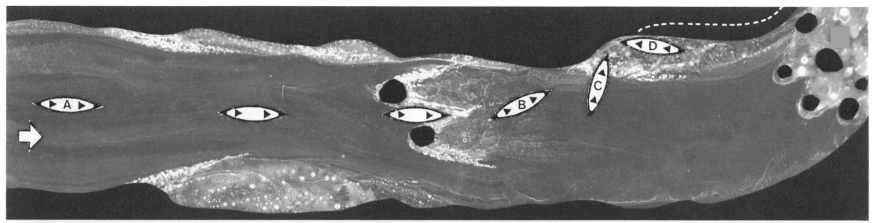

1 Eddy turn landing

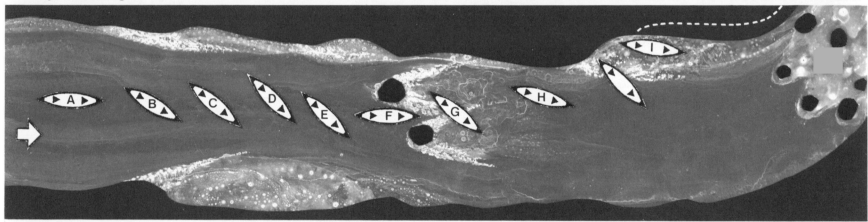

2 Back ferry landing

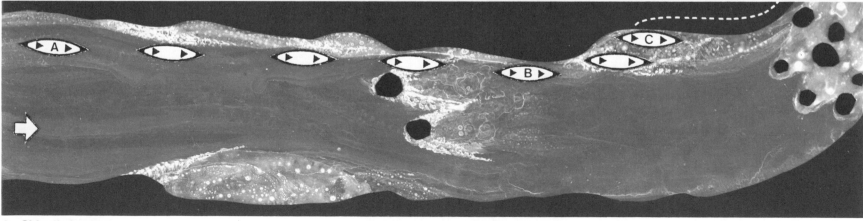

3 Sideslip landing

157

Descending a river with a current

By following a few basic principles, you can keep control of your canoe when running a river with a current. There are also some dangers that you can avoid, if you can anticipate them early enough.

Rounding a bend with the back ferry

As water flows around a bend, most of it swings to the outside to make this the deepest water. For this reason, the outside of the bend is also where you'll find the largest waves.

You are paddling stern on the right (A). The river disappears around the bend to the right. To avoid the waves, and be ready for a landing, drift the corner in the back ferry position by drawing the stern right while the bow paddler draws left. The canoe is now drifting sideways on the current, with the stern closer to shore than the bow (B). To move closer to shore, backpaddle (C). If you begin drifting onto shallows or rocks, paddle forward into deeper water (D). If you see rocks ahead, pivot the canoe so it's aligned with the current, and slips between the rocks (E), then resume the back ferry position (F). The stern is almost always kept close to the shore in the back ferry, except when running difficult rapids.

As you round the bend, the current quickens, and you see that the bank is undercut on the outside of the turn. A tree has fallen into the water (G). This "sweeper" is one of the most dangerous obstacles on a river. A canoe or a swimmer can be pinned against it in the current. In the back ferry position, it is easy to avoid (H). Backpaddling moves you closer to the shore on the inside of the turn (I).

Take note that I haven't said anything about *paddling* downstream; we've been *drifting*. Only a few strokes forward or back are necessary to correct our position in the current and maintain complete control.

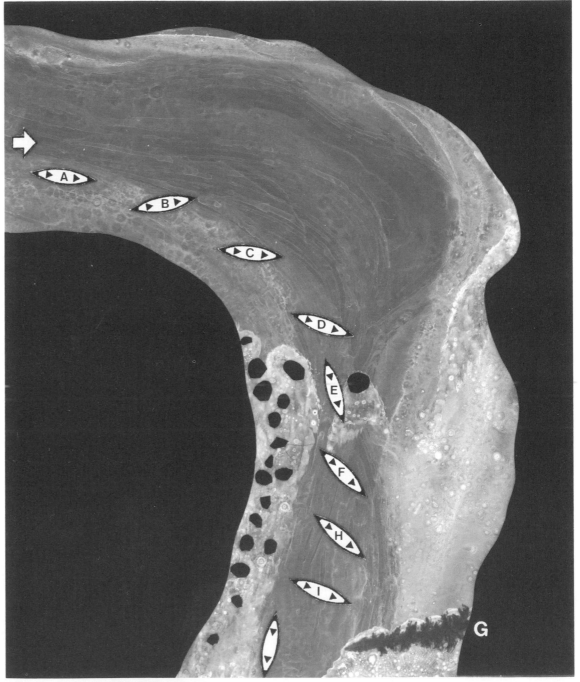

Back ferrying around inside of bend

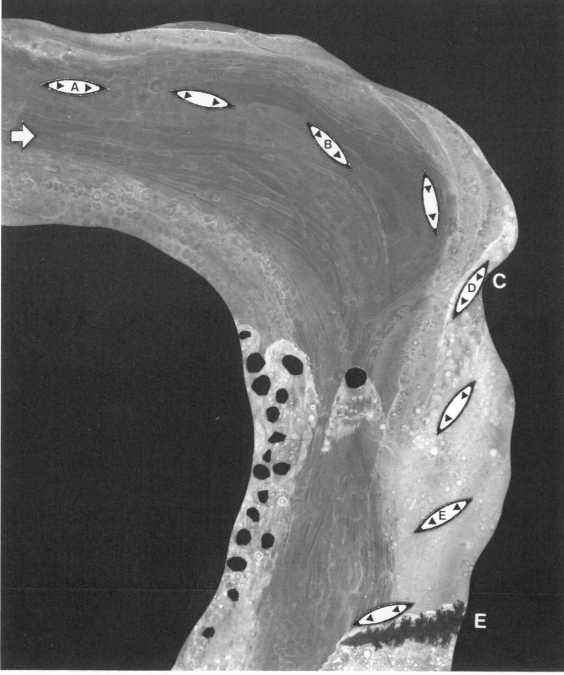

Rounding a bend at the mercy of the river

The possible dangers of paddling forward on the main current

You decide to paddle forward down the outside of the turn to enjoy the waves (A). The speed of the canoe causes the bow to plunge deep, taking in water (B). You look up and see that the river is ploughing into a cliff (C). You power the bow around, barely missing the cliff, but you bang your stern against the rock (D). Then, as you look downstream, you see a sweeper (E). You try to point the bow to shore by paddling harder (F). You are paddling at 4 mph (6 km/hr) in a 4 mph (6 km/hr) current, so you don't have time to miss the sweeper. If you are smart, you leap out of your canoe onto the sweeper. The canoe is carried under and pinned. This is *not* running under complete control.

Back ferry

Recently I received a letter from a paddler who expressed concern that the canoe instruction he had received, and the canoe organization to which he belonged, ignored back ferrying and backwatering (backpaddling). Many other people have expressed the same concerns about aggressive, faster-than-the-current technique, compared to the slow backwater and ferrying techniques for running rapids. In hot dog canoeing and in racing, the slower-than-current techniques are not required in most situations. However, extreme back ferries and reverse entries into eddies can be a lot of fun. I believe that you need both to be a well-rounded whitewater canoeist.

For canoeing very shallow, rock-studded rapids, where the eddies are hardly big enough to get into, backferrying, or at least backwatering, are necessary for a slow descent. In extreme conditions, such as ice-cold water, cold air temperatures and in remote areas, the slow descent and back ferrying are the way to avoid taking on water. On the shallow, rock-studded rapids where the gradient is steep, aggressive backpaddling allows you time to find the channels and to avoid running up on rocks.

I admit that the almost indestructible ABS canoes can be powered through rock gardens like a ball in a pinball game. If you get up speed, the momentum of the canoe often drives the canoe over a rock, past the midway point which keeps the canoe from turning broadside and hanging up, or even worse, pinning. The power method is impossible with aluminum canoes. They stick and pivot broadside onto the rock every time. Light Kevlar canoes and fiberglass canoes can take a limited amount of abuse, if running empty or almost empty. In the school of backpaddling and back ferrying, though, the fun is getting through a rapids without touching a rock.

We also enjoy playing the river by back ferrying across it to catch the big stuff. Of course, you can do this with aggressive eddy turn and S ferry techniques. We like to mix the techniques when conditions — such as a wide, fast river — allow for it.

A while ago I was asked to write an article on running rapids for a large canoe company in the United States. The article was accepted until I sent the accompanying photographs. The canoe shown in the pictures was a wood-canvas canoe. The editors figured that their readers would laugh at the idea of using a traditional, wood canoe for running rapids. I've been doing it for 20 years. Sure, I've hit some rocks, but the trick is to make sure you are moving more slowly than the current. The objective when running rapids is to *miss* the rocks. If you do hit them, the heavy backpaddling technique assures that you don't hit them too hard.

There is no one right way to run rapids. On the one hand, I have seen inexperienced paddlers negotiate the wildest rapids by keeping the canoe pointing downstream and letting the current carry them along. On the other hand, despite all our fancy back ferrying, eddy turns and downstream braces, we have wiped out in a wild set of rapids. I've also seen an empty canoe go through rapids without taking on a drop of water (see page 88). I doubt that any of us will ever know all there is to know about running wild water, but we sure intend to keep trying.

It's a different game when you are running a remote river with all your worldly possessions on board. Most canoe instruction takes place without a load. A loaded canoe is slow, sluggish and stable, but the possibility of swamping is much greater than in an empty canoe. Also, a loaded canoe can't be powered through the big stuff like an empty canoe. Most canoe expeditions begin on shallow, rock-studded headwaters, with a three- or four-week food supply as well as gear. The load gets lighter as the food is consumed but, unfortunately, all the tough stuff is at the top of the river.

Backferry across the current

Crossing a current to reach the other side—front ferry

You are running a river with a strong current and see a rapids coming up. After pulling into an eddy on the right, you realize the portage is on the left shore. To cross to the opposite side, you need a front ferry. The front ferry is easier to do than the back ferry, because the bow is higher out of the water, and less likely than the stern to be grabbed by unexpected currents. The canoe is also easier to paddle forward than backward.

You are sitting in an eddy on the right shore (A). Begin the crossing by sticking the stern out into the current to swing the canoe around so it's facing upstream (B). Because you are not far enough above the rapids, you must wade the canoe upstream in the shallows beside the shore (C). To begin the front ferry, paddle forward, entering the current at a very shallow angle. This gets your stern out into the current right after the bow enters it (D). If you don't manage this, the current will grab the bow and swing you around downstream. If this happens, backpaddle (back ferry) to shore and try again.

Once you are in the current, angle the canoe to the far shore and paddle hard against the current. The current on the upstream side of the canoe will glide it across the current (E). If there are rocks in the current, pass downstream of them, and make use of the quiet water behind them (F). Finish the ferry in an eddy (G) if possible. Otherwise maintain your angle and keep paddling to shore, until the bow paddler can step ashore. As the bow paddler gets out, he or she must hang onto the bow, so it doesn't swing back out into the current. If it does, the stern paddler will end up running the rapids solo.

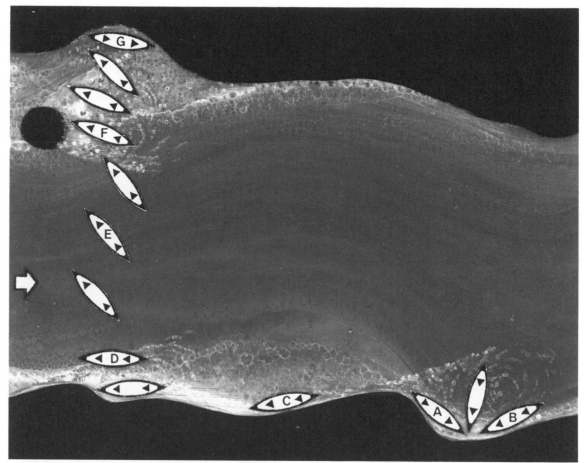

Choosing a safe place for a front ferry crossing

Paddle brace

As you enter the still water of the eddy from the current, you feel the canoe lurch; if the current is extreme, you could upset. The trick is to lean your weight out on the paddle in a high or low brace, before the current grabs your canoe. This helps you to stay upright in a big wave.

High brace
Lean your weight out on the power face of the paddle. The upper hand is high. If you are doing it correctly, your thumb will point toward your nose.

Low brace
Rest your weight on the non-power face of the paddle. The upper hand is very low (level with the gunwale) and your thumb points toward the bow. Practice by paddling the canoe fast, and then going into the brace position.

High brace

Low brace

Currents

Eddy line
Any protrusion into the river from shore has still water behind it. So does any rock sticking above the surface. The "eddy line" is the demarcation between the current and the still water of the eddy. You have to anticipate the violent effect of this current diversion, and be ready with a high or low brace.

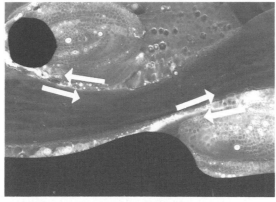

Eddy line or divergent currents

Leaving the eddy

Reading moving water

Rock obstruction
Another essential skill for descending a river with a current is called "reading the water." In calm water, rocks just beneath the surface give no clues to their presence unless you can actually see them. In a current, rocks betray their presence by a wave curling upstream. The water flows over the rock, hits the still water behind the rock and throws up a wave.

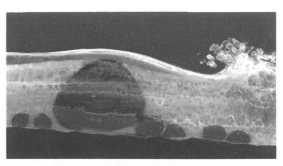

Rock causes wave downstream

Waves caused by rock

Upstream and downstream Vs

Water that doesn't flow over a rock has to flow around it, which causes a wake. This wake looks like a V pointing upstream. Any V pointing upstream is pointing at a rock (A and B). It may be near the surface where you could hit it, or it may be deep enough to pass over, but you know it's there. Two rocks close together will create two wakes. Where they converge between the rocks you will see a V pointing downstream (C). These downstream Vs point to deep water. The idea is to follow the downstream Vs. Rapids are classified as Class 1 if the downstream Vs are not too numerous and are easy to follow. The difficulty rating goes as high as 6. Class 3 is the upper limit for the open canoe.

Haystacks and rollers

A downstream V terminates in a haystack where the two waves meet. In a gentle current, haystacks are only a few inches high. The size of the haystacks increases proportionately with the speed and volume of the water and the size of the rocks creating the downstream V. Even large haystacks can be run by skilled canoeists.

A ledge or sharp drop-off creates a roller and a hole. In large volume rapids they are potentially dangerous.

Unaligned Vs

Watch out for unaligned Vs. If a downstream V terminates in an upstream V, the rapids begins to take on a Class 3 rating. Instruction on negotiating unaligned Vs is beyond the scope of this book. It's time to take to the portage trail, take some whitewater paddling clinics, or delve into *Path of the Paddle* and other books on advanced whitewater canoeing.

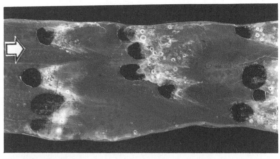
Unaligned Vs

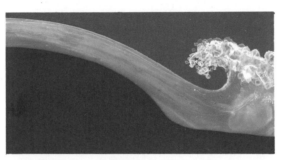
Ledge creates waves

Downstream V terminates in waves

Waves can be run if moderate

Maneuvering down Vs

Downstream V and haystack

Weight difference and staying right-side up

When I canoe with friends, and especially when I am teaching someone how to run rapids, I seem to do an inordinate amount of swimming. If you want to know about canoe recovery, I'm the guy to ask because I get a lot of practice. When you swim as much as I do you have to ask, "Why?" Well, obviously it's because of the guys I paddle with! But then Paul reminds me that he rarely upsets regardless of who is paddling with him. And he teaches many more people to paddle than I do. Becky, like me, has also had a great deal of practice swimming through rapids while instructing.

After much thought I have come up with a theory. The problem isn't necessarily the people I paddle with, but my failure to anticipate their mistakes and prepare myself in advance to compensate for them. Paul does this instinctively, so he rarely swims. Most of my canoeing is solo or with friends or family, so I don't get quite as many surprises dropped on me. As my partner is going for the gunwales and taking the canoe with him, I'm saying to myself, "I should be hanging out there," but it's too late. We're gone!

There is another reason that I spend a lot of time in the water. At 135 lb. (61 kg) I am usually outweighed by my partner. If my 180 lb. (82 kg) partner loses his balance and grabs for the gunwales, he is almost sure to take the canoe and me with him, even if I have anticipated the problem and thrown my weight to the opposite side for a brace. Becky, at about 115 lb. (52 kg), has an even greater problem. Paul, at 155 lb. (70 kg), has a weight advantage on us as he throws all his weight out on his paddle. Often his partner is half-way out of the canoe and heading for a swim, but because of Paul's brace, the canoe doesn't go over. At this point, one of three things can happen. Either his partner's legs come free from under the seat, and he falls in, or his legs catch and hold, and he pulls himself back into the canoe, or Paul can let up on his brace and upset the canoe to free him. At my weight, I haven't had that kind of choice to make. Usually, when my partner goes, I go (photograph 1).

Using weight differences to advantage

Now let's consider two skilled partners, one heavy, one light. If the heavier partner is paddling on the upstream side when leaving an eddy, and the canoe tips to the upstream side to the point where he loses his balance, it is unlikely that the lighter partner can hold the canoe upright with a brace. If the heavy partner is on the downstream side leaving the eddy, and the canoe tips to the upstream side, there is a much greater possibility that the heavier partner can hold the canoe upright (photograph 2). If the lighter partner loses his balance and falls out, he can be picked up downstream. A good canoeist, who knows he has lost his balance past the point of recovery, will kick himself free of the canoe, leaving it, and his partner, upright (photograph 3). The rescue is then very easy. People who are inexperienced usually grab the gunwales and haul the canoe over with them.

1 Partner falls out ——————

2 Heavy partner, downstream brace ——————

3 Man overboard but canoe remains upright ——————

The towering cliffs of the Nahanni River

Portaging

Some people get into canoeing for the challenge, the physical workout or test of endurance. Well, if that's what you are looking for, have I got a deal for you! It's called "portaging." Anyone who tells you portaging is fun is either a liar or crazy, or maybe both. However, whenever you are tempted to curse the portage, remember that it's there to circumvent the rapids and falls that can't otherwise be negotiated, and that its existence forms a barrier that helps to preserve the wilderness. The more portages there are between me and a road, the louder and more clearly I hear the song.

With so much emphasis on whitewater canoeing, it's easy to forget that the majority of people are quite content to take to the portage trail, and have no interest in running rapids beyond Class 1. Many of the rivers I have enjoyed are accessible to people who prefer portaging to running rapids. The exceptions are most of the rivers that flow out of the mountains. They have so much fast water that you would have to walk most of the river if you didn't run the whitewater. On rivers with miles of rapids, you have no choice but to run them or, at the very least, wade and line the canoe, which has its own inherent dangers.

You often hear the saying, "Nobody ever drowned on a portage." True, but many people have come close to drowning while attempting a landing at the portage. Missing the portage, and getting swept into rapids, is one of the major causes of canoe-related drownings. Even canoeists who have no intention of running rapids should be familiar with the basic maneuvers required to make a safe landing in a current.

Landing above a rapids or falls
One November, I was running solo on the White River which flows through Pukaskwa National Park into Lake Superior. The map indicated that there was a falls ahead in a canyon that swung to the left. The land on the left side of the river was lower than that on the right. I had been keeping careful track of where I was to avoid surprises. Although the portage was not marked, I was sure it would be on the left. Portages on most rivers have existed as long as there have been people, and people always take the path of least resistance. There are exceptions, but usually you will find the portage on the inside of the turn, or on the lowest bank. No one wants to walk farther or climb higher than they have to, especially with a load.

I was very near the falls, but I couldn't hear it, because the wind was blowing down-river. Even though I was confident that the head of the portage would be on the left, I watched both sides of the river, just to be sure. Finally I saw it: an unmistakable trail leading into the bush. But, before unloading, I checked along the path to see if there was a low-water portage farther downstream. There was, and I decided to use it. The water was below medium level, so it was safe. In high water, it would be very dangerous to attempt a landing that close to the falls.

A few days later, I was approaching Umbatta Falls. I saw the landing, but was tempted to paddle just a little farther, to a shorter portage. I resisted the urge. After further inspection from the top of the cliff, I discovered that I would have been trapped had I continued downstream. I wouldn't have been able to climb the cliff, and to return upstream against the current would have been difficult and dangerous.

The following spring I was on the Fildegrand River, a wild river in full flood. We were running a rapids that, according to the map, terminated in a falls. Wally Schaber and I were hugging the left shore; Paul and his friend, Derek Brown, were hugging the right shore. Because the river was straight and both banks were the same height, there were no clues as to which side the portage would be on. Finally, we heard the falls above the roar of the rapids. We eddied out to the left shore. Paul and Derek eddied out to the right shore, but there was no possibility of portaging on their side of the river. A ferry to our side this close to the falls would have been very dangerous because of the current. They waded, tracked and portaged their canoe upstream, to put some distance between themselves and the falls, and to give themselves time for recovery in case of an upset. Then they performed a front ferry across the river without difficulty.

Strategies for the portage
There are several strategies for attacking the portage. There's the "get it over with as fast as possible" approach, and there's the "what's the hurry?" approach. If the bugs are bad, I go for the first one; otherwise I pick the second. Sometimes the portage can be a pleasant change from paddling, a chance to stretch the legs. I used to prefer portaging the packs rather than the canoe, but with the light 50 lb. (23 kg) Kevlar canoes, that has changed. Now we fight over who gets to carry the canoe. The ABS canoes have become very popular for river travel but, at close to 85 lb. (38 kg), you don't see people lining up to carry them. Occasionally, I take one of my canvas-covered canoes which weigh in at 85-90 lb. (38 to 40 kg) when wet. Portaging them is strictly a labor of love.

Portaging the packs
I have read an endless number of articles in outdoor magazines badmouthing the tumpline. I think it's one of the greatest inventions known to man. However, there is one secret to using one. You must grip the tump beside your head and pull down to distribute the weight properly. With a tumpline, I can carry more than I can lift once I get it up there. I lift the pack onto one knee, put my arm through the shoulder strap (photograph 1), then swing the pack up and around and slip my other arm in. The tumpline is then placed across the forehead (photograph 2) and a second lighter pack is heaved up over my head (photograph 3) on top of the first pack (photograph 4). If there is someone around, I ask their assistance to get it up there. If the packs are properly loaded and the portage is not too difficult, this is the method I prefer. If I get tired, I drop the second pack and continue to the end of the portage. Sometimes I take the

tumpline off my forehead to rest my neck; at other times I take all the weight on the tumpline by leaning forward to rest the shoulders. It's almost as good as a rest.

The tumpline was never meant for hiking trips. Many hikers who switch to canoeing find it difficult to use one, or don't know how to adjust it. The average portage is not all that long, so it's common to carry twice the load that you would if you were on a hiking trip.

If you really don't like the tumpline, and can't get used to it, don't worry. Just take more trips over the portage. Put all loose items such as bailer, throw bags, cameras, and so on, in the day pack, or secure them to the canoe. When canoeing a river with a lot of portages, the secret to efficient portaging is to avoid carrying anything in your arms. There is less chance of losing something if it is either secured to the canoe or put in a pack.

When I'm travelling with a partner, I try to make it work out so one of us doesn't have to make an extra trip. On the rough portages, I might opt for the single pack rather than doubling up. Except for the really long portages of a mile or more (1.5 to 2 km) I don't mind the exercise. You must know your own limits, and be aware of the possibility of injuring yourself.

If you are not used to portaging, start slowly and work up to bigger loads. You should never carry a heavy load just because you are in a hurry. The canoeist in a hurry, on or off the water, is putting himself and his companions at risk. The ease and comfort with which a soft canvas or nylon pack can be carried depends on the skill of the packer. If you find your pots digging into your back, just make sure the person who packed it gets to carry it on the next portage. I usually have things like tripods and fishing rods tied to the canoe, but they must not unbalance it. I might prefer an empty canoe, however, if it's ABS or wood-canvas.

1 Lift pack onto knee

2 Swing pack up and secure tump

3 Heave second pack up

4 Pull down on tumpline

Tumpline-equipped pack with second on top, Quetico Provincial Park, Ontario

Portaging the canoe

Solo carry

It's inconsiderate to block the trail, so the canoe should be pulled up well above the water and out of the way, in case someone else comes along. There is considerable disagreement as to whether or not the paddles should be tied into the canoe for portaging. Some people claim that it makes the canoe intolerably heavy. Personally, I hate carrying paddles over a portage while carrying a pack, because I like my hands to be free for pulling on the tumpline. If the canoe is equipped with a portage yoke, the paddles aren't needed for the purpose. However, nearly all of my portaging has been done with the paddles serving as a yoke. Even with a yoke, though, my paddles are tied in.

If the paddles aren't tied in properly when you use them as a yoke (photograph 4), you could injure your neck in a fall. Note that the flat of the blade doesn't extend forward any more than necessary, so I can get my head in and out easily. The ropes are tied permanently on the center thwart for ease in securing the paddles. I also tie two short pieces on the bow seat to secure the shafts of the paddles; they should be tied tightly so they don't slip. I even tie in the spare paddle.

Padding is all-important in carrying a canoe. Rather than have a padded yoke, I prefer to put the padding in the life jacket (see page 122). That way, I am ready to carry any canoe, at any time. I have a friend who always carries an old-fashioned keyhole life jacket strictly for use in portaging. It's very thick and provides perfect, immovable padding for the thwart. Some people carry the canoe without padding, with the thwart resting on the vertebrae at the back of the neck, but this can be very painful and, over time, can cause trouble. There is no right way; only a matter of choice. Just don't ask me to carry your paddles!

Solo carry

Lifting a canoe onto one's shoulders without help requires some skill, and moderate strength: it should be practiced before leaving home. For the one-person canoe carry, stand beside the center of the canoe. Let's assume you will be moving down the portage trail to your right. Grasp the near gunwale with your right hand and lift the canoe onto its edge, open side away. Grasp the center thwart with your left hand (photograph 1) and lift the canoe onto your thighs. Flip the canoe up and grab the far gunwale with your right hand. With feet astride and in a half squat, the canoe is balanced on the thighs (photograph 2). Reach down between your legs, cradle the canoe on your left arm and roll the canoe onto your shoulders with your head between the yoke. Pivot right and stand up, all in one motion (photograph 3).

To put the canoe down, the process is reversed. Reach up with your left arm to cradle the gunwales and hull as you roll the canoe to the left. Remove your head from the yoke, and move your right hand from the gunwale to the thwart as the canoe is lowered to the thighs. Then gently lower the canoe to the ground.

If possible, the canoe is carried by one person and the packs by the other. To make a long portage seem shorter, spell each other off. It takes a lot of effort to heave a canoe up onto the shoulders, so change places without putting the canoe down. Say your partner is carrying the canoe. You go to the bow and hold it over your head as your partner squats down until the stern rests on the ground. He or she then steps out and changes places with you (photograph 5). Then you step under the canoe and place the thwart or portage yoke on your shoulders (photograph 6) and stand up. Now your partner can let go of his or her end.

If you are able to carry the canoe, but have difficulty lifting it up, you can have your partner assist you. Both stand at one end. Roll one end up with the other end on the ground. With one person holding it up, you can get into position easily. When you perform this procedure by yourself, and you get the end up over your head, bounce your hands along the gunwales moving backward until the yoke is on your shoulders. To put the canoe down, reverse the procedure.

Solo carry 1

2

3

4

5 Change with partner

6

169

Portaging the canoe . . .

Lunchtime, Magnetawan River, Ontario ————

Two-person carry

For anyone who finds it difficult to carry the canoe alone, the two-person carry is much easier. It must, however, be done properly. Friendships have been destroyed by the two-person carry. It won't work, for example, if people try to lift the canoe up when standing on opposite sides of it. Or if the bow person sticks his or her head right up in the bow and then proceeds to ricochet from tree to tree, blindly leading the way.

The two-person carry works best if the stern person puts the stern thwart on his or her shoulders, while the bow person puts the bow deck on one shoulder. In this position the bow person can see where he or she is going. Lash the paddles in for the yoke on the stern thwart. The stern carrier stands beside the stern thwart, the bow carrier stands on the same side of the canoe beside the bow seat. Both face the bow. Both turn and lift the canoe onto their thighs (photograph 1). They give the canoe a little flip and grasp the far gunwale with their right hands (photograph 2). They roll the canoe over onto their shoulders as they stand up (photograph 3). The stern thwart is on the stern carrier's shoulders and the bow seat is on the bow carrier's. Next the bow person bounces his or her hands along the gunwales until they reach the bow (photograph 4). Raising the bow up, the bow carrier frees his or her head from inside the canoe, then lowers the bow deck onto one shoulder (photograph 5). The stern carrier takes two-thirds of the weight at the stern-thwart position, while the bow carries one-third in the bow position. This enables the bow person to pick the route and steady the canoe over the difficult places.

Changing places

Changing places along the portage is accomplished in the same manner as spelling off one another in the single-person carry. This procedure enables two people of moderate strength and endurance to portage a heavy canoe without undue strain. The procedure must be followed precisely, or the canoe will overbalance and fall. For example, if you have your hands too close to the bow where it is narrow when you are doing the switch, you won't have enough leverage to hold the canoe over your head. Two strong people can throw a canoe up onto their shoulders without these procedures, but if they are that strong, they are better off doing a one-person carry and taking turns.

I confess I have made a few portages that were pure agony, but it has always been worth it. Some of the most spectacular places I have explored have been the reward of a difficult portage.

1 Two-person carry

2

3

4

5

Alternatives to portaging

Wading

When you are running a river in late summer and the water is very low, wading is an interesting and sometimes easier alternative to the portage. It is also an opportunity to study the way water flows around and over rocks. Although the water is shallow, you are looking at rapids in miniature. Look for the upstream and downstream Vs; watch how water flows over rocks and the waves it creates; and look for the eddies and the divergent currents. There are a few dangers in wading. Be careful not to jam your foot between rocks when in waist-deep water. If you fell downstream, the current could hold you underwater and prevent you from getting back up without help.

Lining

Lining takes considerable skill if the current is strong. It's much more risky for the canoe than wading or portaging, but it is an easier way to descend a rapids. Easy rapids can be lined with a stern rope. More difficult rapids require a rope on the stern and the bow. The angle of the canoe is controlled by the two lines. It's the sidewash of the current on the side of the canoe that holds it out in the current. The greater the angle, and the longer the lines, the farther the canoe is forced out into the current. It's easy to become tangled in tracking lines, so when working with them in a current, wear an accessible belt knife. You might have to release the upstream rope if the canoe swings broadside, and recover it with the downstream rope. Practice lining in gentle currents.

Tracking

Pulling a canoe upstream with ropes is called tracking. It's similar to lining, but a little more difficult, because you are pulling the canoe against the current. The angle of the canoe and the length of the ropes determine the distance from shore. You can learn the principle by tracking along a beach in lake water. The faster you run dragging the canoe, the farther it rides out from shore.

Wading

Lining downstream

Tracking upstream

Hot dog canoeing

The purpose behind my book and film series *Path of the Paddle* was to enable canoeists to get down a river and avoid upsetting or swamping. About the time the films and book were completed, canoeists discovered the thrill of following the kayaker into holes, and down the face of standing waves. They began to use the language of the hot dogging kayaker—terms like "air time" (getting as much height as possible off a wave), "surfing" (paddling upstream on the front of a wave), and "enders" (sticking the bow of your canoe into a hole). They also began to appear in the lineup of kayakers waiting to take their turn in the popular surfing holes on local rivers.

Most kayakers welcomed the canoes for comic relief. It was a novelty to see us attempting "air time." Canoes take up more space on the river, though, and aren't as agile. Kayakers sitting in a hole aren't exactly thrilled to see a 16 ft. (4.8 m) canoe descending on them. A canoe equipped with inner tubes for floatation can weigh three times as much as a high-performance kayak, and is three times as unwieldy. So the question, is why not switch to a kayak for fooling around in the holes and rollers and big water? I'm not sure what the answer is, but I do have a few ideas. There is something about the single-bladed paddle that appeals to canoeists. It is a demanding way to paddle in big water, but we accept its limitations and have devised many strokes and methods to compensate for the lack of a double-bladed kayak paddle. Although there are many things a kayaker can do that are impossible to do in an open canoe, there is a great challenge in putting a canoe through places it was never meant to go without getting any water in it. The limits of the open canoe are constantly being diminished. Even the Grand Canyon is being run by the open canoe, with floatation.

The greatest danger that hot dogging presents is the possibility of becoming addicted to it! You find yourself returning again and again to the biggest holes and curling waves. The thrills and spills gradually become an end in themselves, and you begin to look

Surfing on the front of a wave

Hot dog canoeing . . .

for bigger and bigger water, and spend less and less time paddling wilderness rivers and lakes. You have become a hot dogger, which is fine if that's what you really want.

Hot dog canoeing has very little to do with living outdoors or listening to the song. It is great fun, and I have sharpened my skills and made good friends in this gregarious pursuit, but for me there is a more important reason for playing around in the big stuff in a canoe. The canoe is used more frequently for wilderness cruising than the kayak. Many difficult rapids, and sections of rivers that are usually portaged, are now run by skilled canoeists. Often these skills have been developed by hot dogging in big water, where the price of a mistake is nothing more than a brief swim. Most hot dog canoeing takes place at the end of a rapids with quiet water below for easy recovery. Hot dogging builds confidence and sharpens reflexes for fast water. Canoeists find out what it is like to paddle a swamped canoe through haystacks and to swim in them. They also learn how to right a canoe quickly, climb into it (which is easy with floatation) and bail it.

The first thing to know is how to pick your spot. What might look suicidal to the average onlooker could actually be very safe. On the other hand, an innocuous-looking rapids can be a killer. Hot dogging should be done in a group and under guidance. Helmets are a must, since there is a tendency to tip upstream and get carried under the canoe, when surfing. One of the greatest dangers is being led beyond your skill level by an expert who makes it look easier than it really is. You want to push your limits as you develop your skills, but it should be done under responsible and skilled leadership.

Powering through haystacks
The easiest and most common hot dog maneuver is to power down the V, and plough through the towering haystacks or holes (photograph 1). The canoe emerges awash, but the floatation and a strong brace keep it upright.

Surfing
Paddle back up to the eddy facing upstream. Paddling forward as hard as you can, leave the eddy, so the stern exits almost at the same time as the bow. The canoe is angled slightly toward the middle of the river. If you get it right, you are on the face of the first standing wave. Paddle upstream, so you stay stationary in relation to the shore. The current will try to sweep you downstream when you are in its center, but gravity will hold you in front of the wave. You are surfing—one of the greatest thrills in a canoe! If the canoe veers to either side, you will be carried up and over the standing wave or, if unprepared, you will tip upstream. If you upset, hang on to the canoe as it floats through the waves, right it, climb on board, bail it and do it again.

Surfing sideways in a hole
Find a hole where the water is flowing over a drop, with lots of current (photograph 3). It's important to know the difference in types of holes because a keeper can kill you. A safe hole is one where the water surges down a slope, creating a depression, and a wave that falls back on itself. The surge of the current will immediately carry you through the curling wave.

Paddle over and drop down into the hole sideways, leaning downstream so the current can't grip the upstream gunwale and flip you. Gravity will hold you down in the hole, even though the current is trying to carry you out. Bounce around for a while and then, when the good time is over, one of three things happens: you either fill with water and wash out of the hole, paddle out the end, or make a mistake and flip upstream. If you flip upstream, the current will grab you and carry you under the canoe and you will emerge downstream. With luck, the swamped canoe will follow; a canoe with floatation sometimes rolls around in the hole for quite a while.

Rolling the canoe upright
It's so much fun cranking a roll in an open canoe that Paul declares that some of my upsets are contrived. Extra floatation riding above the gunwales near the stern helps to get the roll started, and it can also prevent the canoe from rolling completely upside-down. By hooking your feet under the seat, it is possible to do a roll without thigh straps, but they are an advantage in keeping you in your canoe. Toe blocks that hold your thighs tightly against the straps also help, but it's a matter of preference.

To roll the canoe upright, turn your blade perpendicular and knife it up to the surface. Then turn the blade flat, and beginning with your upper body leaning back, perform a low brace. Make use of the strength of your upper body by bending forward during the roll. Bring your head and shoulders out of the water last, when the canoe is almost upright. While learning, you may have to throw in a little extra sculling or an extra brace. When the canoe is fully upright, you can sit up. The biggest reason for failure is not leaning forward far enough during the roll. Rolling the canoe is more fun than righting it, and climbing back in, or pushing it to shore to empty it. The amount of bailing you do depends on the amount of floatation you have. Too much floatation can make your canoe difficult to roll.

It's taken me years to figure out how to do the open-canoe roll. Now, just when I have it nailed, I've heard about Nolan Whitesell, who is so confident of his roll that he runs places like the Niagara Gorge. I've filmed in that gorge and would never have believed an open canoe could do that. Whitesell has designed a specialized canoe for rolling. It is custom outfitted with full floatation to your height, weight and body build. As with many things, the best canoes and equipment are designed by the people on the leading edge. It was Whitesell who said, "There's no reason why a raft or kayak shouldn't be able to go anywhere an open canoe can go." He has produced a video on rolling the open canoe called *Rollin' with Nolan*. It is available from Nolan Whitesell, P.O. Box 9839, Atlanta, Georgia 30319.

1 Power through haystacks

2 Attempting a Class 4 rapid, Ottawa River

3 Surfing sideways in a hole

4 Surfing

5 Running a small falls, Churchill River

6 Pulling out of the surf

Other tricky maneuvers

Other moves are enders, surfing backward and 180° and 360° turns on the top of the waves.

Crashing through a roller

A floatation-equipped canoe attempts to crash through a roller, fails and turns sideways (photograph 1). It should get trashed, but a heavy-duty brace holds it from going over. A strong high brace pulls the canoe up and over the wave.

The ender

To do an ender, paddle very hard, while surfing on the front of the wave, in order to bury the nose of the canoe in the oncoming current (photograph 2). The bow fills with water, forcing it down, and firing the stern into the air. The canoe might go end over end, throwing you out, or it might do a 180° turn as you brace and exit the wave, while facing downstream and full of water. Kayakers do enders all the time. Canoeists rarely can, and then mostly with luck.

A classic doubles surf

The canoe is surfing on the front of the wave (photograph 3). A couple of paddle strokes drive the bow into the onrushing fast water. Water pours in over the bow.

Trashing in the surf

There are any number of ways to get trashed in the surf (photograph 4). You can even run a small falls, but it takes some experience to know what the hidden dangers are.

The roll

Extra floatation above the gunwales in the stern makes it possible to roll a Kevlar Prospector (photograph 5).

1 Crashing through a roller

2 The ender

3 A classic doubles surf

4 Surfing sideways...sort of

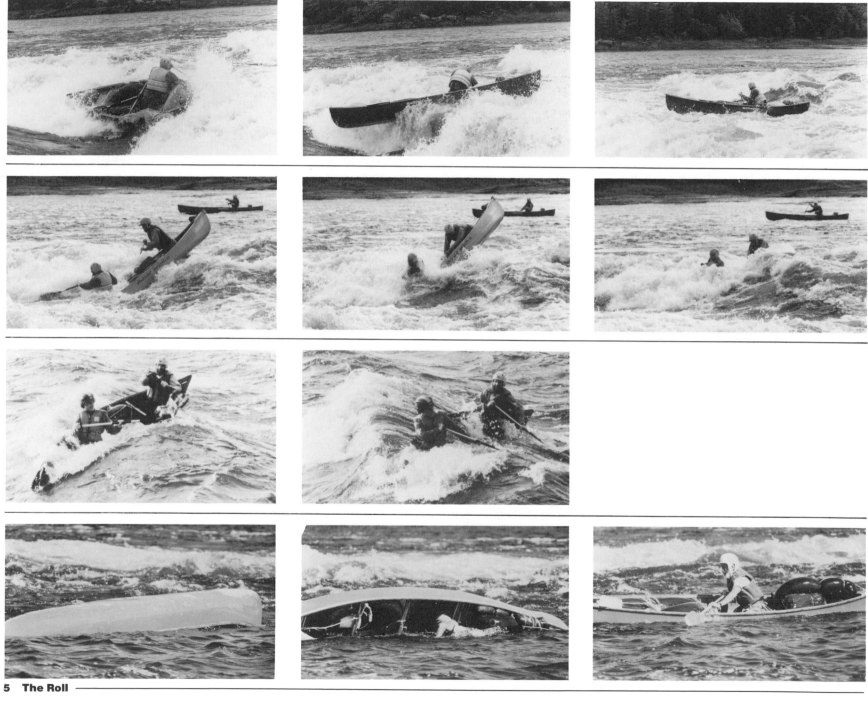

AFTERWORD

The Lakota [Sioux] was a true naturist — a lover of nature. He loved the earth and all things of the earth, the attachment growing with age. The old people came literally to love the soil and they sat or reclined on the ground with a feeling of being close to a mothering power. It was good for the skin to touch the earth and the old people liked to remove their moccasins and walk with bare feet on the sacred earth. Their tipis were built upon the earth and their altars were made of earth. The birds that flew in the air came to rest upon the earth and it was the final abiding place of all things that lived and grew. The soil was soothing, strengthening, cleansing and healing.

The old Lakota was wise. He knew that man's heart away from nature becomes hard; he knew that lack of respect for growing, living things soon led to lack of respect for humans too.

Chief Luther Standing Bear

In our modern world of glass, steel and concrete, it is difficult, if not impossible, to have any sense of where our food, clothing and shelter come from. Everything we eat arrives in bags, boxes, cans or bottles. When we go to the outdoors, it is invariably to have a good time, to relax. For most of us, it's also an escape from the world we have created. After a short visit, though, we return. Not that there is anything inherently wrong with this. It's just that it doesn't lead to much of a relationship with the land.

Chief Luther Standing Bear's words have inspired me to share my love and compassion, or perhaps I should say obsession, for the natural world. I have shared this obsession through painting, film, photography and writing, but not without some trepidation.

Being a wilderness enthusiast is a lot like sitting on an ice floe. Every day the floe gets smaller as pieces break off and float away. You know that it will continue to get smaller day by day, never bigger. That is the reality that all lovers of wild lands have to face. We also have to realize that convincing people to go to what's left of the natural world is like inviting them onto the ice floe. Having spent the better part of my life popularizing the enjoyment of wilderness, I too must accept some responsibility for the floe getting crowded.

If I'm going to encourage people to climb onto it, it would be unthinkable for me not to try to educate them and to encourage them to join one of the various organizations dedicated to preserving what's left of our wilderness.

Unfortunately, environmentalists are often perceived as being against all forms of progress, such as road building, harvesting of trees and mining. The organizations that I belong to are only against stupidity and greed for short-term gain. We all have to make a living, whether it be from logging, mining, tourism, hunting, trapping or employment in a city. What we should be united against is the needless destruction and pollution of the world we live in.

One thing that film making has taught me is that the "bad guys" aren't always all that bad. When I was making my films on wolves, I filmed biologists, trappers and hunters. In some cases the hunters and trappers were more interesting individuals and were more cooperative than the scientists. One trapper kidded me mercilessly about my fascination with wolves. After ten years of friendly correspondence, we haven't convinced each other of anything, but we both enjoy trying! The issue is not that people hunt or trap animals for a living. What really matters is that the creatures that share the earth with us continue to have a place to live. When their habitat goes they go. We are devouring it at an ever-increasing rate.

My motivation in sharing my love of the land through my work is to awaken a love and compassion in people for the land and to encourage them to become involved in the many environmental organizations that are concerned with the preservation of wild places. Each one of the organizations represents a relatively small number of hard-working and deeply concerned individuals who care enough about the natural world to do something about its preservation. They find the problems, research them and give us the facts that we need to make our own decisions. They enable us to write intelligent letters to the governments that are responsible directly or indirectly for what's happening to the wilderness. There are conscientious people in government who welcome letters of complaint and criticism. It provides them with the incentive and the ammunition to do something about a problem. A government minister recently told the board of the Canadian Parks and Wilderness Society that a letter from the public is considered to be just as important as a ten-page position paper released by an environmental organization.

We must create the will within our elected representatives at every level of government to legislate protection for wilderness areas. Politicians tend to think and act in the short term, usually in periods of four years. First we must inform them of the problems, then convince them that we won't re-elect them if they continue to allow the land to be mismanaged. *Mismanage* is a harsh word, but politicians sometimes do cheat, use subterfuge or fail to live up to their promises. For example the logging industry in British Columbia is running out of easily accessible virgin forests to cut and is bringing great pressure to bear on the government to permit cutting in provincial parks. Recently the provincial government designated an area in Strathcona Park, one of the oldest and most beautiful wilderness parks in B.C., as a "recreation zone." It sounds great; however, a "recreation zone" is their term for an area that is open to logging and mining. It is purposely misleading, and it's our responsibility to see that they don't get away with it.

History has shown again and again all over the world that great hardship follows the destruction of the forests. Our forests are being sold off at a rate that is causing severe shortages of logs, but in much of North America reforestation is not taking place at a rate that will sustain the demand. The industry wants what is left, and often it is only environmental organizations that stand in their way.

It amazes me what these organizations accomplish with their relatively small numbers. I dream of what could be accomplished if all the people who enjoy the outdoors belonged to at least one of these organizations and knew what was happening to our wild lands. For starters, try the Canadian Nature Federation. With your membership, you receive a beautiful magazine, *Nature Canada*, which deals with both national and international issues. Another organization that is a must for all canoeists is the Canadian Parks and Wilderness Society. Their newsletter, *Park News*, and magazine, *Borealis*, are also superb. If you are a canoeist living in the United States you might want to start with American Rivers, which deals with the habitat of the canoe—the lakes and rivers of America. The Sierra Club is also a must for anyone who loves the outdoors. I have listed some of my favorites, but there are many more.

In sharing some of my favorite canoe journeys with you, I must face the reality that next time I won't have these places all to myself. However, it's worth it if I have been instrumental in adding one more voice to the cause of wilderness preservation—not just for your sake or mine or that of our children, but for the sake of all the myriad forms of life that live there. We have a responsibility to ensure that they continue to exist because they, like us, were created by God and have a right to exist.

Library and bookstore shelves are loaded with books that claim to be the definitive book on canoeing and camping, but I've never seen one that really is. And this book is no exception. For example, there are books that deal solely with canoe building and canoe repair. Or with first aid or how to paddle. Then there are books on where to canoe or on favorite trips. The best authors deal in detail with what they know best and then refer you to the definitive book on the other subjects.

I have my favorite books on canoeing and camping, but the ones I would recommend most highly are the ones that deal with the aesthetic and spiritual values of wilderness living. The realm of the spirit interests me, because the solutions to our environmental problems must come from there. I see hope in writers like Sigurd Olson, Barry Lopez, Aldo Leopold and some of the native people recorded in *Touch the Earth*. I would like to see them more widely known. Many of the following books make great companions on a canoe trip:

Arctic Dreams by Barry Lopez (Charles Scribner's Sons, New York, 1986). The most intimate portrayal of the Arctic I have ever read.

Canoe by Kenneth G. Roberts and Philip Shackleton (Macmillan of Canada, Toronto, 1983). A scholarly work of the history of the canoe in North America and other places in the world.

Canoe Canada by Nick Nickels (Van Nostrand Reinhold, Toronto, 1976). A great book for assisting in figuring out where to go next. Loaded with pertinent information on each trip, including the required maps.

Canoe Craft by Ted Moores and Merilyn Mohr (Camden House, Camden East, Ont., 1983). A how-to book for making a stripper canoe and information on some old traditional canoe designs, including the Prospector.

Canoeing Wild Rivers by Cliff Jacobson (ICS Books Inc., Merrillville, IN, 1984). One of the best on expedition canoeing. Jacobson has drawn on the experiences and knowledge of many well-travelled canoeists. I was amazed at how often we came to the same conclusions

on so many aspects of canoeing and living outdoors. He's ''out to lunch,'' though, on tents!

Chips from a Wilderness Log by Calvin Rutstrum (Stein and Day, New York, 1978). This is Calvin Rutstrum's last book. He reiterates and expands on much of what he had written earlier, but everything by Rutstrum is worth reading.

The Complete Wilderness Paddler by James W. Davidson and John Rugge (Alfred A. Knopf, New York, 1976). A popular and enjoyable book on how to canoe, canoe camping and canoe tripping. Fun to read and loaded with good stuff.

The Fallacy of Wildlife Conservation by John A. Livingston (McClelland and Stewart, Toronto, 1981). Anything by Livingston is worth reading. This is not your average conservation book. He makes you rethink a lot of your ideas.

Freshwater Saga by Eric W. Morse (University of Toronto Press, Toronto, 1987). The sharing of many years of canoeing, mostly along the voyageurs' routes, will make you long to canoe some routes and probably steer clear of others.

Fur Trade Canoe Routes of Canada—Then and Now by Eric W. Morse (Queen's Printer, Toronto, 1969). A must for anyone who has an interest in the role of the canoe in the exploration and development of Canada.

Guide des Rivières Sportives au Québec by Gilles Fortin (Editions Marcel Broquet, La Prairie, Que. 1980). An excellent book on where to canoe in Quebec. I think Quebec has some of the best whitewater in Canada.

Holy Bible. The *Good News Bible* is the easiest to read. It's a must if you believe God created the world and lived in the person of Jesus Christ. The man portrayed in the gospel bears no resemblance to the soppy portraits we see. It's interesting, he seems to have spent a lot of time going off by himself into quiet places.

Islands at the Edge (Douglas & McIntyre, Vancouver, 1984). A vivid portrayal of a beautiful world and a heartbreaking story of its destruction. The book concludes with a plea to save what is left. It's a story with a happy ending, because South Moresby has been designated as a park.

The Klutz Book of Knots by John Cassidy (Klutz Press, Palo Alto, CA, 1985). This book was written for me. Whenever I have to tie a knot I go and get this book.

Listening Point by Sigurd Olson (Alfred A. Knopf, NY, 1969). Sigurd Olson is one of my favorite authors. He makes me want to go outside and look around. He has taught me how to see.

The Lonely Land by Sigurd Olson (McClelland and Stewart, Toronto, 1961). This book whet my appetite for distant northern rivers. And it introduced me to the name Eric Morse, one of the canoeists in this book.

The Magnetic North by Mike Beedell (Oxford University Press, Toronto, 1983). In this book we get a glimpse of the north through the superb photography of Mike Beedell. He represents for me the true solo adventurer. He goes on his trips, then quietly shares what he has found through his photographs.

Marked by the Wild by Bruce Litteljohn and Jon Pearce (McClelland and Stewart, Toronto, 1973). An anthology of stories about the wilderness. It has accompanied me on many trips.

Nahanni by Dick Turner (Hancock House, Surrey, B.C., 1975). This book made me long to canoe the Nahanni River. I dreamed for fifteen years before I took my first trip down one of the world's most spectacular rivers.

Nahanni Trailhead by Joanne Moore (Deneau and Greenberg, Ottawa, 1980). Every lover of the outdoors dreams about doing what the Moores did. As newlyweds they went off to the Nahanni River, built a log cabin, wintered over and canoed out in the spring.

North American Canoe Country by Calvin Rutstrum (Macmillan, New York, 1964). This is his third book and one of his best. I devoured it when it was first published. It harkens back to a time scarcely thirty years ago when

recreational canoeists were a rare breed.

Second Nature — The Animal Rights Controversy by Alan Herscovici (C.B.C. Enterprises, Toronto, 1985). A book that will make you aware of what's happening to the rest of the creatures that also inhabit the earth.

St. John Ambulance First Aid. There are several of these books and they are worthwhile reading for anyone who goes very far afield.

Touch the Earth by T.C. McLuhan (Pocket Books, NY, 1971). This book is a compilation of excerpts from speeches given by native leaders, at a time when they were being driven from the land. These speeches have affected me in a profound way. I love to read them in some remote place.

Paradise Below Zero by Calvin Rutstrum (Macmillan, New York, 1968). This is an excellent book on winter camping. Possibly dated, but nevertheless informative. His realistic attitude to the acceptance of motorized transport is interesting.

Reflections from the North Country by Sigurd Olson (Alfred Knopf, New York, 1976). One of his most philosophical books.

The Romance of the Canadian Canoe by John Murray Gibbon (The Ryerson Press, Toronto, 1951). Thirty years ago this was one of few books on the Canadian canoe. It's still worth reading.

Runes of the North by Sigurd Olson (Alfred Knopf, New York, 1963). Another beautiful book. This helps you to see things you never saw before and to understand what you are seeing.

Sea of Slaughter by Farley Mowat (McClelland and Stewart, Toronto, 1984). A worthwhile look at what used to be, what could have been, and where we are heading.

Strangers that Devour the Land by Boyce Richardson (Alfred Knopf, New York, 1976). A beautiful glimpse into the Cree culture and how callously it is being destroyed in the name of progress.

Superior: The Haunted Shore by Wayland Drew and Bruce Litteljohn (Gage Publishing, Toronto, 1975). This is about my favorite place,

the north shore of Lake Superior. I didn't realize until I read the book how little I knew about this spectacular land. And as I peruse the photographs in the winter, I feel I am there and I can hardly wait until spring.

To the Wild Country by Janet and John Foster (Van Nostrand Reinhold, Toronto, 1975). A book about some of Canada's more spectacular parks by two people who enjoy the wilderness.

Walden by Henry Thoreau (Anchor Books, Garden City, NY, 1973). First published in 1854, it is one of the all-time classics. Everybody should read it during their lifetime.

Wanapitei Canoe Tripper's Cookbook by Carol Hodgins (Highway Book Shop, Cobalt, Ont., 1982). This little book has just about everything you need to know about eating on a canoe trip.

The Way of the Wilderness by Calvin Rutstrum (Burgess Publishing, MN, 1946). Reprinted in 1958 as *The New Way of the Wilderness*. The first how-to camp and canoe book I ever read. First published in a tough, soft cover with an accompanying canvas pouch, I carried it on all my trips for many years. While some of it is dated, it's still good reading.

The Wilderness Life by Calvin Rutstrum (Macmillan, New York, 1975). I enjoy Rutstrum's tales vicariously as he shares his memories of a lifetime of wilderness travel. It makes me want to finish what I am doing, pack up and get out there.

Wilderness Medicine by William Forgey M.D. (Indiana Camp Supply Books, Pittsboro, IN, 1979). This is the book to carry with you on the remote trips. Unlike many first aid books, it tells you what to do when calling a doctor is not possible.

Wild Waters by James Raffan (Key Porter Books, Toronto, 1986). If this doesn't whet your appetite for some of those remote and distant rivers, then nothing will. I would like to experience all of them. Incidentally, that's Wally Schaber and me on the cover before the long swim.

CONSERVATION AND CANOE ORGANIZATIONS

Conservation Organizations in Canada

Canadian Coalition on Acid Rain
2249 Queen St. E.
Toronto, Ont. M4E 1G1

Canadian Nature Federation
453 Sussex Dr.
Ottawa, Ont. K1N 6Z4
Publication: *Nature Canada*
The CNF represents over 100 naturalists groups at the national level. Membership open to all.

Canadian Parks and Wilderness Society
160 Bloor St. E.
Suite 1150
Toronto, Ont. M4W 1B9
Publication: *Park News*
Promotes the preservation of parks and wilderness areas. Membership open to all.

Friends of the Earth
16-53 Queen St.
Ottawa, Ont. K1P 5C5
Publication: *Infoetox*

Friends of the Stikine
1405 Doran Rd.
Vancouver, B.C. V7K 1N1

Islands Protection Society
Box 688,
Queen Charlotte City, B.C. V0T 1S0

The Nature Conservancy of Canada
2200 Yonge St.
Suite 1710
Toronto, Ont. M4S 9Z9

Pollution Probe Foundation
43 Queen's Park Cres. E.
Toronto, Ont. M5S 2C3

Sierra Club of Ontario Foundation
229 College St.
Suite 303
Toronto, Ont. M5T 1R4

Temagami Wilderness Society
204 Wedgewood Dr.
Willowdale, Ont. M2M 2H9

Valhalla Wilderness Society
Box 224
New Denver, B.C. V0G 1S0

Western Canada Wilderness Committee
1200 Hornby St.
Vancouver, B.C. V6Z 2E2

World Wildlife Fund
60 St. Clair Ave. E.
Suite 201
Toronto, Ont. M4T 1N5
Publication: *Working for Wildlife*
Secures private, corporate and government funding for research projects and educational tools to aid wildlife. Primarily concerned with endangered species.

Yukon Conservation Society
302 Hawkins St.
Whitehorse, Yukon, Y1A 1X6

Conservation Organizations in the United States

American Rivers
801 Pennsylvania Ave.
Suite 303
Washington, DC 2003

Defenders of Wildlife
1244 Nineteenth St., N.W.
Washington, DC 20036
Publication: *Defender*

Friends of the Earth
530 Seventh St., S.E.
Washington, DC 2003

National Audubon Society
950 Third Ave.
New York, NY 10022
Publication: *Audubon*

National Parks and Conservation Association
1701 Eighteenth St., N.W.
Washington, DC 2009

Nature Conservancy
1800 North Kent St.
Suite 800
Arlington, VA 22209

Sierra Club
730 Polk St.
San Francisco, CA 94109
Publication: *Sierra*

Wilderness Society
1400 First St., N.W.
Washington, DC 2005

World Wildlife Fund
1255 Twenty-third St., N.W.
Washington, DC 20037

For other organizations consult *The Conservation Directory* available from:
The National Wildlife Federation
1412 Sixteenth St., N.W.
Washington, DC 20036

Canadian Canoe Organizations

Canadian Recreational Canoeing Association
P.O. Box 500
Hyde Park, Ont. N0M 1Z0
Publication: *Kanawa*

Wilderness Canoe Association
P.O. Box 496, Stn. K
Toronto, Ont. M4P 2G9
Publication: *Nastawgan*

Canadian Canoe Magazines

Che-Mun
Box 548, Stn. O
Toronto, Ont. M4A 2P1

Paddler
157 Silver Birch Ave.
Toronto, Ont. M4E 3L3

Sea Kayaker
1670 Duranlean St.
Vancouver, B.C. V6H 3S4

U.S.A. Canoe Organizations

American Canoe Association
P.O. Box 248
Lorton, VA 22079

The Wooden Canoe Heritage Association
1340 Black Walnut Court
Annapolis, MD 21403

U.S.A. Canoe Magazines

Canoe
P.O. Box 10748
Des Moines, IA 50347-0748

Canoesport Journal
P.O. Box 991
Odessa, FL 33556

INDEX

Acknowledgements

To the native peoples of North America, who conceived the canoe for travelling the lakes and rivers of this vast country.

To my wife Joyce, who took my handwritten notes and translated them into some semblance of a manuscript.

To my family and friends, who have shared and enriched my canoe journeys over the years and who have displayed such patience while I took ''one last shot.''

A special thank you to Pam Gibb-Carsley, Lloyd Seaman, Don Beckett, Becky Mason, Paul Mason, Ric Driediger, Wally Schaber, Neil Hartling, Mike O'Connor and Glenn Fallis who read and contributed to the manuscript.

Thanks to my editor Laurie Coulter for her patience in bringing it all under control despite my protestations that she was dropping all my best stuff.

To Marquis Photographers Limited, who put extra care and effort into the photo finishing.

Front Cover Photo: Paul Mason
Principal Photography: Bill Mason, Becky Mason, Paul Mason
Additional Photography: Ken Buck, Alan Whatmough, Greg Wilber, Judy Seaman Mason, Ric Driediger, Gilles Couët, Michael Peake, Derryl Murphy and Joyce Mason.
Cartoons: Paul Mason, Bill Mason